MASSACHUSETTS

MICHAEL BLANDING & ALEXANDRA HALL

Contents

MASSACHUSETTS

BOSTON

There is something about Boston that seems to set it apart from the rest of the country. To visitors, it often feels more like a European city, with a walkable downtown littered with parks and brownstone buildings. And even while the city has erected skyscrapers to keep pace with its high-tech economy, it has kept its older buildings intact. Businessmen and bicycle messengers race past white-steepled churches and historic houses that played essential roles in the war for American Independence.

While Greater Boston ranks as the seventh-largest urban area in the country, with more than three million people, the city itself barely breaks the top 25, with just 600,000 people. To Bostonians, that makes the city exactly the right size, thank you very much—big enough that you can find most everything you need, but small enough to get to know the major people and places in town quickly. Among them are the cultural institutions that give Boston its identity: the Boston Pops on the Fourth of July, the swan boats in the Public Garden, and the recent world-champion Boston Red Sox at Fenway Park. New symbols mark the city's drive into the 21st century, including the breathtaking Zakim Bridge and the "Big Dig"—the city's ambitious attempt to put the central expressway underground (which unfortunately has been recently beset by engineering problems).

Indeed, the city has come a long way from the days of scrod and clam chowder. The resurgence started in the late 1990s with the dot-com boom, for which Boston, with its educated populace and venture capital companies,

© TIM GRAFFT/MOTT

HIGHLIGHTS

(**Freedom Trail:** Follow the redbrick road from Boston Common to Bunker Hill (page 16).

(**New England Aquarium:** Sharks, penguins, and other ocean-dwellers await at this waterfront museum (page 30).

(**Mapparium:** A 30-foot-wide stained-glass globe of the world is one of the more unusual spaces in the city (page 37).

(**Fenway Park:** From the Green Monster to the bleachers, this ball field is a living shrine (page 38).

(**Museum of Fine Arts:** The French Impressionist paintings and Asian sculpture here are among the best anywhere (page 39).

(**Isabella Stewart Gardner Museum:** This Victorian jewel-box of a museum is as acclaimed for its building as for its art (page 40).

(**Harvard Museum of Natural History:** Meticulously hand-blown glass flowers are just the beginning of the wonders on display here (page 48).

LOOK FOR (TO FIND RECOMMENDED SIGHTS, ACTIVITIES, DINING, AND LODGING.

was especially poised. Even after the dot-com bubble popped, however, the revitalization of downtown has continued, with million-dollar condos springing up on block after block and a bumper crop of inventive restaurants, hip lounges, and international boutiques. The result is a new cosmopolitan air that has improved upon, not replaced, the historic charms of the city and made Boston one of the most enjoyable cities in (or not in) America.

PLANNING YOUR TIME
You could spend a week exploring all that Boston has to offer. The city's small size, however, makes it easy to see different parts of the city on the same trip, no matter how much time you have. The only mandatory sightseeing is a

walk along the **Freedom Trail,** which connects all of downtown's Revolutionary War sites. The city's cultural attractions, for the most part, are grouped on the outskirts of downtown in the Back Bay, South End, and Fenway districts. Art buffs can choose between several very different museums—the world-class **Museum of Fine Arts,** the charming **Isabella Stewart Gardner Museum,** and the cutting-edge **Institute of Contemporary Art.** For sports fans of any age, a tour of **Fenway Park** is essential. And in planning meals, it's important to note that while nearly all restaurants are open year-round, many of the city's upscale dining rooms do not serve lunch and many do not serve breakfast. When in doubt, call ahead.

Even on a short trip, it's worth getting across

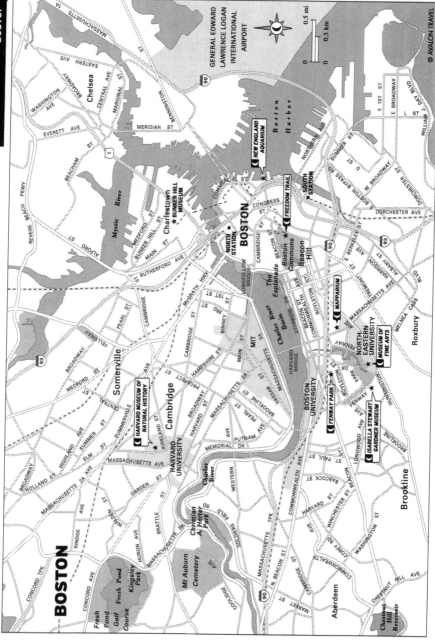

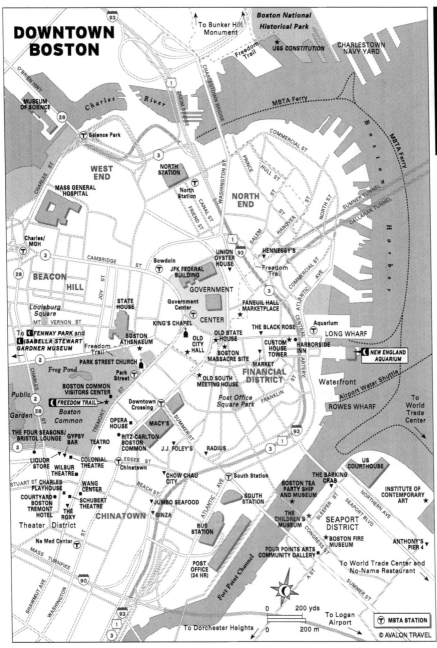

DOWNTOWN BOSTON

To Bunker Hill Monument

Boston National Historical Park

Freedom Trail

USS *CONSTITUTION*

CHARLESTOWN NAVY YARD

MBTA Ferry

Charles River

MUSEUM OF SCIENCE

Science Park

WEST END

NORTH STATION

North Station

COMMERCIAL ST

Boston Harbor

MBTA Ferry

MASS GENERAL HOSPITAL

NORTH END

SUMNER TUNNEL

CALLAHAN TUNNEL

Charles/MGH

CAMBRIDGE ST

BEACON HILL

Bowdoin

UNION OYSTER HOUSE

HENNESSY'S

Freedom Trail

JFK FEDERAL BUILDING

GOVERNMENT

FANEUIL HALL MARKETPLACE

Louisburg Square

STATE HOUSE

Government Center

CENTER

KING'S CHAPEL

OLD STATE HOUSE

THE BLACK ROSE

Aquarium

LONG WHARF

To FENWAY PARK and ISABELLA STEWART GARDNER MUSEUM

BOSTON ATHENAEUM

OLD CITY HALL

BOSTON MASSACRE SITE

CUSTOM HOUSE TOWER

HARBORSIDE INN

NEW ENGLAND AQUARIUM

Freedom Trail

PARK STREET CHURCH

Frog Pond

Park Street

OLD SOUTH MEETING HOUSE

MARKET

FINANCIAL DISTRICT

Waterfront

Airport Water Shuttle

Public Garden

BOSTON COMMON VISITORS CENTER

FREEDOM TRAIL

Downtown Crossing

Post Office Square Park

ROWES WHARF

To World Trade Center

Boston Common

OPERA HOUSE

MACY'S

THE FOUR SEASONS/BRISTOL LOUNGE

GYPSY BAR

TEATRO

RITZ-CARLTON BOSTON COMMON

J.J. FOLEY'S

RADIUS

LIQUOR STORE

WILBUR THEATRE

COLONIAL THEATRE

ESSEX ST

Chinatown

CHOW CHAU CITY

South Station

US COURTHOUSE

THE BARKING CRAB

CHARLES PLAYHOUSE

WANG CENTER

BEACH ST

JUMBO SEAFOOD

SOUTH STATION

BOSTON TEA PARTY SHIP AND MUSEUM

INSTITUTE OF CONTEMPORARY ART

COURTYARD BOSTON TREMONT HOTEL

THE ROXY

SCHUBERT THEATRE

GINZA

BUS STATION

THE CHILDREN'S MUSEUM

SEAPORT DISTRICT

ANTHONY'S PIER 4

Theater District

CHINATOWN

Ne Med Center

BOSTON FIRE MUSEUM

POST OFFICE (24 HR)

FOUR POINTS ARTS COMMUNITY GALLERY

To World Trade Center and No-Name Restaurant

MASS TURNPIKE

To Dorchester Heights

0   200 yds
0   200 m

To Logan Airport

MBTA STATION

© AVALON TRAVEL

the river to Cambridge, Boston's more bohemian "left bank." In addition to a more laid-back vibe, this sister city is home to Boston's most elite cultural institutions—Harvard University and the Massachusetts Institute of Technology.

ORIENTATION

Boston's quirky geography has caused more than a few headaches to visitors trying to keep its twisting roads straight. The bulk of the downtown still takes up the Shawmut Peninsula, with Boston Common as its beating green heart. The downtown neighborhoods are organized around the Common, with Beacon Hill and North End to the north, the Financial District and Downtown to the east, and the Back Bay and South End to the south. East Boston, along with Logan International Airport, is across Boston Harbor to the northeast, while South Boston and the new Seaport District form a peninsula to the southeast. Farther to the south are the city's ethnic residential communities, including Roxbury, Dorchester, and Jamaica Plain. Even farther south is the separate city of Quincy, while west of the Fenway is the chic Brookline, a

separate town despite being almost completely surrounded by Boston. Across the river to the north are intellectual Cambridge and hip Somerville.

SAFETY

Once upon a time it was foolhardy to walk around downtown Boston at night—especially in the blocks between Downtown Crossing and Chinatown colorfully known as the "Combat Zone." Now the Combat Zone is home to a luxury hotel, and with a little common sense it's safe to walk downtown at any hour. Keep in mind that because of Boston bars' early closing times of 1 or 2 A.M., the streets can seem somewhat empty during the early morning hours. It's probably a good idea to avoid crossing Boston Common after midnight. Most of the outlying neighborhoods are also safe to walk in at night, with the exception of parts of Roxbury and Dorchester, including Dudley Square, Grove Hall, Upham's Corner, and Franklin Park (though these areas are safe enough during the day). Most subway lines and stations are safe until closing at 12:30 A.M.; however, use caution for the stations on the Orange Line between Massachusetts Avenue and Forest Hills.

Sights

BEACON HILL

Victorian novelist Henry James and 1990's TV lawyer Ally McBeal felt equally at home on Beacon Hill, which rises steeply on the north side of Boston Common. This is the neighborhood that springs to most people's minds when they think "Boston": gas streetlamps lit 24 hours a day and cobblestone alleyways lined with brick Federal-style townhouses that are home to some of Boston's richest residents.

The most exclusive address on the hill is Louisburg Square, where wrought-iron railings surround a park of beech and alder trees, and wealthy Bostonians including Senator (and 2004 presidential contender) John Kerry make their homes. A block south of the square,

go ahead and snap a shot of the picturesque cobblestone alley of Acorn Street, supposedly the most photographed street in the world. At the bottom of the hill on the east is commercial Charles Street, where doyennes with small dogs shop in a profusion of antiques stores, and young lawyers in the mold of Ally take their laptops to cafés on weekends.

◖ Freedom Trail

It's easy now to look back on the Sons of Liberty as just a bunch of guys in funny hats and breeches, shooting off muskets and complaining about tea. But there is something undoubtedly stirring about visiting the graves of the early revolutionaries and sitting in the

BOSTON

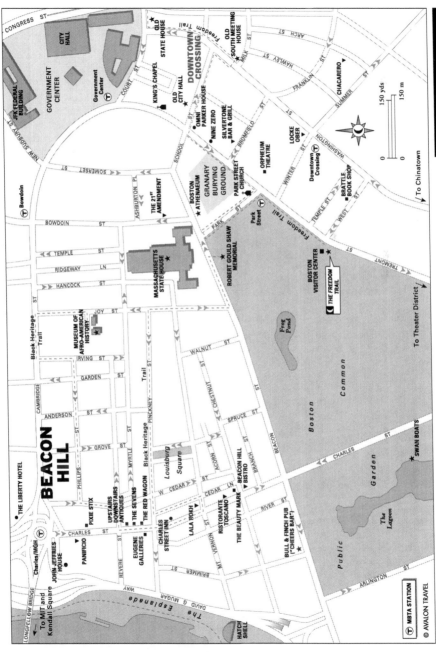

© AVALON TRAVEL

© TIM GRAFFT/MOTT

Acorn Street, Beacon Hill

11 A.M., noon, 1 P.M., 3:30 P.M., and 4:30 P.M. daily, $12 adults, $10 students and seniors, $6 children) that covers the first eleven sites along the route in the company of a costumed actor playing one of the lesser-known patriots such as William Dawes, Abigail Adams, or James Otis.

Perhaps the best way to take in the trail is to book the morning tour, then stop for lunch at the Quincy Market food court or a trattoria in the North End. After lunch, continue along by yourself to the sites in the North End and Charlestown, taking the ferry back to Boston; or return back along the way you came, taking more time to explore the inside of the Old State House, the Old South Meeting House, and the Massachusetts State House. The foundation also offers two-hour self-guided audio tours, with sound effects and voices of historians to bring the trail to life ($15). Since part of the fun of the trail is experiencing the contrast between Revolutionary Boston and the sights and sounds of the modern city, however, the headphone tours can be a bit insulating.

Boston National Historical Park

Seven of the sites along the Freedom Trail, along with the additional site of Dorchester Heights in South Boston, have also been incorporated into a national park (Charlestown Navy Yard, Charlestown, 617/242-5642 or 617/242-5601, www.nps.gov/bost). The park has visitors centers at the USS *Constitution*, Bunker Hill, and 15 State Street, across from the Old State House. From that site, rangers lead 90-minute tours (2 P.M. Mon.–Fri., 10 A.M., 2 P.M., and 3 P.M. Sat.–Sun. mid-Apr.–mid-June; 10 A.M., 2 P.M., and 3 P.M. daily mid-June–Aug.) that take in five sites along the Freedom Trail. The rangers are not quite as entertaining as the costumed actors from the Freedom Trail Foundation, but their tours have the additional appeal of being free.

Boston Common

The Common began its life as a sheep and cow pasture in 1634, just a few years after the city itself was founded. By Puritan law, it was

pews of the church where they first thundered their speeches that brings alive the true passion of the American Revolution. In fact, the days leading up to the War for Independence were less like a noble war for freedom and more like a running mob insurrection. The few passionate men and women who worked to rile up a reluctant populace are very accessible, and it's easy to get drawn into their stories—both those you know and those you don't.

In the 1960s, Boston made it easier to trace the history of the Revolution by connecting 16 historical attractions in downtown Boston with a red line, alternately painted on the sidewalk and embedded in it with a double line of brick. From Boston Common to the Bunker Hill Monument, the trail stretches for two and a half miles, with each site designated by a bronze medallion in the pavement. Visitors can walk the line themselves or hook up with a 90-minute guided tour offered by the **Freedom Trail Foundation** (Boston Common Visitor Information Center, 148 Tremont St., 617/357-8300, www.thefreedomtrail.org,

CHEERS!

© MICHAEL BLANDING

A familiar sign marks Cheers' Faneuil Hall location.

Beware the imposters found in corners all over town: There's only one Boston bar that inspired the hit sitcom **Cheers,** and it's located on Beacon Street (#84, 617/227-0150, www.cheersboston.com, 11 A.M.-10 P.M. or midnight depending on business). For years the bar/restaurant was called The Bull & Finch Pub (as it had been since it first opened), but recently changed its name to Cheers Beacon Hill – one presumes to establish itself as the undisputable, original basis for the show. While the exterior of the bar was used in the show's opening, the interior is almost completely different from the show's set. So while visitors shouldn't come expecting to see Sam or Woody mixing up martinis, they can fully expect to find "Sam's Starters" and "Woody's Garden Goodies" on the menu. That may not be quite as funny, but they certainly can be tasty – just ask the regulars on the other side of the bar. If it's the *feeling* of *Cheers* you're after, then line up with the rest of the nostalgia-seekers at the restaurant's newer Faneuil Hall location (Quincy Market, Southwest Cafe, 617/227-0150, 11:30 A.M.-10 P.M. or midnight depending on business, Mon.-Thu.; opens 11 A.M. Fri.-Sun.), which has been designed to look like an exact replica of the set – right down to the picture of Geronimo hanging on the wall.

legal for any resident of the city to graze their livestock on the common land. Alas, that law was repealed in 1833, so you'll have to leave your cows at home. Within the boundaries of the park, however, are 44 acres of gently hilly grassland, occupied on sunny days by residents lying on the grass or playing Frisbee.

Several monuments within the park are attractions in and of themselves. The stunning fountain located just a few steps down from Park Street towards Boylston is named Brewer Fountain, and is a bronze replica of a fountain exhibited at the Paris World's Fair of 1855. The objects on its base depict sea gods and goddesses

© MICHAEL BLANDING

Francis Parkman Bandstand in Boston Common

Neptune, Amphitrite, Acis, and Galatea. Near the intersection of Park and Beacon Streets, the Frog Pond becomes winter's prime location for ice skating in the center of the city. On the Tremont Street side, at the intersection with Boylston, the Francis Parkman Bandstand is used as the site for summer concerts, political rallies, and Shakespeare in the Park.

Massachusetts State House

On a sunny day, the shimmering gold dome of the state's capitol building can be seen from miles around. The brick building beneath it is a tidy Federal structure (617/727-3676, www.sec. state.ma.us/trs, 10 A.M.–3:30 P.M. daily, free) designed by prominent Boston architect Charles Bulfinch and built in 1798. At the time, fifteen white columns were pulled up Beacon Street in a procession of 15 white horses, one for each state. The wooden dome on top was gilded in copper by Revolutionary renaissance man Paul Revere in 1802, and re-covered with 23-karat gold leaf in 1948. Two marble wings were added at the turn of the 20th century.

An impressive selection of statues graces the park side of the building. The equestrian statue in front of the main entrance depicts Joseph "Fighting Joe" Hooker, a Civil War general from Massachusetts who led the Army of the Potomac for all of six months. (There is no basis, however, to the urban myth that "hookers" are named after his troops, who were supposedly wont to visit brothels while on leave.) Other statues in front of the building are dedicated to 19th-century orator Daniel Webster and educator Horace Mann. In front of the wings are statues of two women martyrs: Anne Hutchinson, a freethinking Puritan who was banished to Rhode Island; and Mary Dyer, a prominent Quaker minister sadly hanged on Boston Common in 1660.

There isn't much to see inside the building, outside of more statues of various Massachusetts politicians. The most appealing item of interest is the "sacred Cod," a five-foot-long pinewood fish that hangs over the chamber of the state House of Representatives. Given to the state by a Boston merchant in 1784, it changes direction depending on which party is in control of the legislature. Free tours of the State House, lasting approximately 40 minutes, are offered daily; advanced reservations are required.

Robert Gould Shaw Memorial and the Black Heritage Trail

Across from the State House is the life-sized bronze bas-relief plaque of Colonel Robert Gould Shaw designed by New England sculptor Augustus Saint-Gaudens. Considered one of the best American sculptures of the 19th century, it depicts the commander of the first all-Black regiment to fight during the Civil War, marching out of Boston with his troops in March 1863. Two months later, Shaw and 271 of his men were killed during a suicide mission on Fort Wagner in South Carolina, galvanizing the country with the bravery of his Black soldiers. (Later, his story was immortalized in the Academy Award–winning 1989 film *Glory*.) The sculpture is a surprisingly realistic depiction of Shaw atop his horse, surrounded by soldiers carrying rifles, backpacks, and bedrolls. Above them is an angel with an olive branch, symbolizing peace, and poppies, symbolizing death.

The Shaw Memorial is the beginning of the Black Heritage Trail, a lesser-known path that traces the separate journey to freedom of Black Americans, nearly one hundred years after the first freedom trail. Plaques at historic houses en route detail the lives of abolitionists and orators who lived on the back side of Beacon Hill, where Boston's free Black community numbered more than a thousand by the turn of the 19th century. The trail ends at the African Meeting House, once headquarters of the New England Anti-Slavery Society and called the "Black Faneuil Hall" for the impassioned speeches by William Lloyd Garrison and other abolitionists heard within. The church now houses the **Museum of Afro-American History** (46 Joy Street, 617/720-2991 x14, www.afroammuseum.org, 10 A.M.–4 P.M. Mon.–Sat., $5 suggested donation), which has exhibits and films dedicated to the story of Boston's abolitionists. The trail is also part of the Boston **African-American National Historic Site** (617/742-5415, www.nps.gov/boaf), run by the National Park Service, which offers free tours on request.

Boston Athenaeum

The center of intellectual life during Boston's golden age in the early 19th century was this private library located near the State House, where scholars such as Ralph Waldo Emerson and Oliver Wendell Holmes gathered to debate the political and philosophical issues of the day. Today, docents offer tours of the renovated building (10 ½ Beacon St., 617/227-0270, www.bostonathenaeum.org, 8:30 A.M.–8 P.M. Mon. and Wed., 8:30 A.M.–5:30 P.M. Tues., Thu., and Fri. year-round; 9 A.M.–4 P.M. Sat. Sept. 12–May 22, free), including the study where Nathaniel Hawthorne reportedly saw the ghost of an old friend. Among the library's more unusual holdings is the private library of George Washington, and one of the world's largest collections of books about the Romany people (commonly known as gypsies). Tours are offered at 3 P.M. on Tuesdays and Thursdays and require reservations.

Park Street Church

The landmark church at the corner of Park and Tremont Streets is one of the most recognizable meeting places downtown. Dating from 1809, the church (1 Park St., 617/523-3383, www.parkstreet.org) touts itself as the location of the first Sunday School and first place where the song *America (My Country 'Tis of Thee)* was publicly sung. During the War of 1812, the church was known as "brimstone corner" for the gunpowder stored in the basement. Later, the brimstone came from the fiery speeches of its ministers, a tradition continued by its current evangelical congregation.

Granary Burying Ground

The bar across the street from this graveyard bills itself as the only place you can drink a Samuel Adams beer while looking out the window at the grave of Samuel Adams. Many of the leaders of the Sons of Liberty are buried in this prime piece of real estate amid the office buildings at Tremont and Park Streets. In addition to Adams, those with a final resting place here include Paul Revere, John Hancock, the victims of the Boston Massacre, and Ben Franklin's parents. (Despite the large Franklin monument, Ben's remains are in Philadelphia.) Also look out for the grave of the original nursery rhymer, Mary "Mother" Goose. The grave markers of the patriots all date from the 20th century—the originals were either stolen or "lost." However, many of the gravestones here date from the 17th century. Their weatherbeaten forms are in a classic "tombstone" shape, often with eerie winged death skulls at their tops.

King's Chapel

A smaller and more crowded burying ground is across the street next to Boston's original Anglican church (Tremont and School Streets, Boston, 617/523-1749 or 617/227-2155, www.kings-chapel.org, 1:30–4 P.M. Sun., 10 A.M.–4 P.M. Mon., Thurs., and Fri.–Sat.,

10 A.M.–11:15 A.M. and 1:30–4 P.M. Tues.–Wed. late May–early Sep.; 10 A.M.–4 P.M. Sat., 1:30–4 P.M. Sun. mid Sep.–late May, 10 A.M.–4 P.M. Fri. Sep. and May, $2 suggested donation), founded in 1686. (Needless to say, it wasn't a popular place in a community founded by Puritans who fled the Church of England.) The current stone church building was built in 1749 and features a bell cast by Paul Revere that is still rung before services. The adjoining graveyard is the oldest in Boston; as such, it contains the graves of some of the original colonists of Massachusetts, including governor John "City on A Hill" Winthrop, and Anne Prine, said to be the real Hester Prynne on whom Nathaniel Hawthorne based his book *The Scarlet Letter*. Along with them are several "B-list" patriots, such as William Dawes, the "other rider" who raised the alarm on the eve of the battles of Concord and Lexington.

DOWNTOWN CROSSING

Few places in Boston are more democratic than the neighborhood known as Downtown Crossing. Down Summer Street from the Park Street T stop, this is an almost entirely commercial district that has been mostly closed to car traffic. After school, teenagers congregate here to flirt and buy clothing and music at the many discount stores lining Washington Street. The bargains here aren't just for schoolkids, however. In-the-know Bostonians raid Filene's Basement, the original "bargain basement" clothing store, for last season's fashions at cut-rate prices.

Architecturally speaking, Downtown Crossing is strikingly uniform in its solid brick-and-granite office buildings, with lovingly detailed sculpted friezes, curlicued cornices, and grand engravings. That uniformity is due to the Great Fire of 1872, when a chance warehouse fire grew to a conflagration that leveled the neighborhood. Flush with money from the China trade, rich merchants rebuilt the neighborhood in a matter of only a few years. One of the buildings that survived the fire is the Old Corner Bookstore, at 3 School Street, which once hosted transcendentalist writers including Ralph Waldo Emerson, Henry David Thoreau, and Bronson Alcott as regular guests.

Old City Hall

Before Boston City Hall was moved to its current location at Government Center, a succession of three different city halls occupied a site on School Street between Tremont and Washington. The last building (45 School Street, 617/523-8678, www.oldcityhall.com), built at the end of the Civil War, is a perfectly preserved example of Second Empire style, with a wedding-cake layer of columns beneath a sloping mansard roof. (It has long been adapted for use as an office building.) In the courtyard is a statue of Benjamin Franklin, looking as if he popped right out of a history book, along with two whimsical statues that represent the mascots of the two political parties—a donkey for Democrats and an elephant for Republicans.

On the sidewalk in front of the building, be sure to note the plaque that designates the original location of the Boston Latin School, the first public school in America, which gave its name to the street and still exists in a new location in the Fenway. Among its graduates are Samuel Adams, Ben Franklin, Ralph Waldo Emerson, and Leonard Bernstein. The plaque itself is in the form of a hopscotch board, surrounded by the letters of the alphabet designated by their appropriate objects (apple, bird, cat…). Particularly Bostonian is the grasshopper representing G, which is copied from the weathervane on top of Faneuil Hall.

Old South Meeting House

The Boston Tea Party may have ended in the harbor, but it started at this brick church building with a grey-shingled tower (310 Washington St., 617/482-6439, www.oldsouthmeetinghouse.org, 10 A.M.–4 P.M. daily Nov.–Mar., 9:30 A.M.–5 P.M. daily Apr.–Oct., $5 adults, $4 students and seniors, $1 children 6–18, free children under 6) dating from 1729. Led by Samuel Adams, some 6,000 patriots gathered here on the night of December 16, 1773, flooding out into the street. After fiery

© MICHAEL BLANDING

Old South Meeting House

who were all members of the Old South's congregation.

Old State House

Before construction of the new state house on Beacon Hill, British and American governors alike used this small brick building (206 Washington Street, 617/720-1713, www.bostonhistory.org, 9 A.M.–6 P.M. daily Jul.–Aug., 9 A.M.–4 P.M. daily Jan., 9 A.M.–5 P.M. daily Feb.–Jun., Sep.–Dec., $7 adults, $6 seniors and students, $3 children 6–18, free children under 6) as the headquarters for the Massachusetts government. Now dwarfed by the office towers around it, the cupola atop the center of the building used to be the highest point in Boston. On one side of the building are replicas of the standing lion and unicorn that signified the crown of England (the originals were torn down during the Revolution), while on the other is a gold-covered eagle signifying the new United States. On the second floor of the building is the headquarters for the Bostonian Society, which runs a small museum full of artifacts including tea from the Boston Tea Party, weapons from the Battle of Bunker Hill, and clothing worn by John Hancock. It also exhibits a Boston Massacre "sound and light show."

Boston Massacre Site

In front of the Old State House, on a traffic circle in the busy intersection of Congress and State Streets, an unadorned circle of grey bricks marks the site of the Boston Massacre, where five colonists were killed by a British soldier in 1770. (The actual site is in the middle of the intersection, but, as guides are wont to tell tourists, don't visit it unless you want to fall victim to "another Boston massacre.") The first victim of the Revolution was arguably Christopher Snider, a 12-year-old boy shot by a British loyalist after a protest over the trade acts. Two weeks later, on March 5, 1770, a mob protesting Snider's death converged on the Old State House, throwing snowballs laced with stones and oyster shells at the soldiers, and later returning with bats and sticks. Soldiers answered by firing their rifles into the crowd,

speeches, Adams spoke the code words, "This meeting can do no more to save our country." Those words were a signal to certain members of the audience to don face paint and feathers and head down to Griffin's Wharf, where three ships stood loaded down with bins of loose tea. In all, $33,000 of tea was thrown into the harbor, setting the stage for the battles that followed. (As a postscript, when Queen Elizabeth II visited Boston for the Bicentennial in 1976, the mayor of the city presented her with a check for $33,000 to cover the cost of the tea—not counting interest.)

The Old South still serves as a meeting place of sorts, offering lectures and classical music concerts of a less revolutionary nature. It is also home to a museum that traces the events surrounding the tea party through an "audio exhibit" that features actors reading the words of Sam Adams and the other patriots along with sound effects to re-create the time period. A separate multimedia exhibit dubbed "Voices of Protests" focuses on Adams, statesman Ben Franklin, and abolitionist Phyllis Wheatley,

A circle of bricks in front of the Old State House marks the Boston Massacre site.

and when the smoke cleared, five colonists lay dead, including Crispus Attucks, a former slave and whaler of Black and Native American descent. The soldiers were later exonerated of the charges on the basis of self-defense. But the image of the "massacre" that stuck in the minds of the people was an engraving made by Paul Revere, which shows the soldiers firing unprovoked into a defenseless crowd.

GOVERNMENT CENTER

Further up Tremont Street, the neighborhood around Boston City Hall was once known as Scollay Square, an area synonymous with debauchery for its mix of bars and burlesque clubs that entertained soldiers returning from World War II. All good things come to an end, however, and Scollay Square met its end in the 1960s, when the entire area was razed for a massive urban redevelopment scheme to create a new center of city government. The result is generally agreed to be a disaster, a windswept plaza of concrete, with the hulking modernist form of Boston City Hall shipwrecked in the center. In recent years, city planners have attempted to improve the area with the addition of a new T station and a covered arcade, but the area is what it is: ugly and depressing.

A considerably more pleasing example of urban renewal is down behind city hall in the bustling center of Quincy Marketplace. Once a derelict collection of old fish warehouses behind the historic Faneuil Hall, the area was transformed in the 1970s to become a pedestrian paradise along the lines of London's Covent Garden. The gamble was wildly successful, and the marketplace is still crowded at all times of the day and night with shoppers poking into the many upscale chains or watching the street performers who juggle and do magic tricks on the flagstone plaza in front of the main market building. That building is also home to an immense "food corridor" that seems to stretch forever with stalls on either side offering clam chowder, pizza, rotisserie chicken, and anything else your hunger pangs might ask for. Many of the stalls are branches of restaurants elsewhere in the city, making the quality of the offerings better than most food courts.

Faneuil Hall

Spelling the name of this landmark public building is a rite of passage for Boston schoolchildren. Named after one of the wealthiest of Boston's merchants, Peter Faneuil, the building (Congress St, 617/523-1300, www.cityofboston.gov/freedomtrail/faneuilhall.asp, 9 A.M.–5 P.M. daily, free) demonstrated Yankee thrift and mercantile ingenuity by serving two purposes. Downstairs was a public food market, full of stalls for meat, vegetables, milk, and cheese, while upstairs was a meeting hall for discussion of pressing local issues. When the hall was built in 1742, the most pressing issues were taxation on goods by the British government, and Faneuil Hall became the main meeting space for protests and discussions by the Sons of Liberty—earning it the nickname the "Cradle of Liberty." After it was expanded in size by architect Charles Bullfinch, the hall was also the main venue for talks by William

Lloyd Garrison, Frederick Douglass, and other anti-slavery activists. Public talks and citywide meetings are still held in the upstairs hall, lent more gravitas by the huge mural of Daniel Webster arguing against slavery that overlooks the stage. During the day, historic talks are given by National Park rangers every half hour. Downstairs, the stalls still exist, even though they have long since stopped selling food products; most are now the venue for souvenirs and other made-in-Boston goods.

NORTH END

The scent of marinara sauce wafts inescapably over the neighborhood that juts out into the harbor on the north side of the city. Congested and lively, the North End is Boston's answer to New York's Little Italy, with dozens of Italian restaurants, grocers, pastry shops, and small businesses such as tailors and cobblers lining every inch of storefront space. The area is the oldest part of the city, and claims as its own a number of Puritans and revolutionaries, including Paul Revere, whose house still stands.

At the turn of the 20th century, however, it became the firm territory of a new wave of Italian immigrants who made the neighborhood over in the image of Napoli. Even while it has slowly gentrified over the years, it has retained its ethnic identity, with third- and fourth-generation Italians choosing to age in place or returning on Italian Feast Days, which usually occur on Sundays during the summer and feature churches and community clubs attempting to outdo each other with lavish parades full of floats, bunting, and sizzling Italian sausage.

To the east of the North End proper is North Station, one of the main transit hubs of the city. Built partially over the station, the TD Banknorth Garden is the official home of the Boston Celtics and Bruins—though many still lament the passing of the original Boston Garden that was located next door, the site of the many championship banners that Boston brought home with the help of a few Larry Bird three-pointers.

Paul Revere House

Every town in New England, it seems, claims

© MICHAEL BLANDING

Paul Revere House

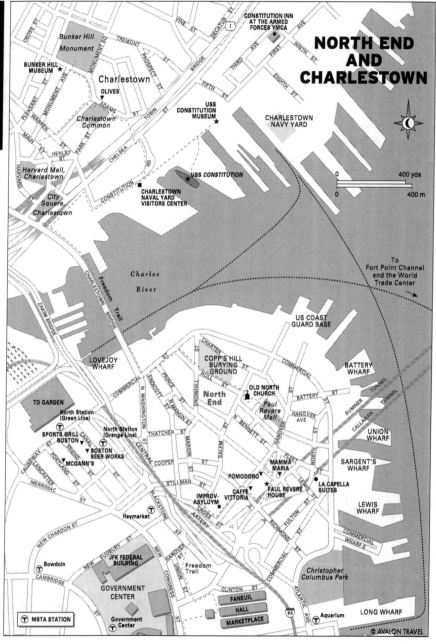

NORTH END AND CHARLESTOWN

CONSTITUTION INN
AT THE ARMED
FORCES YMCA

Bunker Hill
Monument

BUNKER HILL
MUSEUM ★

Charlestown

OLIVES

USS CONSTITUTION
MUSEUM ★

CHARLESTOWN
NAVY YARD

Charlestown
Common

Harvard Mall,
Charlestown

City
Square,
Charlestown

★★ USS CONSTITUTION

CHARLESTOWN
NAVAL YARD
VISITORS CENTER

0   400 yds
0   400 m

Charles
River

To
Fort Point Channel
and the World
Trade Center

US COAST
GUARD BASE

COPP'S HILL
BURYING
GROUND

BATTERY
WHARF

LOVEJOY
WHARF

OLD NORTH
CHURCH

North
End

Paul
Revere
Mall

TD GARDEN

North Station
(Green Line)

SPORTS GRILL
BOSTON ▼

BOSTON
BEER WORKS

MCGANN'S ▼

North Station
(Orange Line)

UNION
WHARF

SARGENT'S
WHARF

MAMMA
MARIA

POMODORO ▼

LA CAPELLA
SUITES

LEWIS
WHARF

IMPROV-
ASYLUYM

CAFFÈ
VITTORIA

★ PAUL REVERE
HOUSE

Haymarket

COMMERCIAL
WHARF E

NEW CHARDON ST

Bowdoin

CAMBRIDGE

JFK FEDERAL
BUILDING

Freedom
Trail

Christopher
Columbus Park

GOVERNMENT
CENTER

Government
Center

CLINTON   ST

FANEUIL

HALL

MARKETPLACE

Aquarium

LONG WHARF

MBTA STATION

© AVALON TRAVEL

ZAKIM BRIDGE

Despite the construction debacle Boston's "Big Dig" has become, the project does have one soaring success story: the stunning double-wishbone towers of the Leonard P. Zakim Bunker Hill Bridge. Raised in 2002 to connect Boston to Charlestown, the bridge provides a beautiful backdrop to the North End, and serves as a bona fide engineering marvel as well. Building it in a tangle of highways that was notoriously difficult to bridge, engineers solved the conundrum by running eight lanes between the center of the wishbones, and cantilevering an extra two lanes on one side. The resulting asymmetrical design is the widest cable-stayed bridge in the world, and has quickly formed a stirring of attachment and pride akin to what San Franciscans feel for the Golden Gate. Its asymmetrical mouthful of a name, however, is a result of classic Boston infighting. Liberal Bostonians wanted to name the bridge after Jewish civil rights activist Lenny Zakim, while working-class conservatives from Charlestown felt strongly about honoring the nearby site of the Battle of Bunker Hill. In the end, lawmakers split the difference by combining the two monikers with the result that, depending on which side of the bridge you are standing on, you may hear it called by a different name. So much for bridging over divides!

Zakim Bridge

© MICHAEL BLANDING

---

to have a bell cast by Paul Revere in its belfry, if not a genuine piece of Revere silver in its historical museum. The patriot who made the famous midnight ride to warn the suburbs of the British march, however, was virtually unknown until before the Civil War, when Massachusetts poet Henry Wadsworth Longfellow made him the subject of a poem to stir up passion for the Union cause. Contrary to the poem (and many simplified history books), however, Revere never made it to Concord to warn the minutemen of the British approach; he was arrested by the British after warning John Hancock and Sam Adams in Lexington. Nor did he shout "The British Are Coming!" from his horse— probably a whisper of "The regulars are out tonight" was more like it. And he wasn't the only

rider out that night. At least two other riders, William Dawes and Dr. Samuel Prescott, were also out warning the colonists.

Whatever the details of Revere's famous night, however, he was by any measure a veritable Leonardo da Vinci of the colonial world, who won acclaim as a silversmith, coppersmith, bell ringer, dentist, and father of 16 children. Many of them were raised in the house that still bears his name (19 North Square, 617/523-2338, www.paulreverehouse.org, 9:30 A.M.–4:15 P.M. daily Nov.–mid-Apr., closed Mon. Jan.–Mar.; 9:30 A.M.–5:15 P.M. daily mid-Apr.–Oct., $3.50 adults, $3 seniors and students, $1 children 5–17, free children under 5), a typical example of 17th-century architecture and the oldest house still standing in the city.

© MICHAEL BLANDING

"One if by land, two if by sea" was the signal that went out from the Old North Church.

If you are looking for an exhibit of Revere silver, you are better off going to the Museum of Fine Arts; the house has only a small collection of artifacts relating to the patriot, contained in a few poorly labeled cabinets (though a case full of Revere-inspired tchochkes, including a whisky bottle in the shape of the patriot on his horse, is amusing).

The house is more interesting as a window into the living quarters and implements of a typical family in colonial urban America. Interpretive guides are on hand to lead guests up creaking narrow staircases into the surprisingly snug quarters where Revere and his wife slept and entertained guests. On Saturday afternoons, artisans demonstrate such arts as silversmithing and gilding in the outdoor courtyards.

Old North Church
Situated right in the middle of the oldest neighborhood in town, the Old North Church was one of the most recognizable landmarks in colonial Boston. So it was the perfect vantage

point if, say, one wanted to hang a lantern to warn that the British were on the march. As a pre-teen, Paul Revere was a bell ringer in the church. Thus, on the night of April 18, 1773, he was able to convince the church's sexton to climb into the belfry and hold two lanterns up for under a minute, a signal to the patriots that the British were moving by sea across to Charlestown, thence to march on to Concord and Lexington. The sexton, Robert Newman, was the unsung hero in the story—arrested by the British the following morning, he was held in prison until freed by General George Washington in an exchange. Inside the church, reproductions of colonial flags hang from the ceiling, and every half hour a guide tells Revere's story from the pulpit.

Between Old North and Hanover Street is the Paul Revere Mall, with a huge bronze statue of Revere upon his horse by local master sculptor Cyrus Dallin, usually lorded over by wizened Italian women feeding the pigeons. Look for the plaques along the wall that honor other patriots who grew up in the North End and reach back into history to tell the stories of some of the original Puritan settlers of the neighborhood, including theologians Cotton and Increase Mather, governor John Winthrop, and Ann Pollard, the first White woman to disembark onto Boston soil.

CHARLESTOWN
The original settlement of the Puritans was named after the king they left behind. A swampy mess of a place without much access to fresh water, Charlestown was eventually abandoned when John Winthrop and the gang were invited over to the Shawmut Peninsula to found Boston. Charlestown, which is incorporated as a neighborhood of Boston, grew to be an important port in the 18th century. Then tragedy struck during the Revolutionary War, when the British fired cannonballs filled with incendiary oil across the channel and burned the city to the ground as a retaliation for their losses at the Battle of Bunker Hill.

The city was rebuilt in the early 19th century, about the same time as the brick mansions and brownstones were going up on Beacon Hill, and it shares a similar colonial feel with that neighborhood. Gas lamps, black shutters, and window boxes give an antique feel to much of the neighborhood, especially in the area around Monument Square, at the top of the hill surrounding the Bunker Hill Monument. In the 20th century, the area became home to an Irish working-class community known by the rest of the city as "townies." They still come out to celebrate on Bunker Hill Day, a special neighborhood holiday to commemorate the battle. Charlestown has changed in recent decades, as young professionals priced out of Beacon Hill and the Back Bay in the 1980s descended upon its quaint streets and carved its townhouses into thousands of luxury condos. Boutiques and gourmet restaurants sprang up to serve the new crowd, giving the neighborhood a feel similar to Georgetown in Washington, D.C. The isolation of the enclave gives its residents, whether recent arrivals or townies, a sense of community few other neighborhoods match.

Bunker Hill Monument

High on the top of Breed's Hill stands a 221-foot granite obelisk (Monument Square, Charlestown, 617/242-5641, www.nps. gov/bost/historyculture/bhm.htm, exhibit: 9 A.M.–5 P.M. daily, monument: 9 A.M.–4:30 P.M. daily, free) to mark the misnamed first major battle of the Revolutionary War. In it, the patriots—while defeated—inflicted such high casualties upon the British Army that thousands rushed to the colonist cause to begin a protracted siege of Boston. The monument itself has some 300 steps inside that lead up to one of the best views of the Boston Harbor and the city skyline.

Across the street, the impressive new **Bunker Hill Museum** (43 Monument Square, 9 A.M.–5 P.M. daily, free) opened in 2007 with two floors of exhibits about the battle. In addition to artifacts such as a British cannonball, the museum features two dioramas with miniature figurines that perpetually fight the battle over again with the help of a sound and light display. The highlight, however, is the beautifully painted "cyclorama" on the second floor, depicting the battle in breathtaking 360 degrees.

USS Constitution

The oldest commissioned ship in the American Navy, the USS *Constitution* has earned many nicknames over the years, including "Old Ironsides" and the "Eagle of the Sea." Originally designated as simply "Frigate D," the frigate was built in Portsmouth Navy Yard in Maine, named by President Washington, and launched in 1798. In 17 years of active duty, it racked up a battle record as celebrated as any ship of its time, defeating the heavier British ships *Guerrière* and *Java* during the War of 1812, and leading a blockade of Tripoli during the War of the Barbary Coast.

The ship is now docked at Charlestown Navy Yard, where navy sailors wearing funny hats give tours every half hour. Fans of *Master and Commander* will be thrilled to stand behind a long gun cannon on the gun deck or sit at the gambrel table in the captain's quarters. Even casual visitors will snicker at the toilet seats located on the aptly named poop deck. Some of the stones in the bilge are the originals placed there for ballast more than 200 years ago. The last time the *Constitution* detached from a tugboat to sail freely under its own power was in 1997 during its 200th anniversary; the ship, however, is towed out into Boston Harbor and turned around with a 21-gun salute every year on July 4. (Members of the public can sign up on the ship's website for a lottery to board the ship for these cruises.)

To get to the ship, visitors first pass through the newly renovated **Charlestown Naval Yard Visitors Center** (Charlestown Navy Yard, Building 5, 617/242-5601, www.nps.gov/bost/historyculture/cny.htm, 9 A.M–5 P.M. daily), which features a 10-minute video on the history of the Yard, along with ropes, chains, uniforms, and other artifacts. Near the ship is a much-larger **USS Constitution Museum** (Charlestown Navy Yard, 617/426-1812, www.ussconstitutionmuseum.org, 10 A.M.–5 P.M.

daily Nov.–Apr., 9 A.M.–6 P.M. daily May–Oct., free) that displays swords, pistols, and cannonballs captured from the *Constitution*'s various engagements, along with a giant-sized model of the ship under full sail. Several short films give more information about the ship and its history. Kids love the upper floor of the museum, which features a cannon they can swab, wad, and "fire" against an enemy ship; and a rudimentary video game in which they can engage the HMS *Java* while learning the basic principles of battle under sail.

FINANCIAL DISTRICT

The financial engine of the city—and indeed the whole region of New England—can be found in a skyscraper forest that takes up just a few dozen blocks between downtown and the waterfront. While many of the banks and companies that once made their headquarters in Boston have left for other cities, the area is still anchored by the office buildings of powerhouses Fidelity Investments and State Street Bank. Most of the neighborhood's office towers were built during the second half of the 20th century, and reflect an eclectic (a better word might be random) mix of styles, some beautiful and some, well, not so much. The area is worth a ramble just to take in the variety—especially the older buildings sprinkled into the mix. The Richardson-Romanesque Flour & Grain Exchange Building at 177 Milk Street, for example, looks like the fanciful castle of a feudal lord, while the Batterymarch Building at 89 Broad Street employs 30 different colors of bricks in its art deco facade. At the center of the neighborhood is Post Office Square, an oasis of flowers and grass where businesspeople bring their bag lunches to enjoy a brief respite from the rat race.

Custom House Tower

Close to the waterfront is Boston's oldest "skyscraper," the 500-foot tall Custom House Tower (3 McKinley Square, 617/310-6300, www.marriott.com, 7 A.M.–11 P.M.). Built in 1915, the distinctive Beaux Arts tower features a 22-foot-wide clock, and a pair of peregrine

Custom House Tower

© MICHAEL BLANDING

falcons who nest at its top during the summer. You can try to catch a glimpse of them, along with knockout views of the harbor, on the 26th-floor observation platform (tours 10 A.M. and 4 P.M. Mon.–Thu., 4 P.M. Fri., year-round, free). Inside the tower is also a small museum with a few paintings and American historical artifacts on loan from the Peabody Essex Museum in Salem. The building was recently converted into one of Marriott's more interesting urban hotels.

◖ New England Aquarium

Fish have always loomed large in Boston, from their role as the foundation of the city's early maritime economy, to their position grilled or buttered at the top of most restaurant menus. So it is only fitting that the city should also have a world-class aquarium (Central Wharf, 617/973-5200, www.neaq.org, 9 A.M.–5 P.M. Mon.–Fri., 9 A.M.–6 P.M. Sat.–Sun., $21 adults, $13 children 3–11, free children under 3, IMAX: 9:30 A.M.–9:30 P.M. daily, $10 adults, $8 children 3–11, whale watch: $40 adults, $32 children 11 and under) that pays homage to the wonders of the sea.

The literal centerpiece of the massive waterfront museum is a 200,000-gallon tank full of sharks, sea turtles, and giant ocean fish that rises like a watery spinal column through the center of the building. A long walkway spirals around the tank, giving viewers a chance to see sealife on all levels of the ocean, from the toothy pikes that float on the surface to the 45-year-old sea turtle, Myrtle, who often sleeps on the floor. Other crowd-pleasers are the harbor seals in the courtyard and the enormous open-air penguin pool, filled with three dozen rockhopper, little blue, and African penguins who fill the building with their raucous cries.

The aquarium is not just a museum, but also a research-and-rescue organization that finds stranded seals, dolphins, and other animals and nurses them back to health. You can see the aquarium's latest convalescents in a hospital ward on the second floor. The aquarium also ventures out into the harbor itself for whale watch trips, seeking out the humpbacks and right whales that make their way into Massachusetts Bay. The aquarium's exterior was renovated in the late 1990s, and the IMAX theater opened in 2001 along with a revitalized series of special exhibits. There is also an interactive children's center, where you can drop off the tykes for sea-related projects.

CHINATOWN

Like most major U.S. cities, Boston has a bustling Chinatown, where Asian immigrants shop at crowded markets with the pungent smells of strange roots and dried fish, while restaurants with live-seafood tanks draw hungry tourists and residents from other neighborhoods. Also in the mix of a bewildering array of storefronts are shops selling discount cookware and electronic items, shiny red facades of Buddhist temples, and banks and businesses with Cantonese characters over the doorways. The main drag of the neighborhood is Beach Street, the site every February of a colorful and loud Chinese New Year parade. At the foot of the street, the Chinatown Gate signals the

official entrance to passing motorists. In recent years, Southeast Asian immigrants—particularly those from Vietnam—have outnumbered the ethnic Chinese, so that the corner cafés are more likely to be serving *pho* than chow mein.

The neighborhood is also one of the few in the city that stays up into the early morning hours. Top-name chefs often meet over sushi or egg rolls at back-alley restaurants long after their own eateries have closed. Restaurants in Chinatown have long had the reputation for being the only place that you can still get served alcohol after 2 A.M., the ridiculously early closing time of most bars in Boston. Night owls in the know ask for "cold tea" to get a discreet mug of beer—though you didn't hear that from us. For years, the residents of Chinatown have also had to fight off the bad reputation of an encroaching red-light district once known as the Combat Zone. Nowadays, the "zone" has all but disappeared, with only a pair of strip clubs and a few tired-looking XXX bookstores remaining on Washington Street.

THEATER DISTRICT

Boston has always been a great town for theater. Back in the golden days of the Great White Way, shows would debut in Boston weeks before they went on to Broadway, often tweaking the performances based on the reviews of the literate local critics and audiences of the day. The tradition has been revived somewhat in the last decade, with many of the old classical theaters getting facelifts and new shows trying their luck in Beantown before retooling for New York. When they do, they come to one of the grand theaters in this neighborhood, an extension of Tremont Street sandwiched between the Back Bay and the South End. During the day, the area can be one of the seedier parts of town, where suspicious characters linger around the doorways of convenience stores and dive bars. Like much of downtown, however, the area has gotten spiffier in the last decade, especially since Emerson College moved some of its classrooms in to imbue it with a lively dose of student energy.

On weekend nights, however, all the glamour of the neighborhood's heyday returns, with the corner of Tremont and Stuart Streets becoming a morass of cabs and limousines disgorging young lovelies in strapless black dresses and men with camel-hair overcoats into the brightly lit mouths of the Wang, Colonial, Wilbur, and Schubert. After the performances let out, the restaurants and nightclubs along the street raise their own curtains to keep the show going.

BACK BAY

The most fashionable neighborhood of Boston, the Back Bay is also one of the most easily navigated. Grand boulevards in the style of Paris are lined with brownstones and large Victorian-style apartment buildings, linked by short side streets that are ordered alphabetically (Arlington, Berkeley, Clarendon…). Ironically, given how swanky the neighborhood has become, the area used to be one big disease-spreading swamp—it's no accident that

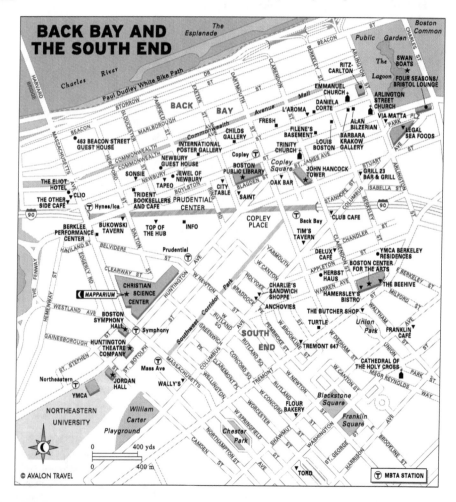

BACK BAY AND THE SOUTH END

© AVALON TRAVEL

the neighborhood's main drag, Boylston Street, is named after a doctor. In the days when Boston used to be a peninsula, the Back Bay was literally a bay in the Charles River, where refuse would wash up with the tides, and men and boys—including a young Ben Franklin—would fish from shore. As the city expanded in the 1800s, the earth from Beacon Hill and other high ground was used for landfill to fill up the bay, and a new neighborhood was born, quickly filling with larger and more impressive houses built for the glitterati of the day.

The heart of the neighborhood, if not the city, is Copley Square. The large plaza, which is half brick and half grassy lawn, is named after the Victorian-era painter John Singleton Copley, and is often the site of classical music concerts in the spring and summer. A statue of the painter, complete with pantaloons and artist's palette, stands at the southwest corner of the square. From Copley, each of the boulevards of the neighborhood has its own character. Boylston Street is the main commercial drag, lined with towering office buildings,

along with convenience stores and coffee shops. Newbury Street, by contrast, is the ritziest street in town, where you are more likely to hear Spanish or Italian than a Boston accent. Along the street are branches of national chains from Armani to Zegna, along with a few local clothing boutiques and jewelry designers.

Next in line, Commonwealth Avenue is a boulevard in grand Parisian style, with a large pedestrian mall lined with statues running down the center, and trees festooned with lights in the winter. Quaint Marlboro Street has a purely residential feel, enhanced by the legions of flowering dogwoods that spawn floating petals in the springtime. Lastly, Beacon Street lines the river with more giant brownstones, along with the parkland of the Esplanade.

Public Garden

In contrast to the Boston Common, which has an open, park-like feel, the Public Garden is an intimate outdoor space, full of leafy trees and flower beds. Built on landfill in the 19th century, the garden was America's first public

© MICHAEL BLANDING

Public Garden

botanical garden, envisioned by its creators as a respite from urban life. A stroll through the park at any hour makes an ordinary day instantly romantic, at no time more than sunset, when the trees cast mysterious shadows over the walkways. The centerpiece of the garden is a lagoon, which is crossed by a fairy-tale bridge and surrounded by willow trees that trail their branch tips in the water. Tracing lazy circles around the lagoon during the day are Boston's famous **swan boats** (617/522-1966, www. swanboats.com, 10 A.M.–4 P.M. Apr.–mid-Jun., 10 A.M.–5 P.M. late Jun.–Labor Day, 12–4 P.M. Mon.–Fri., 10 A.M.–4 P.M. Sat.–Sun. $2.75 adults, $2 seniors, $1.25 children 2–15), a flotilla of six large paddleboats with large white cygnets at the stern. The boats are a mandatory attraction if you are in Boston with children (even if you have to borrow some). Children are also big fans of the nearby bronze statues of Mrs. Mallard and her seven little ducklings. The statues pay homage to the children's book *Make Way for Ducklings*, which was partially set in the Public Garden.

Arlington Street Church

Located on the corner of Boylston and Arlington Streets, Arlington Street Church is where the sect of Christianity known as Unitarianism reached its full flower. (In fact, it was once known as the "Boston religion," based on its association with the social and political elite of the time.) Among other social causes, Unitarianism threw its weight early on behind the abolitionist movement, led by preachers Theodore Parker and William Ellery Channing, who has a statue dedicated to him across the street from the church. The sect, now known as Unitarian Universalism, still has its headquarters in Boston on Beacon Hill, and was recently one of the strongest religious voices supporting gay marriage. (Arlington Street Church itself has for a long time had an openly lesbian minister.)

Inside the church, the highlight is a collection of Tiffany stained-glass windows. Installed over thirty years at the beginning of the 20th century, the windows are subtly breathtaking, with light from outside filtering through multiple layers of opalescent glass and skin tones so real they might as well be warm to the touch.

Trinity Church

In the heart of Copley Square stands the undisputed masterpiece of architect H. H. Richardson, one of the most-photographed buildings in Boston. Richardson cultivated a bold style, which after his success with Trinity became all the rage in the 1870s and 1880s. Called "Richardson Romanesque" in honor of its creator, the style featured massive blocks of stone, often worked in a contrasting "checkerboard" pattern, along with sweeping Romanesque arches and towers. The inside of the Presbyterian church (206 Clarendon St., 617/536-0944, www.trinitychurchboston.org, 9 A.M.–6 P.M. Tues.–Sat., 7 A.M.–7 P.M. Sun., $6 for tours) is calculated to impress, with a vaulted ceiling and a huge carved wooden pulpit in front of the altar. Classical music concerts are regularly offered inside the church,

Trinity Church, reflected in the windows of the John Hancock Tower

© MICHAEL BLANDING

especially around the holidays, and tours of the church are led several times a day from the bookshop inside.

John Hancock Tower

When it was first proposed in the 1970s, the 790-foot Hancock Tower was met with fierce resistance by residents who feared it would wreck the historic ambience of Copley Square. In a stroke of genius, architect I. M. Pei covered the outside of the building with reflective glass, thereby enhancing rather than overshadowing the architectural beauty of Trinity Church, the Boston Public Library, and other nearby buildings. Not everything ended happily, however—due to a design flaw, many of the 10,344 panes of glass began falling out and shattering on the sidewalk below before the building was completed. Pei later corrected the technique for hanging the glass (which he also used on the pyramid for the Louvre) and the building is now one of the most striking in the city skyline. The observation deck on the 60th floor was closed to the public due to security

concerns after 2001, and is only opened for special events.

Nearby, the much smaller "old" John Hancock building features a beacon on top that changes color depending on the weather forecast. Many older Bostonians can still recite the rhyme that cracks the code: "Steady blue, clear view / Flashing blue, clouds due / Steady red, rain ahead / Flashing red, snow instead." During summer and fall, flashing red means the Red Sox game is cancelled (though snow isn't out of the question at that time of year either).

Boston Public Library

Added to Boston's long list of firsts in 1848 was the nation's first municipal public library. The library (700 Boylston St., 617/536-5400, www.bpl.org, 9 A.M.–9 P.M. Mon.–Thurs., 9 A.M.–5 P.M. Fri.–Sat., closed Sun., free), which fills two city blocks on the south side of Copley Square, consists of two buildings. The original, designed by Charles McKim and opened in 1895, is now the research library,

© MICHAEL BLANDING

Boston Public Library

with a more modern building next door holding the circulating collection. Aside from its collection of hundreds of thousands of books, magazines, and videos, the library is full of art and architectural flourishes that make the building as much of an attraction as its contents. The outside exterior is built on pleasing classical proportions and covered with names of great thinkers down through the ages; twin female statues of Art and Science keep guard outside. One of the best-kept secrets of the city is the library's central courtyard, an Italianate plaza accented by a fountain that makes a peaceful asylum from the busy streets around.

Inside the McKim Building, you can feel smarter just by stepping into the impressive Bates Reading Room, a 200-foot-long testament to scholarship, with a 50-foot-high barrel ceiling, high arched windows facing Copley Square, and long tables full of scholars sitting at green banker's lamps and thinking great thoughts. Those in need of further inspiration can step into the 80-foot-long Sargent Gallery, which features painter John Singer Sargent's fantastical mural sequence "Triumph of Religion," a sensual, often tempestuous journey through the gods, goddesses, and prophets of the ancient world. Other artistic works in the library are a mural sequence dedicated to the story of the search for the Holy Grail by American artist Edwin Austin Abbey, and a painting of George Washington at Dorchester Heights by Emanuel Gottlieb Leutze (who also did the famous painting of Washington crossing the Delaware). Free hour-long tours of the library's art and architecture are offered at various times daily; call for times.

SOUTH END

As the city of Boston expanded outwards from Beacon Hill and the North End, the next logical place to populate was the southern end of the Shawmut Peninsula. In the late 19th century, then, the South End quickly became *the* place to see and be seen, and rich merchants and ship captains built large brownstones on its waffle-iron layout of streets. Literally made of large brown stones, these homes were distinguished from the smaller brick buildings on Beacon Hill by their larger rooms and high ceilings, frequently with tall stairways leading up to the entrance door on the second floor (an assurance against flooding). Nearly as quickly as they colonized it, however, the fickle abandoned the South End in favor of the Back Bay, which was newly reclaimed from landfill in the river and built on an even grander scale than its neighbor.

For more than 100 years, the neighborhood was a melting pot of various immigrant groups who occupied the buildings left behind by the bourgeoisie, and it achieved a reputation for being a rough-and-tumble area. That reputation is hard to imagine now as the neighborhood reaches the height of a long, slow gentrification that began in the 1970s when it was rediscovered, primarily by artists and middle-class gay men and lesbian women. The neighborhood is still the center of Boston's GLBT population, and it's not unusual to see rainbow flags proudly fluttering from the upper stories of brownstones. The neighborhood also has a pleasing mix of residential and commercial uses, with the busiest streets of Tremont and Columbus lined with intimate (and expensive) neighborhood restaurants and storefronts occupied by boutiques selling $100 T-shirts and cutting-edge alternative fashion.

In the late 1990s, the South End expanded even farther southward past its historical boundary of Washington Street to create a brand-new neighborhood cheekily called SoWa (South of Washington). All of the available land in one of downtown's last frontiers has quickly been snatched up by modern loft apartment buildings that give the street an in-the-moment vibe. The area appeals to a certain intersection of art and commerce, with some of the city's edgier galleries cheek-by-jowl with its hotter new restaurants. Thus far, however, it has retained a certain grittiness that has forestalled its complete gentrification.

Boston Symphony Hall

The acoustics in this elegant concert hall are generally recognized as among the top three in the world (only Vienna and Amsterdam can compare). The home of both the Boston Symphony Orchestra and the Boston Pops, the hall (301 Massachusetts Ave., 617/638-9390, www.bostonsymphonyhall.org) was built in 1900 with a minimum of ornamentation. For many Bostonians, it's an annual holiday rite to see a performance of Handel's *Messiah* utilizing the impressive Aeolian Skinner organ behind the stage. Free tours of the hall, which include an explanation of its legendary acoustics, are offered every Wednesday at 4 P.M. and the second Saturday of the month at 2 P.M., from October to early December and early January to mid-June.

Christian Science Center

The towering dome of the "mother church" is the centerpiece of the sprawling headquarters for the worldwide religion of Christian Science. Founded in 1879 by Mary Baker Eddy, the religion is best known for its practice of "faith healing" that forbids its practitioners to take medicine for illnesses. Eddy, however, was once a larger-than-life figure in American culture who was a leader of the early women's movement and a pioneering publisher. Visitors can learn more about Eddy's life at the eclectic **Mary Baker Eddy Library** (200 Massachusetts Ave., 617/450-7000, www.marybakereddylibrary.org, 10 A.M.–4 P.M. Tues.–Sun., $6 adults, $4 seniors, students, and youth 6–17, free children under 6). A series of multimedia exhibits encourages visitors to develop their own life philosophies while at the same time tracing the evolution of its matriarch's ideas with refreshingly little proselytizing. Another exhibit within the museum literally provides a window into the newsroom of the *Christian Science Monitor,* which has its headquarters in the complex.

◀ Mapparium

Within the Christian Science Center, one hidden gem deserves special mention. The Mapparium (200 Massachusetts Ave., 617/450-7000, www.marybakereddylibrary.org, 10 A.M.–4 P.M. Tues.–Sun., $6 adults, $4

seniors, students, and youth 6–17, free children under 6) is like nowhere else on the world—maybe because it's literally inside of it. Visitors are ushered along a bridge into a 30-foot-diameter globe with the countries of the world (circa 1935) displayed in vibrant stained glass around the walls. For map geeks, it would be possible to spend an hour tracing the outlines of countries and continents, reflecting on their changes over the years. Every twenty minutes, a seven-minute light show explores the spread of ideas around the globe through the voices of Nelson Mandela, Eleanor Roosevelt, and other seminal thinkers.

Cathedral of the Holy Cross

At the turn of the 19th century, the famine Irish spent nine years constructing New England's largest Catholic church. The cruciform neo-Gothic edifice (1400 Washington St., 617/542-5682, www.angelfire.com/ma4/cathedral/home.html) rivals the largest in Europe. The city's Yankee forefathers, of course, promptly hid it behind the screaming tracks of an elevated railway, which drowned out homilies for almost 90 years. Now not only are the tracks gone, but also lights have been added to illuminate the facade. The seat of the Archdiocese of Boston, the cathedral on Washington Street features rare Munich stained glass and a (supposed) relic of the true cross in the base of a crucifix. For years, eleven o'clock Sunday Mass was said by Bernard Cardinal Law, who stepped down in disgrace in 2003 after a prolonged scandal of molesting children that had been covered up for years. Now mass is said by the new archbishop, Sean O'Malley, a former Capuchin friar who has rehabilitated the church in the eyes of many Bostonians. Occasional organ concerts featuring the reconstructed Hook & Hastings are the closest thing to divine transport in Boston.

FENWAY

Upon first glance, the area of the city known as the Fenway doesn't seem to offer much. A gritty network of streets lined with pubs and discount stores, the neighborhood has traditionally been

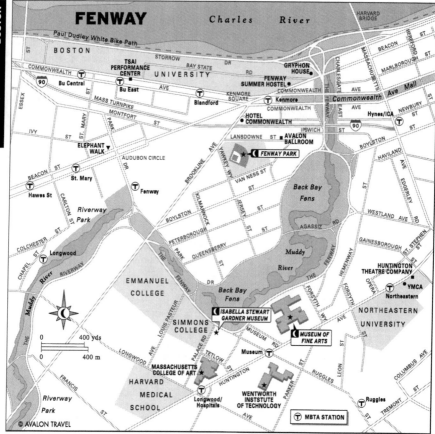

the stomping grounds for students of nearby Boston University. Scratch beneath the surface, however, and you'll find several of the city's premier cultural attractions, including the Museum of Fine Arts and the jewel box Isabella Stewart Gardner Museum. The neighborhood gets its name from the Back Bay Fens, a winding, swampy greensward that serves as the drainage channel for the city. Today, The Fens is a rambling parkland, lined with ball fields and community gardens, including the hidden Kelleher Rose Garden, a dreamy garden full of vine-covered trellises and over 100 varieties of roses. The center of the neighborhood

is Kenmore Square, a lively crossroads of student bars, discount stores, and burrito joints, just down the street from the historic home of the Boston Red Sox: Fenway Park. Behind the baseball stadium, Landsdowne Street is lined with the city's flashiest dance clubs, where international students shake their stuff after midnight.

◖ Fenway Park

A new banner was flapping in the breeze here after the Red Sox's come-from-behind race to win the 2004 World Series, after 86 years of trying. While the high of that victory has

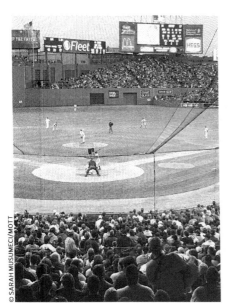

historic Fenway Park

works—posters of which have been decorating college dorm rooms for decades. But it also has outstanding Asian and Egyptian collections, as well as many celebrated early American paintings and artifacts. The museum (465 Huntington Ave., 617/267-9300, www.mfa. org, 10 A.M.–4:45 P.M. Sat.–Tues., 10 A.M.– 9:45 P.M. Wed.–Fri., $17 adults, $15 seniors and students, $6.50 youth 6–17 but free on weekends, holidays, and after 3 P.M. on weekdays, free children under 6) began its life as the painting collection of the Boston Athenaeum, the private library located on Beacon Hill. Over the years, it benefited from Brahmin patronage to amass a fine collection of both classical and modern art objects. Under its current leadership, the museum has taken some gambles to bring more modern viewers into the galleries, staging artistic exhibitions on guitars and racecars alongside show-stopping special exhibits on the likes of Monet, Van Gogh, and Gauguin. A new addition to the museum, currently being designed by internationally renowned architects Foster and Partners, will provide even more space for exhibition of the museum's 350,000 works of art. When completed in 2010 or 2011, the renovation will include an entire new wing for American art, glassed in over the current wing of the museum, as well as spiffed-up European galleries and more room for contemporary artwork.

infused the park (4 Yawkey Way, 617/226-6666, www.redsox.com, $12 adults, $11 seniors, $10 children) with a new energy, Fenway has long been one of the most electric places to catch the national pastime. First opened in 1912, Fenway has a soul that none of the more modern parks can match. For the uninitiated, the geography of the park—with its Green Monster, Pesky's Pole, and Ted Williams' seat—can seem more complicated than many whole cities. Thankfully, true believers lead tours of the park daily from 9 A.M. to 4 P.M. (or until three hours before the game). As good as those tours may be, however, nothing quite beats taking a seat in the bleachers, grabbing a Budweiser, and waiting for the first crack of the bat.

◖ Museum of Fine Arts

Quite simply, behind the neoclassic marble facade of this grand art museum is one of the best and most beloved art collections in the country. The MFA, as it's known, is particularly noted for its collection of French Impressionist

At present, most visitors to the MFA make a beeline for the 2nd floor, which is home to several jaw-dropping rooms dedicated to works by French impressionists Monet, Manet, Renoir, Van Gogh, and others. Particular highlights are Renoir's *Dance at Bougival,* and Gauguin's *Where Do We Come From? What Are We? Where Are We Going?,* the centerpiece of a recent Gauguin exhibit that was one of the museum's most successful shows ever. Less trafficked but equally rewarding are the American galleries. On display is arguably the most famous American painting ever: Gilbert Stuart's original unfinished painting of George Washington, which was used as a model for more than 100 paintings of the first president, including the one that appears (in reverse) on the one dollar

© SARAH MUSUMECI/MOTT

bill. The collection includes several paintings by John Singer Sargent, including the arresting *Daughters of Edward Darley Bolt,* as well as those by Boston's own adopted artist, John Singleton Copley, including his portrait of Paul Revere. Several examples of the patriot silversmith's work are on display in adjoining galleries of colonial artifacts and furniture.

John Singer Sargent is also the master behind the Sargent murals that cover the ceiling of the museum's grand rotunda with rich classical imagery. The murals, which Sargent considered the culmination of his life's work, have caused more than one visitor to develop a crick in the neck from looking up at them in amazement for so long. The rotunda marks the crossroads of culture, separating galleries dedicated to Egypt and Asia. The Egyptian galleries contain many items that were unearthed in a fruitful museum-sponsored exhibition at Giza that began in 1905; the towering statue of *Pharaoh Menkaure and his Queen* is one of the finest Egyptian pieces on display anywhere. The entire Asian collection meanwhile is hands down one of the best in the world. Many of its galleries were filled through the enterprising efforts of William Sturgis Bigelow and Ernest Fenollosa, who were known as the "Boston Buddhists" for their contribution in bringing Buddha into the West. Among the highlights of the collection is a "Japanese temple room" that features three exquisite life-size stone Buddhas, along with other Japanese sculpture contemplatively arranged in a dimly lit alcove.

Tours of various collections within the museum are offered free with admission throughout the day. Introductory tours to the entire museum run at 10:30 A.M. and 3 P.M. Monday through Friday, 6:15 P.M. on Wednesday, and 11 A.M., 12:30, and 3 P.M. during weekends. On the first Friday of every month, the museum also hosts a popular singles event where the artsy and amorous mingle over red wine and jazz while they ogle the art and each other.

Isabella Stewart Gardner Museum

This small museum (280 The Fenway,

617/566-1401, www.gardnermuseum.org, 11 A.M.–5 P.M. Tues.–Sun., $12 adults, $10 seniors, $5 students, free youth and children under 18) is filled with priceless European and American paintings. The most cherished work of art, however, may be the building itself, which is constructed around a plant-filled Italianate courtyard that may be the most pleasing indoor space in the city. The namesake socialite who built the museum was known as something of a brilliant eccentric, who wore Red Sox caps with her ball gowns and scandalized polite society by posing for an eroticized portrait by John Singer Sargent. (On display in the museum, the portrait was exhibited only once in Gardner's lifetime due to the wishes of her husband.) The museum keeps alive Gardner's eccentric spirit by allowing any woman named Isabella free admission to the museum at all times. Other works of art in the collection include Titian's *Europa,* which may be the single most important work of art in Boston; Sargent's dynamic *El Jaleo;* Boticelli's *Virgin and Child with an Angel;* and an early Rembrandt self-portrait.

The building, which was also Gardner's residence, has four floors of artwork organized as a living house museum, with some of the original typed labels still in place. Gardner's will stipulated that nothing in the museum be moved, or else the entire collection would be sold and the proceeds donated to Harvard's art faculty. That requirement presented particular problems after the night of St. Patrick's Day, 1990, when two thieves broke into the museum and cut thirteen paintings out of their frames. Among the priceless works of art stolen were two rare Rembrandt paintings, including a later self-portrait, and one of only about 35 Vermeers in the world. The theft, which some have called the largest art heist in history, still remains unsolved despite a $5 million reward offered by the museum; the frames for the stolen paintings still hang in a room called the Dutch Room. Next door, a room called the Tapestry Room provides a beautiful background for periodic chamber music concerts. Ms. Gardner's collection isn't all that is on display at the museum; a small exhibition space hosts contemporary shows.

Not to be left behind in the Boston art museum renovation sweepstakes, the Gardner too plans a major expansion, which will include a new building adjacent to the museum designed by award-winning architect Renzo Piano, further increasing the space for contemporary work and traveling exhibitions. The renovation recently passed a major hurdle when the Massachusetts Supreme Judicial Court ruled that it was consistent with Gardner's will and could proceed.

SEAPORT DISTRICT

Located across Fort Point Channel from downtown, the South Boston waterfront district is a neighborhood in transition. For years, it has been home to New England's largest community of artists, who have taken advantage of the solid warehouses that once housed the stores for Boston's wool trade to build artist studios and performance spaces. The neighborhood itself is a visual artist's dream, with open spaces broken by iron girders and views of the harbor. As downtown has become built up however, the newly christened Seaport District is the next development frontier, with cranes and bulldozers furiously breaking ground on new hotels, condo buildings, and a gargantuan new convention center. After years of negotiating, the artists have been worked into the plan, and a new urban neighborhood is taking shape that retains its urban edge and allows conventioneers to walk to stores and galleries sprouting up in old buildings.

Boston Tea Party Ship and Museum

The original three British ships that provided the dance floor for the Boston Tea Party were moored at Griffin's Wharf, which was later buried in landfill during the expansion of the city. The best estimate of the location is near the present-day corner of Atlantic Avenue and Congress Street, near South Station. Not far from that spot, this newly renovated museum (Congress Street

BOSTON BY SEA

No matter how many tours visitors to Boston go on, many miss seeing the city from one very important angle: the ocean. Viewed from in and around the harbor, the city's skyline is not only immense, but astoundingly peaceful, and offers an entirely new perspective and sense of place. To that end, there are a number of ways of getting out on the harbor that don't require a private charter. One of the easiest means is the Lighthouse Cruises offered by **Boston Harbor Cruises** (departing from Long Wharf, 617/227-4321, www. bostonharborcruises.com). The voyages last five hours, are narrated by members of the American Lighthouse Foundation, and pass numerous lighthouses – including Boston Light, the oldest lighthouse station in America, and Thacher Island, the only operational twin lighthouses in the country. Rather do your wining and dining offshore? **Spirit of Boston dancing and dinner cruises** (departing from World Trade Center, 617/748-1450,www. spiritofboston.com) lays out candlelit tables, an enormous buffet, and live music on its enormous boat. Likewise, the huge dinner cruises offered by **Odyssey Cruises** (departing from Rowes Wharf, 866/307-2469, www.odysseycruises. com) play everything from live jazz to pop dance tunes while you dig into dinner and take in the ever-changing water view. On a more hands-on note, passengers are encouraged to participate in sailing when they cruise aboard the schooners *Liberty* or *Liberty Clipper* (depart Long Wharf, 617/742-1422,www.libertyfleet.com/) – replicas of early-1800s schooners used by New England fishermen.

Bridge, www.bostonteapartyship.com), scheduled to be opened in 2010, will feature replicas of the three original ships—the *Beaver,* the *Dartmouth,* and the *Eleanor*—along with other artifacts to bring alive the cold night of December 16, 1773, when 342 chests of British tea were broken open and hurled into the harbor, the tipping point for the American Revolution. Among the items on display is the so-called "Robinson Tea Chest," which was recovered by a participant the day after the event, and one of only two original tea chests known to survive.

Institute of Contemporary Art

Once upon a time, Boston's Institute of Contemporary Art (ICA) was viewed as being on par with New York's Museum of Modern Art (MoMA) on the vanguard of experimental modern art. While MoMA decided to collect the artists it exhibited, and now boasts the likes of Jackson Pollock and Jasper Johns, the ICA felt that it could better remain on the cutting-edge by continually exhibiting new work. Oops. Making up for lost time, however, in 2006 the ICA opened a new home on the waterfront (100 Northern Ave., 617/478-3100, www.icaboston.org, 10 A.M.–5 P.M. Tues.–Wed. and Sat.–Sun., 10 A.M.–9 P.M. Thurs. and Fri., $15 adults, $10 seniors and students, free children under 17, free to all Thurs. after 5 P.M.) in a space-age glass building that triples the size of the museum's old home in the Back Bay, and more importantly adds a permanent collection for the first time. In its old location, the museum garnered a reputation for staging explosive exhibitions such as the first U.S. exhibition of the photos of Robert Mapplethorpe in the 1980s; in recent years, however, its exhibits of contemporary multimedia installations and photography has had a more uneven reception. The new building, designed by edgy architectural firm Diller Scofidio + Renfro, has reinvigorated the museum, providing dramatic views of the waterfront from flexible gallery spaces, and adding a 325-seat performing arts theater overlooking the harbor. It has already set tongues wagging in the art world with its successful exhibition of pop graffiti artist Shepard Fairey, best known for the enigmatic Andre the Giant tags in cities all over the country, and more recently, for the iconic Barack Obama campaign poster that was ubiquitous during his presidential campaign. On his way to the opening exhibition, Fairey was arrested by Boston police for vandalism—only adding to the publicity of the show.

Boston Children's Museum

Back in the 1970s this waterfront museum (308 Congress St., 617/426-6500, www.bostonkids.org, 10 A.M.–5 P.M. Sat.–Thurs., 10 A.M.–9 P.M. Fri., $12 adults, $9 seniors and children 1–15, free children under 1) pioneered the kind of messy, hands-on learning that is now de rigueur in children's museums. In 2007, it underwent a renovation to update the exhibits to the 21st century. Budding construction workers can build skyscrapers and jackhammer them down in the Construction Zone; little monkeys can tackle a brightly colored maze of tunnels, towers, and walkways called the Climb; and the nautically inclined can float their boats in a 28-foot-long model of the Fort Point Channel (visible outside the museum's walls) called Boats Afloat. Word to the wise: get there early or come late on weekends to avoid playing referee to dozens of kiddie skirmishes that break out when the exhibits reach capacity. Better yet, come mid-week when you and the kids will have the best exhibits to yourself!

Boston Fire Museum

Boston has always has had a tempestuous relationship with fire—from the great fire of 1872 to the infamous 1942 Cocoanut Grove conflagration (a fiery tragedy that killed almost 500 people in a crowded nightclub and led to important changes in the fire code). This small museum in a historic old firehouse (344 Congress St., 617/482-1344, www.bostonfiremuseum.com, 11 A.M.–4 P.M. Thurs., 11 A.M.–9 P.M. Fri., 11 A.M.–3 P.M. Sat., free) is calculated to thrill the under four-foot-high set with displays of shiny antique fire engines and memorabilia from Boston's fiery history, including items from the Cocoanut Grove itself. The museum is run by the Boston Sparks Association, a group of several hundred fire fanatics who still listen to scanners late at night and show up at fire scenes to watch the jakes do their thing.

OTHER NEIGHBORHOODS
East Boston

To most Bostonians, the peninsula known as East Boston is synonymous with Logan Airport. Alongside the planes, however, is a residential community that has changed its ethnic makeup over the years. The spaghetti restaurants and pizza joints of an old Italian neighborhood are still bustling, but they've been joined by taquerias and *pupuserias* of a vibrant new Central and South American population. More recently, developers have taken interest in the brick warehouse buildings on the harbor, transforming them into high-priced luxury condos that promise (or threaten) to remake the neighborhood. If you take some time to explore here, you'll note that the streets are all named after battles in the Revolutionary War. The vantage point from the waterfront in front of Maverick Square is also one of the best views you could have of the city skyline without being on the water—especially during fireworks on New Year's Eve.

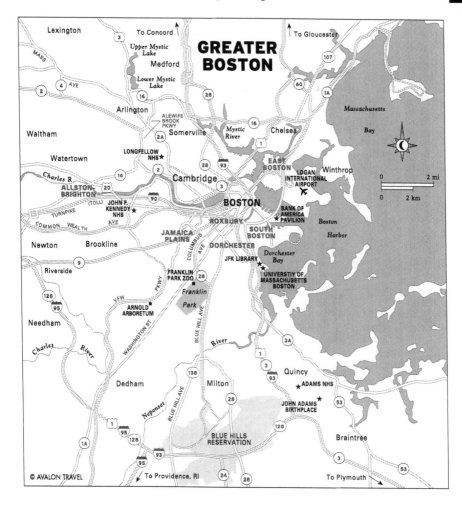

South Boston

Every year, the sidewalks of Broadway are lined with spectators for the annual St. Patrick's Day parade, the annual outpouring of pride in this heavily Irish enclave. Set apart on a peninsula, South Boston—or "Southie" as it's called by residents—has always been a tight-knit, insulated community that has kept to a code of family and neighborhood alliances. Much of the life of the community still transpires in the pubs that line the streets, including the famous L Street Tavern, which served as Robin Williams's neighborhood bar in the movie *Good Will Hunting*. (The movie's Oscar-winning screenwriters, Matt Damon and Ben Affleck, grew up across the river in Cambridge, a neighborhood that South Boston residents love to deride.) The best way to really get the flavor of the community is to pop into one of these throwbacks to Boston's Irish past, order a Guinness and fish-and-chips, and talk to the guy next to you at the bar.

Dorchester Heights

South Boston is also home to this little-visited historic site (G St., S. Boston, www.nps. gov/bost/historyculture/dohe.htm Sat–Sun noon–6 P.M., free), where in 1776 the siege of Boston was finally lifted. Despite the battles of Concord and Bunker Hill, the British and Americans were in a long stalemate, with the colonists controlling the west bank of the Charles, and the British blockading the harbor. During the winter of 1775, Bostonian General Henry Knox braved snow and cold in an epic 300-mile journey to drag the cannons of New York's Fort Ticonderoga to Boston. Wrapping their wheels in straw, colonists moved the cannons up onto the high ground at Dorchester Heights during the night of March 4, 1776, when a British attack was thwarted by storms. With the cannon pointing down at them, the British position was untenable, and they deserted Boston under a gentleman's agreement with Washington a week later. While the heights have since been leveled for landfill, the high ground is capped by a monument and offers an impressive and unusual vantage of Boston Harbor. Call ahead to determine opening hours for the monument, as they can be capricious due to recent National Park staff cuts. In one recent year, it was only open on weekend afternoons from June to Labor Day.

Roxbury and Dorchester

Roxbury was once its own town connected to Boston by a narrow isthmus. As the sea filled in, however, the boundary between it and Boston blurred until it was sucked up and annexed by its northern neighbor. In the 20th century, African Americans displaced from downtown settled around Dudley Square and on the heights of Fort Hill. The area is still the heart of Boston's Black community, where you can find African clothing stores and soul food along with Caribbean grocers. Between Roxbury and South Boston is the sprawling plain of Dorchester, a true melting pot of African Americans, Asian Americans, and Irish, among other ethnicities. Upham's Corner is home to a vibrant community of immigrants from the African islands of Cape Verde, while Field's Corner is a little Saigon of Vietnamese restaurants and cafés.

John F. Kennedy Library

Located on the campus of University of Massachusetts–Boston, this underrated library and museum (Columbia Point, Dorchester, 866/535-1960, www.jfklibrary. org, 9 A.M.–5 P.M. daily, $12 adults, $10 seniors and students, $9 youth 13–17, free children under 13) is dedicated to Boston's modern political hero, with artifacts and exhibits that bring alive the 1960 Democratic National Convention in which Kennedy was nominated, his service during World War II, and other periods of his life. The Kennedy Museum was also the site of a public viewing of the casket of JFK's brother and longtime Massachusetts Senator Ted Kennedy, who died in 2009. The museum plans to install a new exhibit relating to the life and accomplishments of the younger Kennedy in upcoming years.

In addition to the Kennedy paraphernalia, the museum is also the unlikely home to the

Hemingway Collection, the largest collection of Ernest Hemingway memorabilia located in one place. The bulk of the holdings are manuscripts, letters, and other papers available for research; however, the Hemingway Research Room also contains items belonging to the adventurous writer, including his hunting bag, shrapnel taken from his leg during World War I, and an impala shot by Mary Hemingway on safari in 1954. History buffs should also check out the **Commonwealth Museum** (220 Morrissey Blvd., Dorchester, 617/727-9268, www.sec.state.ma.us/mus/museum, 9 A.M.–5 P.M. Mon.–Fri., free) across the street, which contains archaeological items unearthed during the building of the Big Dig, including "America's oldest bowling ball."

Allston-Brighton

Sandwiched between Boston University and Boston College, the twin neighborhoods of Allston-Brighton have become the quintessential student ghetto. Run-down apartments are often filled over capacity by slumlords willing to look the other way. Along the main drags of Harvard and Brighton Avenues is a riot of student bars that feature live bands and lively flirtation. The number of struggling rock-band members who have lived in the neighborhood has given it the slightly tongue-in-cheek name of "Allston Rock City."

Jamaica Plain

One of the only Boston neighborhoods that is genuinely racially integrated, Jamaica Plain includes remnants of a sizeable "lace curtain" Irish population living side-by-side with a lesbian community and Boston's largest Latino enclave. Centre Street is one of the funkier shopping districts in town, with hipster clothing and record stores interspersed with coffee shops and bakeries. The neighborhood is also surrounded by green space, with the large Jamaica Pond on one side and gargantuan Franklin Park, designed by landscape architect Frederick Law Olmsted, on the other. On the southern rim of the neighborhood is the **Arnold Arboretum** (125 Arborway, Jamaica

© MICHAEL BLANDING

Samuel Adams Brewery in Jamaica Plain

Plain, 617/524-1718, www.arboretum.harvard.edu, sunrise–sunset daily, free), owned by Harvard University and containing more than 200 acres of rambling hillside covered with rhododendrons, lilacs, and other flowering plants and hardwood trees.

No one is quite sure how Jamaica Plain got its unusual name—some speculate it comes from the rum distillers who settled there during colonial times. The neighborhood certainly made its fortunes through alcohol, as German brewers set up shop along the fresh water of Stony Brook. One of their breweries is now occupied by **Boston Beer Company** (30 Germania St., Jamaica Plain, 617/368-5080, www.samueladams.com), the makers of **Samuel Adams** beer. Founded in 1984, the company began the revolution that turned American beer from watery pilsners to full-bodied microbrewed lagers and ale. The company offers tours (10 A.M.–3 P.M. Mon.–Thurs., 10 A.M.–5:30 P.M. Fri., 10 A.M.–3 P.M. Sat., year-round, $2 suggested donation) of the brewing process along with a historical presentation on the history of beer in Boston—including the early efforts by patriot Sam Adams himself.

CAMBRIDGE AND SOMERVILLE

Few places are defined as much by intellect as the city of Cambridge. To folks across the river, it's where the "smaht kids" are. To scholars around the world, it's equivalent to academic excellence. University culture permeates the axis of Massachusetts Avenue, which runs roughly from Harvard University to the Massachusetts Institute of Technology (universally referred to as MIT) and is awash in bookstores, pubs, and cafés. At even the grungiest bar you are apt to find earnest patrons debating Friedman and Keynes. Despite the high-powered intellectualism, however, the populace of Cambridge exudes a more relaxed vibe than the business chic of downtown Boston. Flannel and jeans outnumber suits, and even the fine-dining restaurants have a whimsical or downbeat feel.

Cambridge justly has a reputation as one

of the country's two "people's republics" (the other being its Californian soul sister, Berkeley), and the city has been a hotbed of student activism on issues from the Vietnam War to anti-globalization. As rents have risen over the years, however, many say that the real spirit of Cambridge has drifted north to the more proletarian Somerville, a working-class community that has picked up the slacker overflow, especially in the neighborhood of Davis Square.

Harvard Square

The geography of Cambridge is inexplicably organized into more than a dozen "squares," which are actually anything but. The heart of them all is Harvard Square, a spider web of streets outside the walls of the university that is crowded at all hours with students, parents, professors, and tourists. Gone are the days when the square was a downbeat mecca of bars and used record stores; the chain stores have long since swallowed up all but a few struggling independents. Still, there's something about strolling the brick sidewalks or people-watching from an outdoor table that is quintessential Cambridge. When the weather turns

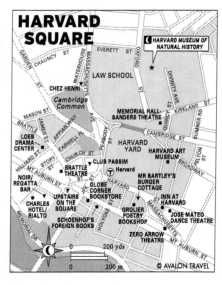

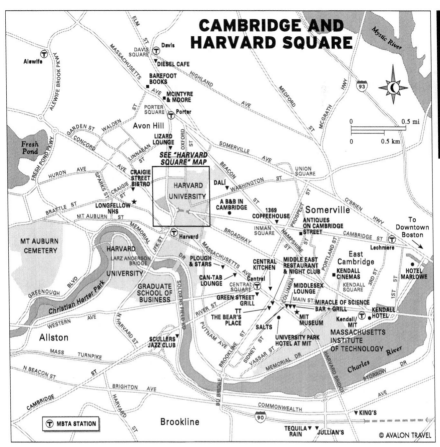

CAMBRIDGE AND HARVARD SQUARE

© AVALON TRAVEL

balmy, street performers flood nooks and crannies, offering everything from folk music sets to magic acts, and turning the area into a spontaneous carnival. Equally satisfying is a stroll down Brattle Street, the heart of Cambridge literati, where John Kenneth Galbraith, Robert Reich, and other leading political lights inhabit miniature colonial mansions.

Harvard University

Harvard is the kind of place people love to hate—most often out of jealousy. For some, it's synonymous with snobbery and effeteness; for others it represents the culmination of a

lifelong dream. Whatever your feelings, the campus itself doesn't disappoint. It is filled with important-looking brick buildings with actual ivy clinging romantically to their marble friezes. Most have stories, which the tour guides at the **Harvard Events & Information Center** (Holyoke Center Arcade, 1350 Massachusetts Ave., Cambridge, 617/495-1573, www.harvard. edu, 10 A.M. and 2 P.M. Mon.–Fri., 2 P.M. Sat., free) are happy to divulge. If you venture into Harvard Yard yourself, be sure to touch the foot of the statue of John Harvard for luck. It's known as the "statue of three lies" since it doesn't depict Harvard; wrongly calls him the founder; and gets the date of the founding wrong (it was 1636, not 1638). So much for the university's motto, *Veritas*—Latin for truth.

◖ Harvard Museum of Natural History

Before there was science, there was "natural history," and for decades Harvard sponsored naturalist exhibitions to catalog the animals, plants, and minerals of the world. The naturalists brought their booty back home, cataloged it, and ensconced it in one of the more endearing and eclectic museums in the area (26 Oxford St., Cambridge, 617/495-3045, www.hmnh.harvard.edu, 9 A.M.–5 P.M. daily, $9 adults, $7 students and seniors, $6 children 3–18) in the area. The bulk of the museum is taken up by gallery after gallery of real stuffed animals—taxidermy beasties of all shapes and sizes, from elephants to a pair of pheasants once owned by George Washington. Even more impressive is the rock-and-mineral collection, full of geodes, crystals, and precious stones the size of a small child. The pièce de résistance of the museum, however, is undoubtedly the glass flowers. Created by a father-and-son team from Germany, the flowers are meticulous representations of almost 900 species, made entirely from glass. The models are so exacting that they seem real, from the petals on a coneflower to the hairs on the leg of a tiny glass bee.

Harvard Art Museum

The paintings at Harvard's underrated art museum (485 Broadway, Cambridge, 617/495-9400, www.artmuseums.harvard. edu, 10 A.M.–5 P.M. Mon.–Sat., 1 P.M.–5 P.M. Sun., $9 adults, $7 seniors, $6 students, free Sat. before noon, every day after 4:30 P.M., and children 17 and under) were mostly acquired through random donations by rich alumni. Thus, it has pretty much one of everything, and everything is exceptional. Alas, much of it is also not available for viewing at present, since the museum is undergoing a major renovation that will combine Harvard's three disjointed art museums (the Fogg, Busch-Reisinger, and Sackler museums) into one glorious new space

designed by Renzo Piano, the busy beaver who is also designing the Isabella Stewart Gardner Museum addition across the stream. Until the new museum opens in 2013, visitors will have to content themselves with a rotating exhibition of the highlights of the museum—including a large number of Impressionist and post-Impressionist paintings, including a Van Gogh self-portrait, Degas' dancers, and several Picassos—that will be on view at the Sackler.

Longfellow National Historic Site

Today, Americans may not remember "The Song of Hiawatha" or the "Midnight Ride of Paul Revere," but back in the Victorian era, Henry Wadsworth Longfellow was the literary equivalent of George Clooney—a poet who transcended his art to become a genuine celebrity. Rangers lead tours of his former residence (105 Brattle St., Cambridge, 617/876-4491, www.nps.gov/long, 10:30 A.M.–4 P.M. Wed.–Sun. June–Oct., $3 adults, free children 15 and under), which features elegant Victorian furniture and the study where the poet composed many of his works. Other exhibits detail the home's earlier history as headquarters to George Washington during the siege of Boston in 1775–1776. Throughout the year, the site often offers performances of actors portraying other famous writers, including Walt Whitman and Louisa May Alcott. Longfellow devotees can see the poet's final resting place a short walk away at **Mount Auburn Cemetary** (580 Mt. Auburn St., Cambridge, 617/547-7105, www.mountauburn.org, 8 A.M.–5 P.M. daily Oct.–Apr., 8 A.M.–7 P.M. daily May–Aug., free), a grand Victorian burial ground that also holds the graves of other Victorian intellectuals, such as Mary Baker Eddy, Oliver Wendell Holmes, Buckminster Fuller, and "Battle Hymn of the Republic" composer Julia Ward Howe.

Central Square

As Harvard Square "jumped the shark," the alternative crowds moved to the next square down Massachusetts Avenue, which became the unwashed center for Boston's 1990s rock renaissance. Bands including the Lemonheads,

Morphine, Juliana Hatfield, and the Pixies all got their start at the legendary Middle East and other rock clubs in this stretch. Even as some chain stores have filled in the gaps (and The Gap), this section of Cambridge is still seen as more "real" by the tattooed and tongue-pierced crowd. Ethnic restaurants, art stores, and dance studios line the avenue, while the rock clubs still pack them in at night.

Massachusetts Institute of Technology

Cambridge's "other university" is, if anything, more acclaimed among the segment of society that wears pocket protectors and horn-rimmed glasses. The first computer was invented here in 1928, and the inventor of the World Wide Web is now a scientist-in-residence. The center of the school is known as the Infinite Corridor, a hallway that runs like a spine through the central buildings. If you are worried about inadvertently stepping into a particle reactor, you can join a free tour that leaves from Lobby 7 (77 Massachusetts Ave., Cambridge,

617/253-4795, www.mit.edu, 11 A.M. and 3 P.M. Mon.–Fri., free). Maps for self-guided tours are also available there. For the inner geek in all of us, the nearby **MIT Museum** (265 Massachusetts Ave., MIT Museum Bldg N51, Cambridge, 617/253-5927, web.mit.edu/museum, 10 A.M.–5 P.M. daily, $7.50 adults, $3 seniors, students, and youth 17 and under, free 10 A.M.–12 P.M. Sun.) has photographs and working specimens of everything from slide rules to robots. Holograms and kinetic sculptures explore the uneasy intersection of art and technology. The same could be said about one of MIT's newest and most striking buildings. The **Ray and Maria Stata Center** at 42 Vassar Street was designed by architect Frank Gehry, of Guggenheim Bilbao fame, and looks like a row of skyscrapers after getting a workout by Godzilla. Inside are unusually shaped communal spaces, designed to help scientists get out of their labs and actually talk to one another.

Davis Square

Once the subway was extended up to Somerville in the 1980s, Davis Square went through a dramatic transformation from forgotten gulch of dollar stores and newsstands to a funky hipster heaven. The neighborhood has no fewer than five cafés, and come Saturday afternoon all of them are overflowing with Tufts students or recent grads, with real or computerized notebooks propped open. True, the attempts by the Somerville Theater to brand the neighborhood the "Paris of the '90s" fizzled, but the theater still anchors a vibrant cultural scene, and bars along Elm Street keep the streets hopping after dark.

BROOKLINE

Despite being completely surrounded by Boston, the large town of Brookline maintains a clearly separate identity. As soon as you cross the town line, the streets get leafier and the houses get bigger. Brookline residents pride themselves on living a quasi-urban lifestyle while still enjoying the suburban benefits of good schools and green space. Sophisticated but proudly unhip, the neighborhood's

© TIM GRAFFT/MOTT

MIT's unmistakable Stata Center

crossroads of Coolidge Corner is like a more adult Harvard Square, where you are more apt to run into a professor than a student. The town is also home to one of the largest Jewish populations outside of Israel and Palm Beach—a fact evident from all of the kosher delis, temples, and Hebrew bookstores that line its streets.

John F. Kennedy
National Historic Site

Just steps up from Coolidge Corner is the birthplace of the 35th president, where John F. Kennedy took his first steps and said his first words. The home (83 Beals St., Brookline, 617/566-7937, www.nps.gov/jofi, 10 A.M.– 4:30 P.M. Wed.–Sun. mid-May–Sept., $3 adults, free children under 17) is now filled with furniture, photographs, and other memorabilia collected by Kennedy's mother, Rose, who also provided an audio tour describing life in Brookline in 1917. Rangers also occasionally lead tours to the Kennedys' second home up the street, as well as St. Aidan's, the Catholic church where JFK and his family worshipped.

QUINCY

South of Boston and accessible by the T, Quincy is actually the fourth-largest city in the state, and might be thriving if it were located anywhere else. As it is, the city tends to be overshadowed by its larger neighbor. Apart from an area of old historic homes, the city is mostly dilapidated and depressed. For a brief time in the 19th century, Quincy was the center for granite quarrying in the region, and many of the monuments in Boston were mined from quarries that still stand open (and are used by rock climbers). The city is better known, however, as the birthplace of two American presidents—John Adams and his son John Quincy Adams.

Adams National Historic Site

The second president of the United States always got short shrift—not as acclaimed as Washington (#1) or as controversial as Jefferson (#3). That all changed a few years ago when David McCullough published his blockbuster biography *John Adams*, and showed its title character to be a forthright scholar swept into greatness by the historic tides of war. Even after the Revolution, Adams was able to stay above the sectarian wrangling of his time to put the interests of the country foremost. Much of his moral center can be attributed to his wife, Abigail Adams, who was a brilliant thinker and early feminist in her own right. The family headquarters was in a palatial home called the "Old House," at 135 Adams Street, which was home to four generations of the Adams family. Two-hour guided trolley tours take visitors literally from cradle to grave, starting at the birthplaces of Adams and his son, proceeding to the Old House, and ending at the church where the two are buried along with their wives. Trolleys leave from the National Park Visitors Center (1250 Hancock Street, Quincy, 617/770-1175, www.nps.gov/adam, 9 A.M.–5 P.M. daily mid-Apr.–mid-Nov., 10 A.M.–4 P.M. Tues.–Fri. mid-Nov.–mid-Apr., $5 adults, free children under 17, $10 family pass). Alternately, you can walk to the Old House from Quincy Center and tour the home and the grounds, which still include some of Adams' beloved apple trees.

Entertainment and Events

As a city that has always prided itself on culture, Boston rarely lacks for interesting arts and entertainment offerings. Performances range from meticulous renderings of chamber music to offbeat theater productions in experimental studios. Both major papers, the *Boston Globe* and *Boston Herald,* run comprehensive arts listings on Thursdays and Fridays, while the *Globe* also provides a roundup of events in its daily "Go!" section. A more alternative take on the week's events, including previews for upcoming rock shows, can be found in the weekly newspapers *The Boston Phoenix* and *The Weekly Dig.* For tickets to theater performances, a great resource is **BosTix** (617/262-8632, www.bostix.org), which offers half-price tickets the day of the show. Booths are located in Quincy Marketplace (10 A.M.–6 P.M. Tues.–Sat., 11 A.M.–4 P.M. Sun.) and Copley Square (10 A.M.–6 P.M. Mon.–Sat., 11 A.M.–4 P.M. Sun.) and only accept cash.

CLASSICAL MUSIC

In addition to **Boston Symphony Hall** (301 Massachusetts Ave., 617/266-1492, www.bso. org), Boston has many excellent smaller halls that regularly offer classical concerts. These include: New England Conservatory's acoustically refined **Jordan Hall** (30 Gainsborough St., 617/585-1260, www.newenglandconservatory.edu/concerts); Boston University's **Tsai Performance Center** (685 Commonwealth Ave., 617/353-8725, www.bu.edu/tsai); and Harvard's intimate **Sanders Theatre** (45 Quincy St., Cambridge, 617/496-2222, www. fas.harvard.edu/tickets).

Boston Symphony Orchestra

Since its founding in 1881, the BSO (888/266-1200, www.bso.org) has been one of the country's premier classical orchestras. In 2006, classical aficionados were clapping vigorously (their version of cheering) when modern legend James Levine ascended to the BSO's podium as conductor of both Boston's orchestra and the New York Metropolitan Opera.

Boston Pops

From the very beginning of its existence, the BSO has interspersed classical music with lighter fare. In 1900, the latter became the specialty of Boston Pops, which reached national prominence under the baton of march-master Arthur Fiedler in the 1970s and further acclaim with movie-theme composer John Williams. The current manifestation of the Pops is under the direction of the boyishly exuberant Keith Lockhart, whose lineups might feature show tunes, movie themes, or vocal pop music. The orchestra performs in Symphony Hall in May and June, and then stages free outdoor concerts through July.

Handel and Haydn Society

Dedicated to the performances of choral works from the 19th century and earlier, H&H (617/262-1815, www.handelandhaydn.org) regularly performs at Symphony Hall, Jordan Hall, and the Sanders Theatre. The highlight of the year is its Christmastime performances of *Messiah,* a Boston tradition.

Boston Lyric Opera

In addition to classics by Rossini, Mozart, and other masters, the BLO (617/542-6772, www. blo.org) regularly stages modern works, such as a recent opera based on the children's book *The Little Prince.* Performances take place at the Shubert Theatre.

Chamber Music

The eight-person **Boston Chamber Music Society** (617/349-0086, www.bostonchambermusic.org) performs classics by Mozart, Beethoven, and other composers. The **Pro Arte Chamber Orchestra** (617/779-0900, www.proarte.org) is a co-op orchestra that presents relatively more daring fare.

Church Concerts

A little-known choral gem, **Emmanuel Music** (15 Newbury St., 617/536-3356, www.

emmanuelmusic.org) performs entire Bach masses on Sundays at Emmanuel Church. **Trinity Boston** (206 Clarendon St., 617/536-0944, www.trinitychurchboston.org) performs half-hour recitals on Fridays at noon, as well as occasional choral concerts in one of the most beautiful settings in Boston—Copley Square's Trinity Church.

ROCK AND POP CONCERTS

The biggest names in rock and pop come to the **TD Garden** (100 Legends Way, 617/624-1050, www.tdbanknorthgarden.com), which is converted to a concert auditorium when the Celtics and Bruins aren't in town. Acoustics are about what you'd expect from a sports arena. During the warmer months, a much nicer place to see a show is the **Bank of America Pavilion** (290 Northern Ave., 617/728-1600, www.livenation.com), an open-air auditorium in the Seaport District with the twinkling lights of the harbor as a backdrop to folk and pop performers. During the summer months, many area radio stations also sponsor shows with of-the-moment pop stars at the **Hatch Memorial Shell** (617/626-4970, www.mass.gov/dcr/hatch_events.htm) on the Charles River Esplanade.

The **Orpheum Theatre** (1 Hamilton Pl., 617/679-0810) is run-down, hot, and cramped, but still provides a sufficiently grungy venue for alternative-rock shows. A much more exciting place to see mid-size performers is the **House of Blues** (15 Lansdowne St., 888 /693-2583), which despite its name hosts mostly indie rock performers such as Regina Spektor and The Bravery in a huge amphitheatre with multiple balconies. Shows are general admission, so get there early to get close to the stage.

JAZZ CONCERTS

The "Harvard of jazz," Berklee School of Music sponsors performances of both modern legends and up-and-coming prodigies at its **Berklee Performance Center** (136 Massachusetts Ave., 617/747-2261, www.berkleebpc.com), which also occasionally has folk and pop acts.

THEATER
Citi Performing Arts Center

The most opulent performance space in Boston is the **Wang Theatre** (270 Tremont St., 617/482-9393, www.citicenter.org) in the Citi Performing Arts Center. It's a 3,000-seat theater in the European tradition, with a grand lobby, marble-column proscenium, and giant crystal chandelier. Most of the performances here are not terribly original, however, tending towards traveling Broadway musicals and spectaculars like Riverdance and the Ten Tenors. Recently, the Wang has experimented with rock acts, the likes of Death Cab for Cutie and The Pixies. Citi saves its (relatively) more artsy theater fare for its sister property, the 1,800-seat **Shubert Theatre** (265 Tremont St., 617/482-9393, www.citicenter.org).

Broadway Across America

Since coming to town a decade ago to revive Boston as a tryout town for New York, this organization (866/523-7469, www.broadwayacrossamerica.com) has breathed new life into the Theater District, staging plays that always garner buzz, even if they don't always deliver. Its flagship theater is the **Colonial Theatre** (106 Boylston St., 617/246-9366, www.bostoncolonialtheatre.com/), a restored space with colorful history that now stages exciting Broadway-bound productions.

In addition, the newly renovated **Opera House** (539 Washington St., 617/259-3400, www.bostonoperahouse.com/) is giving the Wang a run for its money with a 2,500-seat venue for mainstream musicals such as *The Lion King* and *The Phantom of the Opera*.

Theater Companies

For two decades, the **Huntington Theatre Company** (264 Huntington Ave., 617/266-0800, www.huntingtontheatre.org) has been regarded as Boston's top professional theater company. Under the tutelage of artistic director Nicholas Martin, several of its performances have recently gone on to Broadway. The company's works tend toward well-crafted dramas with emotional storylines. In addition to its main stage at the Boston University Theatre, it also performs at the BCA's Calderwood Pavilion.

Across the river in Cambridge, the **American Repertory Theatre** (617/547-8300, www. amrep.org) has earned an enthusiastic following for its more avant-garde performances that often feature elaborate post-modern stage design. In addition to two stages at Harvard's Loeb Drama Center (64 Brattle St., Cambridge), the company recently opened the Zero Arrow Theatre (2 Arrow St., Cambridge, 617/495-2668), which has a flexible stage for even more cutting-edge productions.

The multistage **Boston Center for the Arts** (539 Tremont St., 617/426-5000, www. bcaonline.org) is a South End complex that features several modern resident theater companies. In addition to the 360-seat Calderwood Pavilion, the complex has four smaller stages of varying sizes.

Affiliated with the Wang Center, the **Commonwealth Shakespeare Company** (617/426-0863, www.commshakes.org/) has

been performing the Bard outdoors for the past decade. The free summertime performances take place in July and August at the Parkman Bandstand in Boston Common.

Last but not least, the **Charles Playhouse** (74 Warrenton St., www.charles-playhouse. com) is home to two long-running Boston favorites, the bizarrely comic Blue Man Group (800/982-2787, www.blueman.com) and the interactive whodunnit *Shear Madness* (617/426-5225, www.shearmadness.com), a cheesy Boston tradition for more than 25 years and 12,000 performances.

DANCE

Few ballet companies are as respected as the **Boston Ballet** (19 Clarendon St., 617/695-6950, www.bostonballet.org), which has been performing classic and modern interpretations of the form for 40 years. Its annual productions of *The Nutcracker,* performed at the Opera House, are internationally famous. A younger ballet company, which puts its emphasis on the dancing rather than costumes or sets, is the **Jose Mateo Dance Theatre** (400 Harvard St., Cambridge, 617/354-7467, www. ballettheatre.org). It performs in the Sanctuary Theatre, a beautifully restored Gothic church in Cambridge.

FILM

The revivals of Humphrey Bogart classics during Harvard's exam period long ago put the **Brattle Theater** (40 Brattle St., Cambridge, 617/876-6837, www.brattlefilm.org) on the map. It sill runs Bogey marathons along with foreign films, New Wave cinema, and more recent independent fare in a delightfully shabby Harvard Square theater. Film directors regularly show up to introduce shows. Also in Cambridge, **Kendall Cinemas** (1 Kendall Sq., Cambridge, 617/499-1996, www.landmarktheatres.com) shows first-run art-house and foreign films in a well-appointed theater serving espresso at the candy counter.

The large, art deco **Coolidge Corner Theatre** (290 Harvard St., Brookline, 617/734-2500, www.coolidge.org) anchors its

© KINDRA CLINEFF/MOTT

Boston Center for the Arts

LECTURES AND READINGS

As befits an intellectual populace, Boston and Cambridge's many colleges and universities often open their doors to the public for lectures by speakers at the top of their academic games. The **Harvard University Gazette** (www.news.harvard.edu/gazette) publishes a full schedule of talks, as do the websites of **Boston University** (www.bu.edu/calendar) and **Massachusetts Institute of Technology** (http://events.mit.edu). Public lectures, often on topics relating to the city's history, geography, or various ethnic cultures, are also held periodically at **Boston Public Library** (700 Boylston St., 617/536-5400, www.bpl.org/news/comingevents.htm) and **Old South Meeting House** (310 Washington St., 617/482-6439, www.oldsouthmeetinghouse.org). Contemporary readings and talks by authors are held at several noteworthy bookstores, including **Harvard Bookstore** (1256 Massachusetts Ave., Cambridge, 800/542-7323, www.harvard.com) and **Brookline Booksmith** (279 Harvard St., Brookline, 617/566-6660, www.brooklinebooksmith.com), which for popular authors takes over the **Coolidge Corner Movie Theater** (290 Harvard St., Brookline, 617/734-2500, www.coolidge.org) across the street.

neighborhood with a gorgeous space for second-run and cult movies, as well as concerts and lectures by best-selling authors. It also has a smaller video screening room for DV (digital video) films and local work.

Free films, tending towards the classics, are shown in the Rabb Lecture Hall of the **Boston Public Library** (700 Boylston St., 617/536-5400, www.bpl.org), usually on Mondays. During the summer, **Free Friday Flicks** (617/787-7200, www.wbz1030.com) brings family-friendly blockbusters outdoors to the Hatch Shell on the Esplanade. The **Museum of Fine Arts** (465 Huntington Ave., 617/369-3306, www.mfa.org) also regularly screens contemporary foreign films and movies relating to current art exhibitions.

COMEDY

After years in a cramped spot in Quincy Market, the **Comedy Connection** (The Wilbur Theatre, 146 Tremont St., 800/745-3000, www.thewilburtheatre.com, $12–24) has hit the big time with a move into the Theater District. In addition to local up-and-comers, it routinely books the biggest names in yuks, recently including Bill Maher, Janeane Garofalo, and Mike Bribiglia. (The Wilbur Theatre also occasionally hosts rock acts such as Neko Case and Sonic Youth.) Quick-thinking young comics incorporate audience suggestions into improvisational sketches à la *Whose Line Is It Anyway?* at the North End's **ImprovAsylum** (216 Hanover St., 617/263-6887, www.improvasylum.com).

EVENTS

Boston's events calendar starts on New Year's Eve with **First Night,** a citywide celebration featuring concerts, kid's activities, and artistic events throughout the day of December 31. The night is capped off by two fireworks celebrations, one in the early evening and another at midnight. Just after the holiday bulge disappears, Bostonians fatten up again with the **Boston Cooks!** festival in late January and early February, during which celebrity chefs offer cut-rate meals with the proceeds donated to charity. Around the same time **Boston Wine Expo** takes over the World Trade Center for samplings of thousands of vintages from more than a dozen countries.

If that's not enough partying for you, **St. Patrick's Day** is right around the corner on March 17. The main event is a parade on the nearest Sunday through South Boston, whose streets are bedecked with green for the occasion. To work off all of the weight they've put on in the winter, residents turn out for the **Boston Marathon,** the oldest (and some say toughest) marathon in the United States. Spectators start lining the route to cheer along

Beacon and Boylston Streets, all the way to Copley Square. The race is held on the second Monday in April, which is also known in Massachusetts as **Patriot's Day** to celebrate the early victories of the Revolutionary War.

Patriotism continues when the neighborhood of Charlestown celebrates its own holiday, **Bunker Hill Day,** on June 17. The celebration features military demonstrations by colonial re-enactors, along with a parade and street vendors. Boston's patriotic triptych concludes with the gala celebrations on the **Fourth of July.** Residents wake up early to hear the reading of the Declaration of Independence from the balcony of the Old State House. The main event is the concert by the beloved Boston Pops on the Esplanade, which is televised nationally every year and draws hundreds of thousands to hear musical medleys accompanied by celebrity performers. Get there early if you have any hope of snagging a patch of grass.

The fall in Boston is dedicated to the arts, with theaters commencing their new seasons of plays, and neighborhoods including the South End, Cambridge, and Jamaica Plain holding annual **open studios** to showcase local artwork. The holidays officially begin with the **Holiday Tree Lighting** at the Prudential Center, which brings out politicians and celebrities along with the mayor to throw the switch.

Nightlife

After hours, Boston has a rambunctious mix of old-time Irish bars, dance clubs, and newer upscale lounges. As a remnant of the blue laws, "happy hour" drink specials are forbidden here—though many bars offer free food for the after-work crowd. Smoking is also illegal in all bars, though a few may quietly let you light up in back. Bars in Boston and Somerville generally close at 1 A.M. during the week and 2 A.M. on weekends. Cambridge bars close at 1 A.M. nightly.

BARS AND LOUNGES
Beacon Hill
Catch up on political gossip at **The 21st Amendment** (150 Bowdoin St., 617/227-7100, www.21stboston.com), a beat-up watering hole across from the State House. Named after the amendment that ended prohibition, it caters mostly to a draft-beer crowd. Down the hill, **The Sevens** (77 Charles St., 617/523-9074, 11 A.M.–11 P.M. Mon.–Sat.; 12 P.M.–11 P.M. Sun., www.sevensalehouse.com) is the closest thing Beacon Hill has to a neighborhood bar, where well-mannered brahmins and well-coifed business consultants share wooden booths and watch the flow of people on Charles Street.

Government Center and Faneuil Hall
The laid-back **Hennessy's** (25 Union St., 617/742-2121, 11 P.M.–1 A.M. Mon.–Sat.; 12 P.M.–12 A.M. Sun., www.somerspubs.com/) is carefully crafted to evoke a Victorian roadside tavern, with a selection of Irish whiskies and occasional Celtic music that draws an expat Irish crowd. A reliable pour of Guinness and raucous live fiddlers can be found at **The Black Rose** (160 State St., 617/742-2286, 12 P.M.–2 A.M. Mon.–Sat.; 12 P.M.–1 A.M. Sun., www.irishconnection.com/), an Irish pub near Faneuil Hall that is a favorite with tourists. Pictures of Hibernian writers line the walls, and hearty fare such as corned beef and fish-and-chips is served. Located inside the Omni Parker House, **The Last Hurrah** (60 School St., 617/725-1888, 10 A.M.–1 A.M. Mon.–Sat.; 1 P.M.–1 A.M. Sun., www.omnihotels.com) is named after a book about one of Boston's most notorious politicians, "Rascal King" James Michael Curley. Its elegant, plant-filled room is a hangout for City Hall types and Financial District suits, who trade favors and stock tips over martinis.

Downtown Crossing
Cops, reporters, businessmen, and hipsters

can all be spotted ordering boilermakers at **J. J. Foley's** (21 Kingston St., 617/695-2529, 4 p.m.–2 a.m. Mon.–Sat.; 3 p.m.–12 a.m. Sun.,), one of the last great downtown neighborhood bars. The lighting is dim, the jukebox exceptional, and the crowd usually quite thirsty.

North End

If you couldn't get into the game at the Garden, or if you're just a multitasker, you'll enjoy the **Sports Grille Boston** (132 Canal St., 617/367-9302, 5 p.m.–1 a.m. Mon.–Sat.; 4 p.m.–11 p.m. Sun.,), which has 140 TVs, all tuned to one thing: sports. The bar's mammoth interior has a bit of a soulless feeling, offset slightly by the authentic memorabilia of Boston sports legends on the walls. As an antidote to all those plastic Paddy pubs that serve beer green, the Irish pub **McGann's** (197 Portland St., 617/227-4059, 11 a.m.–1 a.m. daily) is the real thing, with a decor straight from County Clare, and the likes of Belhaven and Tetley's on tap. Sinead O'Connor once even played a (very) intimate show on stage here. The industrial decor and smell of roasted malts at **Boston Beer Works** (112 Canal St., 617/896-2337, 11 a.m.–1 a.m. Mon.–Sat.; 12 p.m.–11 p.m. Sun., www.beerworks.net) harken back to the days when brewpubs were king. If the fad has paled, the beer at least hasn't—brews like Boston Red and Back Bay IPA hit the spot, while TVs show all the action at the arena next door.

Financial District

Working stiffs clock out of their cubicles and become human again at **Market** (21 Broad St., 617/263-0037, 4 p.m.–2 a.m. Mon.–Sat.; 12 p.m.–11 p.m. Sun., www.mktboston.com) A round wooden bar and rough-hewn wooden pillars create a rustic vibe to chill out the after-work crowd, while crafted cocktails with lychee and blackberries help stir up a juicy singles scene.

Back Bay

There could be a raging nor'easter outside, but inside the legendary **Oak Bar** (138 St. James St., 617/267-5300, 11 a.m.–2 a.m. Mon.–Sat.; 11 a.m.–12 a.m. Sun., www.theoakroom.com) in the Fairmont Copley Plaza, it's always 70 degrees, with the sun just setting over the Indian Ocean, and the distant whack of a cricket bat audible over the veldt. The crisp service of the gold-vested bartenders bespeaks civilization, while the generous martinis whisper pure decadence. In the basement of the nearby Copley Square Hotel, **Saint** (90 Exeter St., 617/236-1134, 4:30 p.m.–2 a.m. Mon.–Sat.; 5 p.m.–1 a.m. Sun.,) is like a grown-up version of a "heaven and hell" party—cool and opalescent in one room and devilish red velvet in the other. Insouciant patrons spend their time sampling a fusion tapas menu, listening to cool techno, and making provocative glances across the room. On Newbury Street, the young and lovely hang out at **Sonsie** (327 Newbury St., 617/351-2500, 8 a.m.–1 a.m. Mon.–Sat.; 8:30 a.m.–12 a.m. Sun., www.sonsieboston.com), where French doors open up onto the street, the better to check out the handbags and clothing labels of passersby.

South End

The neighborhood living room for the South End's gay scene, the **Club Cafe Lounge & Video Bar** (209 Columbus Ave., 617/536-0966, 4 p.m.–2 a.m. Mon.–Thurs.; 12 p.m.–2 a.m. Thurs.–Fri.; 11 a.m.–1 a.m. Sun., www.clubcafe.com) is clean and well-lit, all the better to check out the attractive stranger at the next table. Groups of people play musical chairs while trading gossip before and after clubbing. Located on two levels beneath the Boston Center for the Arts, **The Beehive** (541 Tremont St., 617/423-0069, 5 p.m.–2 a.m. daily, www.beehiveboston.com) buzzes with a bohemian crowd who come for laid-back jazz and a potent drink list that tastes of blood orange and apricot nectar. The space itself is a knockout, designed within an inch of its life from an eclectic mix of influences ranging from Spanish bordello to New York pop art. Upstairs, tables serve a bistro menu of bouillabaisse and steak frites.

The hole-in-the-wall **Delux Cafe & Lounge** (100 Chandler St., 617/338-5258, 5 p.m.–1 a.m.

daily) is one of the most trippy bar scenes in the city, where a heterogeneous crowd downs pints beneath Christmas lights and Elvis album covers. Snack food includes the best grilled cheese sandwich in the city. **The Butcher Shop** (552 Tremont St., 617/423-4800, 11 A.M.–11 P.M. Sun.–Mon.; 11 A.M.–12 A.M. Tues.–Sat., www. thebutchershopboston.com) is only a meat market in the most literal sense. Butchers prepare cuts of meat during the day; at night, however, the giant butcher block table is taken over by the young and metrosexual, who toy with an extensive by-the-glass wine list and nosh on honey-soaked figs and panini sandwiches.

Other Neighborhoods

Boston's only drag-queen bar, **Jacque's Cabaret** (79 Broadway, 617/426-8902, 11 A.M.–12 A.M. Mon.–Sat.; 12 P.M.–12 A.M. Sun., www.jacquescabaret.com) is like a pomegranate: deliciously seedy. Anything goes and frequently does at shows in which female impersonators lip-synch for cat-calling audiences that usually include at least one bachelorette party. Located in the neighborhood of Bay Village, behind the Theater District, the bar has a small room downstairs that hosts indie bands and cabaret acts. The local hangout for Fort Point Channel's artists community, **Lucky's Lounge** (355 Congress St., South Boston, 617/357-5825, 11 A.M.–11 P.M. Mon.–Thurs.; 10 A.M.–11 P.M. Sat.–Sun., www.luckyslounge.com) rewards those who can find it. A basement door without a sign opens up onto a retro-cool cocktail lounge where kitschy landscapes line the walls and Frank Sinatra is in regular rotation.

A true Jamaica Plain institution, **Doyle's Cafe** (3484 Washington St., Jamaica Plain, 617/524-2345, 9 A.M.–11 P.M. Mon.–Sat.; 11 A.M.–9 P.M. Sun., www.doyles-cafe.com) is a temple to more than 100 years of city politics, with memorabilia on the wall dedicated to politicians from John F. Kennedy to John Kerry—and a new generation of politicos writing history over pints or single malts in the corner booths. Beer lovers make regular pilgrimages to Allston to sample the more than 112 brews on tap at **Sunset Grill & Tap** (130 Brighton Ave., Allston, 617/254-1331, 4 P.M.–2 A.M. Mon.–Sat.; 11 A.M.–1 A.M. Sun., www.allstonsfinest.com). Another 400 are served in bottles; if you are really thirsty you can order it by the yard.

Cambridge

The black leather couches and velvet curtains of **Noir** (1 Bennett St., Cambridge, 617/661-8010, 4 P.M.–2 A.M. daily, www.noir-bar.com) could easily serve as the backdrop for an illicit affair. Located in Harvard Square's Charles Hotel, the lounge does its best to stir up intrigue with cocktails named for classic film noir movies. The more rambunctious **Grendel's Den** (89 Winthrop St., Cambridge, 617/491-1160, 11:30 A.M.–11 P.M. daily, www.grendelsden.com) is a subterranean lair where surly waitstaff serve pints and finger food to a heavily Harvard-saturated crowd.

In Central Square, the **Plough & Stars** (912 Massachusetts Ave., Cambridge, 617/576-0032, 11:30 A.M.–12 A.M. daily, www.ploughandstars.com) is an Irish bar with a working-class feel. It features an eclectic mix of live music and European soccer matches on the telly. The New York–cool **Middlesex Lounge** (315 Massachusetts Ave., Cambridge, 617/868-6739, 11:30 A.M.–1 A.M. Mon.–Wed.; 11:30 A.M.–2 A.M. Thurs.–Fri.; 5 P.M.–2 A.M. Sat., www.middlesexlounge.com) puts its couches on wheels, the better to convert from techno lounge to dance floor with the shake of a booty. The zen minimalist vibe attracts a cross-section of Cambridge pseudo-literati. At MIT's neighborhood bar, **Miracle of Science Bar + Grill** (321 Massachusetts Ave., Cambridge, 617/868-2866, 7 A.M.–1 A.M. Mon.–Fri.; 9 A.M.–1 A.M. Sat.–Sun.; www.miracleofscience.us), the menu is modeled after the Periodic Table of Elements. Amorous nerds use their laptops to send instant messages across the room.

Somerville

An Irish bar on steroids, **The Burren** (247 Elm St., Somerville, 617/776-6896,

11:30 A.M.–12 A.M. Mon.–Fri.; 11 A.M.–1 A.M. Sat.–Sun.; www.burren.com) nevertheless manages to keep it real with Irish *seisiuns* and step-dancing on a stage in the back room. On other nights, patrons drink their stout while listening to open-mic poetry.

Brookline

The **Coolidge Corner Clubhouse** (307A-309 Harvard St., Brookline, 617/566-4948, 4 P.M.–1 A.M. Mon.–Fri.; 11:30 A.M.–12:45 A.M. Sat.–Sun.; www.thecoolidgecornerclubhouse. com) is a curious hybrid of French brasserie and neighborhood sports bar. Its 22 TVs ensure that there is always a game on worth watching.

LIVE MUSIC
Rock

The center of Boston's rock scene is actually in Central Square in Cambridge. The legendary **Middle East Restaurant & Nightclub** (472–480 Massachusetts Ave., Cambridge, 617/864-3278, www.mideastclub.com) is a complex of three rooms with different styles. Larger bands play in the grungy basement downstairs, while local acts and indie bands play the cozier upstairs. Belly dancers and the occasional singer-songwriter take the stage in the Middle Eastern restaurant upstairs. Word to the wise: skip the food. Named 30 years ago for a pet hamster, **TT The Bear's Place** (10 Brookline Ave., Cambridge, 617/492-2327, www.ttthebears. com) is the hangout of choice for the city's own rock stars, groupies, and wannabes. Bookings tend heavily toward the local, but also include touring bands on their way up. Several rooms allow rockers to talk or shoot pool until their friend's band takes the stage.

U2 made their first legendary U.S. performances at **Paradise Rock Club** (967–969 Commonwealth Ave., 617/562-8800, www. thedise.com), a mid-sized club with good views from several tiers of balconies (each with its own bar). Next door, the Paradise Lounge is a smaller space decked out with modern art that stages everything from acoustic performances to erotic poetry. Outside of Harvard Square,

the **Lizard Lounge** (1667 Massachusetts Ave., Cambridge, 617/547-0759, www.lizardlounge-club.com) is the place to go for esoteric rock, neo-burlesque, or poetry readings in its small basement.

Jazz and Blues

The cream of the jazz and Latin crop come to the **Regattabar** (1 Bennett St., Cambridge, 617/395-7757, www.regattabarjazz.com), a 225-capacity room in Harvard Square. Tables are arranged around a stage floor in a simple space with no distractions from the music—which in the past has included the likes of Branford Marsalis and Joshua Redman. Booked by legendary jazz club promoter Fred Taylor, **Scullers Jazz Club** (Doubletree Guest Suites, 400 Soldiers Field Rd., 617/562-4111, www.scullersjazz.com) is impressive both for the quality of its talent and the expansiveness of its view of the Charles River. The 200-capacity room has hosted everyone from Lou Rawls to Chris Botti.

The South End's **Wally's** (427 Massachusetts Ave., 617/424-1408, www.wallyscafe.com) hosts jazz the way it was meant to be played, in a closet-sized room that heats up both on and off stage. It is one of the few places in Boston that brings people of all backgrounds together to worship at the altar of syncopation. Don't expect big names—just talented performers. The **Can-Tab Lounge** (738 Massachusetts Ave., Cambridge, 617/354-2685, www.cantab-lounge.com) is a joint in the classic sense of the word, where R&B and blues acts alternate nights with multi-ethnic poetry slams. Crooner and minor legend Little Joe Cook performs on weekends here, as he has for the past 25 years.

Folk

The intimate **Club Passim** (47 Palmer St., Cambridge, 617/492-7679, www.clubpassim. org) has a history many times its small size. Many great names have gotten their start in this Harvard Square folk institution, including Joan Baez, Suzanne Vega, and Shawn Colvin. Now, it has a talented group of regular performers who have developed a singer-songwriter style known as the "Boston Sound" for its catchy harmonies and erudite lyrics. Every Memorial Day and Labor Day weekend, it stages a three-day marathon of music. No alcohol is served, but good vegetarian cuisine is.

DANCE CLUBS
Downtown

The beautiful people shake their thing at **Gypsy Bar** (116 Boylston St., 617/482-7799, www.gypsybarboston.com), a plush downtown dance club decked out in deep-brown leather, dark wood, and pulsing red lights. It draws an international crowd who mingle at the long wine bar before they take the plunge onto the dance floor to dance to house music as the night wears on. At the other end of the spectrum, the fraternity brothers who frequent **Liquor Store** (25 Boylston St., 617/357-6800, www.liquorstoreboston.com) are more randy than the mechanical bull featured in a bikini bull-riding competition every Friday night. The club does have some standards, however—no sneakers or shorts are allowed.

The Roxy (279 Tremont St., 617/338-7699, www.roxyplex.com) used to be a grand ballroom, and the opulent decor sets the stage for its air of modern decadence. High-energy and heavily European crowds come here to dance to hip-hop and '80s music. Occasionally the stage also hosts rock bands and Chippendale's male reviews.

Fenway

Behind Fenway Park, it's always Mardi Gras at **Tequila Rain** (3 Lansdowne St., 617/437-0300, www.tequilarainboston.com), a testosterone-filled dance club that features Top 40 music and periodic hormonal tomfoolery like wet T-shirt contests and dunk tanks. It caters to a post-game and suburban crowd.

Two different tastes can be found at the co-joined gay clubs **Ramrod/Machine** (1254 Boylston St., 617/266-2986; 1256 Boylston St., 617/536-1950; www.ramrod-boston.com, www.machine-boston.com). Ramrod is a cruisy leather bar with a back room open only to those wearing leather or not wearing a shirt. Next door, Machine is a more casual hangout with a large dance floor and a hot, hot Friday-night scene. The two mix over a pool table that connects the two spaces.

BILLIARDS AND BOWLING

Flat Top Johnny's (1 Kendall Square, Cambridge, 617/494-9565, www.flattop-johnnys.com) feels like a 1940s pool hall, updated with a punk-rock soundtrack and a Roy Lichtenstein–esque mural on one wall. The crowd consists of the hipper denizens of Cambridge, who seem like they've taken time off from their art or recording studio to rack a few.

The computerized scorekeepers at **Kings** (50 Dalton St., 617/266-2695, www.kingsbackbay. com) keep track of the pins so you don't have to. The self-consciously retro Back Bay bowling alley is a favorite with after-work leagues. The balls are the regular size—not the smaller candlepins common in New England. A small side room has eight vintage pool tables.

The Fenway area's **Jillian's** (145 Ipswich St., 617/437-0300, www.jilliansboston.com) is an homage to attention deficit disorder, with a 16-lane bowling alley and what seems like miles of the latest arcade games and pool tables on three different floors. If you can't have fun here, you probably don't know how.

Shopping

Several shopping malls are connected in the center of the city, allowing shoppers to browse for a mile without suffering so much as a raindrop. Near Copley Square, the **Shops At Copley Place** (2 Copley Place, 617/369-5000, www.simon.com) include upscale clothing designers such as Neiman Marcus, Barneys New York, and Louis Vuitton, and jewelry stores Montblanc and Tiffany & Co. They are connected through a pedestrian walkway to the **Shops at Prudential Center** (800 Boylston St., 617/236-3100, www.prudentialcenter. com), which has a diverse selection of upscale and casual stores. In Cambridge, the two-story **Cambridgeside Galleria** is filled with books, music, and clothing stores. (100 Cambridgeside Place, Cambridge, 617/621-8666, www.cambridgesidegalleria.com).

ANTIQUES

Charles Street has some 40 antiques stores along its one-third-mile length. While pricey, they offer a selection you won't find anywhere else in the city. One of the best is **Upstairs Downstairs Antiques** (93 Charles St., 617/367-1950, 10 A.M.–6 P.M. daily) a warren of rooms stuffed with tableware, glassware, and other knickknacks from a dozen decades. Armchair historians and explorers alike thrill at the selection of antique maps and charts at **Eugene Galleries** (76 Charles St., 617/227-3062, 10 A.M.–5 P.M. Mon.–Sat.; 11 A.M.–5 P.M. Sun.), which cover Boston, New England, and the rest of the world. Worth making a trip out to Cambridge for the prices alone, **Antiques on Cambridge Street** (1076 Cambridge St., Cambridge, 617/234-0001,

© MICHAEL BLANDING

Quincy Market is a former fish warehouse turned upscale mall.

9:30 A.M.–5:30 P.M. daily) is filled with the wares of more than 100 sellers—furniture, artwork, vintage clothing, housewares, and more.

ART GALLERIES

The most prestigious art galleries are in the high-rent district of Newbury Street. The biggest name on the street is the **Barbara Krakow Gallery** (10 Newbury St., 617/262-4490, 10 A.M.–5 P.M. Mon.–Sat.; or call for an appointment, www.barbarakrakowgallery.com), which draws nationally known contemporary artists. More traditional paintings and prints are on display at the venerable **Childs Gallery** (169 Newbury St., 617/266-1108, 10 A.M.–5:30 P.M. Mon.–Fri; 11 A.M.–5 P.M. Sat.–Sun.), www.childsgallery.com), which focuses on pre-WWII American and European work. The **International Poster Gallery** (205 Newbury St., 617/375-0076, by appointment only, www.internationalposter.com) is a treasure trove of original French liquor prints and Russian propaganda posters.

Anchoring the cutting-edge SoWa arts district, the **Carroll and Sons Gallery** (450 Harrison Ave., 617/482-2477, 10 A.M.–5 P.M. Mon.–Fri; or by appointment, www.carrollandsons.net) is the place to spot new and often local talent. You can't get much closer to the source of creation than the **Fort Point Arts Community Gallery** (300 Summer St., 617/423-4299, 10 A.M.–7 P.M. Mon.–Fri; weekend hours vary), www.fortpointarts.org), which exhibits the work of New England's largest and oldest artists community in a building where many of them have their studios.

BATH AND BEAUTY

Boston is the original home of **Fresh** (121 Newbury St., 617/421-1212, 10 A.M.–7 P.M. Mon.–Fri.; 10 A.M.–6 P.M. Sat.; 11 A.M.–5 P.M. Sun., www.fresh.com), a luxury bath boutique that features milk, tea, and sake among its natural ingredients. Hard-to-find hair and makeup products line the shelves at **The Beauty Mark** (33 Charles St., 617/720-1555, 10:30 A.M.–6 P.M. Mon.–Fri.; 11 A.M.–5 P.M.

Sat., closed Sun.), www.thebeautymark.com), a tiny store with a cult following.

BOOKS
New

Professors and students alike shop at **Harvard Book Store** (1256 Massachusetts Ave., Cambridge, 617/661-1515, 9:30 A.M.–8 P.M. Mon.–Sat.; 10 A.M.–5 P.M. Sun., www.harvard.com), which has been named one of the best in the country for its combination of erudite bestsellers and brainy staff. **Brookline Booksmith** (279 Harvard St., Brookline, 617/566-6660, 10 A.M.–8:30 P.M. Mon.–Sat.; 10 A.M.–7 P.M. Sun., www.brooklinebooksmith.com) anchors the neighborhood of Coolidge Corner with an attractive bookstore well laid out for browsing. **Trident Booksellers and Cafe** (338 Newbury St., 617/267-8688, 8 A.M.–12 A.M., www.tridentbookscafe.com) has a good selection of magazines along with books focusing on philosophy and Eastern spirituality.

Used

The owner of the **Brattle Book Shop** (9 West St., 617/542-0210, 9 A.M.–5:30 P.M. daily, www.brattlebookshop.com), Ken Gloss, scours estate sales for rare and antique page-turners, then dusts them off for browsing. In Porter Square, the large and musty **McIntyre & Moore** (1971 Massachusetts Ave., Cambridge, 617/229-5641, 10 A.M.–8 P.M. Mon.–Wed.; 10 A.M.–10 P.M. Mon.–Wed.; 12 P.M.–8 P.M. Sun., www.mcintyreandmoore.com) has a great selection of literary criticism and cultural theory, along with shelves of fiction and nonfiction books.

Specialty

You've heard about Curious George and Snow White, but what about Herb the Vegetarian Dragon? A "thinking child's bookstore," **Barefoot Books** (1771 Massachusetts Ave., Cambridge, 617/349-1610, 10 A.M.–6 P.M. Mon.–Sat.; 12 P.M.–5 P.M. Sun., www.barefootbooks.com) offers decidedly imaginative titles. In Harvard Square, **Grolier Poetry Bookshop** (6 Plympton St., Cambridge,

MAP QUEST

Traveler, tourist, victim of wanderlust – whatever you call yourself, don't bypass the **Globe Corner Bookstore** (90 Mt. Auburn St., Cambridge, 617/497-6277, www.globecorner.com, 9:30 A.M.–9 A.M. Mon.–Sat., 11 A.M.–7 P.M. Sun.). With some 15 years amassing a dedicated following for its excellent stock of in-depth travel information (one of the largest in North America), it offers mesmerizing oversized atlases, an epic selection of travel guidebooks, regional cookbooks, nautical books, recreational guides, and a huge case of geographical survey maps of locales in New England. Even more books and maps are available on the website of the shop, which will place a special order for any item it doesn't have readily in stock.

617/547-4648, 10 A.M.–8 P.M. Mon.–Sat.; 11 P.M.–5 P.M. Sun., www.grolierpoetry-bookshop.com) is one of only two bookstores in America devoted completely to poetry. Nearby, **Schoenhof's Foreign Books** (76A Mount Auburn St., Cambridge, 617/547-8855, 10 A.M.–8 P.M. Mon.–Fri.; 10 A.M.–7 P.M. Sat.; 10 A.M.–6 P.M. Sun., www.schoenhofs.com) offers the largest selection of foreign books in North America. Art scholars worldwide go to **Ars Libri** (500 Harrison St., 617/357-5212, 9 A.M.–6 P.M. Sat.–Fri.; 11 A.M.–5 P.M. Sat.; closed Sun.,www.arslibri.com), full of rare and out-of-print tomes on art and sculpture.

CLOTHING AND ACCESORIES

The place to shop for clothes is stylish **Newbury Street,** which carries outposts of international designers from Armani to Zegna, alongside local boutiques. Other neighborhoods have their own local clothing shops that range from style-conscious to bargain-conscious.

Unisex

A techno-powered emporium inside a classy old museum building, **Louis Boston** (234 Berkeley St., 617/262-6100, 11 A.M.–6 P.M.

Mon.–Wed.; 11 A.M.–7 P.M. Thurs.–Sat.; closed Sun., www.louisboston.com) is where "proper Bostonians" shop for Loro Piana cashmere and clubbers stay abreast of the latest European fashions. The pages of *Vogue* and *GQ* leap into the retail world at **Alan Bilzerian** (34 Newbury St., 617/536-1001, 10 A.M.–7 P.M. Mon.–Sat.; 11 A.M.–6 P.M. Sun., www.alan-bilzerian.com), Boston's supplier of the most of-the-moment labels.

The myth. The legend. The bahgains. Even if you don't find what you are looking for at **Filene's Basement** (497 Boylston St., 617/424-5520, 9 A.M.–9 P.M. Mon.–Sat.; 11 A.M.–7 P.M. Sun., www.filenesbasement.com), you'll find something irresistible at the original designer discount store.

Women's

Emerging urban designers spruce up the rack at **Turtle** (619 Tremont St., 617/266-2610, 11 A.M.–7 P.M. Tues.–Fri.; 10 A.M.–6 P.M. Sat., noon–5 P.M. Sun., closed Mon., www.turtle-boston.com), a boutique with all of the style at a fraction of the price. International flair and old-world elegance meet at **Daniela Corte** (91 Newbury St., 617/262-2100, www.daniela-corte.com, by appointment only), an Argentine clothing designer who constructs one-of-a-kind designs.

Men's

The Ivy League clothier of choice for over 100 years, **J.Press** (82 Mt. Auburn St., 617/547-9886, 9 A.M.–5:30 P.M. Mon.–Sat.; www.jpressonline.com) will outfit you with argyle and herringbone worthy of Harvard Yard. The South End's **Market** (558 Tremont St., 617/338-4500, 9 A.M.–5:30 P.M. Mon.–Sat.) stocks the latest fashions from Dolce & Gabbana and Paul Smith.

Children's

High-powered moms shop for too-cute-for-words ensembles at **The Red Wagon** (69 Charles St., 617/523-9402, 10 A.M.–7 P.M. Mon.–Sat.; 11 A.M.–5 P.M. Sun., www.thered-wagon.com), which carries both American and

European labels. Tween fashions fill **Pixie Stix** (131 Charles St., 617/523-3211, 10 A.M.–7 P.M. Mon.–Sat.; 11 A.M.–5 P.M. Sun., www.pixiestixboston.com), a pink-and-aqua emporium of designer jumpsuits, T-shirts, and skirts.

Vintage

Cowboy hats, cocktail dresses, or leather jackets, you'll find everything you need for Halloween—or just Saturday night—at the closet-sized vintage shop **Oona's** (1210 Massachusetts Ave., Cambridge, 10 A.M.–8 P.M. Mon.–Fri.; 10 A.M.–6 P.M. Sat., noon–5 P.M. Sun., 617/491-2654). The gargantuan **Garment District** (200 Broadway, Cambridge, 617/876-5230, 11 A.M.–midnight Sun.–Fri.; 9 A.M.–midnight Sat., www.garment-district.com) has threads for every style, whether it's the Mod Squad or the Jimi Hendrix Experience.

Jewelry

The **Jenny's Jewelry** (345 Washington St., 617/523-0610, 10 A.M.–9 A.M. Mon.–Fri.; 10 A.M.–7 A.M. Sat.; noon–5 P.M. Sun., www.jewelryexchange.com) is an emporium of gold, pearls, and gemstones, with dozens of discount jewelers vying for your hand. Modern jewelry as well as a wide selection of estate pieces can be found at **E. B. Horn** (429 Washington St., 617/542-3902, 9:30 A.M.–6 P.M. Tues., Wed. and Fri.; 9:30 A.M.–5:30 P.M. Mon. and Thurs.; closed Sun., www.ebhorn.com), a downtown jeweler with 165 years of history in the same location. State-of-the-art timepieces take center stage at **Ross-Simons** (800 Boylston St., 617/236-3100, www.ross-simons.com).

FOOD

Alligator, rattlesnake, or ostrich meat might not be what you had in mind for dinner, but they might tempt you at **Savenor's Market** (160 Charles St., 617/723-6328, 11 A.M.–8 P.M. Mon.–Fri.; 10 A.M.–8 P.M.Sat; midnight–7 P.M.Sun; www.savenorsmarket. com). Chefs themselves shop at this gourmet shop which also carries more pedestrian fare like *kobe* beef and truffle oil. **Cardullo's**

Gourmet Shoppe (6 Brattle St., Cambridge, 617/491-8888, 10 A.M.–9 P.M. Mon.–Sat.; 11 A.M.–7 P.M.Sun., www.cardullos.com) is a Harvard Square institution, stocked with international and New England foodstuffs. Take the North End home with you at **Salumeria Italiana** (151 Richmond St., 800/400-5916, 8 A.M.–6 P.M. Mon.–Sat.; www.salumeriaitaliana.com), an old-world storefront packed with fresh pasta, sauces, and oils.

HOME DECOR

Funky and functional touches for the hip homebody make **Bliss Home** (225 Newbury St., 617/421-5544, 10 A.M.–8 P.M. Mon.–Fri.; 10 A.M.–7 P.M.Sat., midnight–5 P.M.Sun., www. blisshome.com) one-stop gift shopping—for others or yourself. Inventory includes glasses, dinnerware, bar sets, and bath items. Dutch for "alluring," **Lekker** (1317 Washington St., 10 A.M.–7 P.M. Tues.–Sat.; noon–6 P.M.Sat., closed Sun., 617/542-6464, www.lekkerhome.com) sells a combination of clean and contemporary furniture from Germany and the Netherlands, antique armoires from Asia, and textiles and other unique home accessories. Plastic has been given a new life at **Kartell** (10 St. James Ave., 617/728-4442, 10 A.M.–7 P.M. Mon.–Sat.; noon–5 P.M.Sun.) an ultra-modern furniture store featuring European "it"-designers such as Phillipe Starck.

MUSIC

For more than 25 years, **Newbury Comics** (332 Newbury St., 617/236-4930; 36 JFK St., Cambridge, 617/491-0337; and other area locations; 10 A.M.–9 P.M. daily, www.newburycomics.com) has been the music store of choice for area aficionados, with a terrific selection by local artists, regular in-store appearances, and hard-to-find singles and imports. For used CDs, it's hard to beat the selection at **CD Spins** (324 Newbury St., 617/267-5955; 54 Church St., Cambridge, 617/497-7070; and other area locations; 10 A.M.–7 P.M. Mon.–Fri.; noon–5 P.M. Sat.–Sun., www.cdspins.com), a local chain with everything from punk rock to show tunes.

BOSTON

ODDITIES

Part one-of-a-kind shop, part museum of shipbuilding history, the **Lannan Ship Model Gallery** (99 High St., 617/451-2650, www. lannangallery.com) honors Boston's maritime past with more than 300 historical ship models and antique bells, and navigational devices. Coin and baseball card collectors, take note: It gets no better than at **Kenmore Collectibles** (466 Commonwealth Ave., 617/482-5705, 11 A.M.–6 P.M. Mon.–Fri.; 11 P.M.–4 P.M.Sat.; closed Sun., www.kenmorecollectibles.com), where every genre and era are amply represented. Pick up rare and vintage coins, alongside sports memorabilia you never thought you'd see again.

SOUVENIRS

Bostonians may know **Shreve, Crump & Low** (440 Boylston St., 617/267-9100, 10 A.M.–6 P.M. Mon., Wed., and Fri.; 10 A.M.–7 P.M.Thurs., noon–5 P.M.Sun., www.shrevecrumpandlow. com) as one of the city's luxury jewelers, but it also carries a classy line of made-in-Boston souvenirs, from swan-boat pins to ceramic cod pitchers. Cross off everyone on your list at once at the stalls at Faneuil Hall, which are filled with Boston mugs, magnets, keychains, and T-shirts. The **Bostonian Society Museum Shop** (Faneuil Hall, 617/720-3284, 10 A.M.–7 P.M. Mon.–Fri.; 11 A.M.–5 P.M.Sat., closed Sun.) carries colonial-style quilts and ties, and even tea that purports to be the kind thrown overboard at the Boston Tea Party. For sports lovers, **The Brearly Collection** (Faneuil Hall, 800/563-6544, 10 A.M.–8 P.M. Mon.–Sat.; 10 P.M.–6 P.M. Sun., www.brearley.com) offers framed and signed photos of great Boston sports moments. The perfect birthday or anniversary gift: a framed copy of any day's paper from the **Boston Globe Store** (135 Morrissey Blvd., Boston, 617/929-3000, 9 A.M.–4 P.M. Mon.–Fri; closed Sat.–Sun). Known locally as "the Coop," **Harvard Cooperative Society** (1400 Massachusetts Ave., Cambridge, 617/499-2000, 9 A.M.–6:30 P.M. Mon.–Fri.; 10 A.M.–6 P.M. Sat.; closed Sun., www.thecoop.com) anchors Harvard Square with a bookstore and souvenir emporium filled with products emblazoned with the crimson *Veritas* logo. Finally, what's a more delicious souvenir of New England than its trademark delicacy—lobster? Before you board the plane at Logan, snag a few ice-packed crustaceans to go at the airport's branch of **Legal Sea Foods** (Logan International Airport Terminal B, 857/241-2000; Terminal C, 617/568-2800; 10 A.M.–11 P.M. daily, www. legalseafoods.com).

SPORTING GOODS

The city's recognized leader for everything outdoors, **City Sports** (480 Boylston St., 617/267-3900, 10 A.M.–7 P.M. Mon.–Sat.; noon–6 P.M. Sun., www.citysports.com) has active clothing and sports equipment. Straight from the four-time winner of the Boston Marathon, the **Bill Rodgers Running Center** (North Market Bldg., Quincy Marketplace, 617/723-5612, 10 A.M.–7 P.M. Mon.–Sat.; 10 A.M.–5 P.M. Sun., www.billrodgers.com) will suit you up in sweats, sneakers, and advice from its runners turned sales staff. Perfect for stocking up before venturing to Great North Woods, **Joe Jones Wilderness House** (1048 Commonwealth Ave., 617/277-5858, 11 A.M.–6 P.M. daily,) carries skis, fishing rods, tents, crampons, and anything else you could need to tackle the elements.

Sports and Recreation

SPECTATOR SPORTS

Red Sox

On October 27, 2004, sportswriters from around New England dusted off columns they had written long ago, but never thought they'd have a chance to use in their lifetimes. After 86 years, the Boston Red Sox had done the impossible and won the World Series. For most fans of the team (877/733-7699, www.redsox.com), their entire lives had been an exercise in frustration, blaming a supposed curse visited on their team when the Red Sox traded Babe Ruth to their archrivals, the New York Yankees, in 1918. Despite that, the team has some of the most rabid fans in baseball, who became if anything even more enthusiastic (and title-hungry) after breaking their long World Series drought. They were rewarded again in 2007 when the Sox bested the Colorado Rockies to once again win the Series and prove that lighting can strike twice.

Bruins

After the Red Sox, the Bruins come next in the hearts of most true Bostonians (though the Super Bowl–winning Patriots have supplanted them in some). Names like Ray Borque and Bobby Orr are still quick to the tongue of hockey fans, though the Stanley Cup has eluded the team (617/624-2327, www.bostonbruins.com) since 1972. (Few Bostonians begrudged Borque's decision to leave for Colorado, where he won the title in 1996.) When the rival Montreal Canadiens play in town, tickets can still be hard to come by.

Patriots

Though based 30 miles southeast in Foxboro, and officially belonging to the entire region, the New England Patriots are an honorary Boston sports team—and one the city is only too happy to claim. After decades of drought and heartbreaking games against rivals Miami Dolphins and New York Jets, the team (800/543-1776, www.patriots.com) hit upon a winning formula with quarterback Tom

Championship banners proudly hang outside Fenway Park.

© MICHAEL BLANDING

Brady and a team-oriented style of play that earned it three Super Bowl titles in four years, from 2001–2005, and official bragging rights as a "dynasty."

Celtics

For most Bostonians, the heyday of the Celtics (866/423-5849, www.nba.com/celtics) will always be the 1980s, when players like Larry Bird, Kevin McHale, and Robert Parrish racked up title after title against their nemesis, the Los Angeles Lakers. The C's struggled throughout the 1990s under a string of coaching changes and player changes—but like their cousins the Sox and the Pats, they too finally hit pay dirt in 2008 when they hit upon a winning formula with veteran players Paul Pierce, Kevin Garnett, and Ray Allen schooling the leagues youngsters to grab the championship banner and make Boston once and for all the undisputed "winningest" city in the country.

College Sports

Perhaps because of the success of its pro teams, Boston has never seen itself as much of a college sports town. Several annual events are worth seeing however, including the **Head of the Charles Regatta** (617/868-6200, www. hocr.org), which fills the river near Harvard with hundreds of rowing sculls every October. Despite both Harvard and Yale generally fielding lackluster football teams, the annual match-up between them is internationally known as **The Game** (www.the-game.org) due to its fierce competition for Ivy League bragging rights. Now more than 125 years old, the Game is played at Harvard stadium in Allston on alternating years. Perhaps the most eagerly awaited college sporting event is the annual **Beanpot Tournament,** a hockey matchup between Harvard, Boston College, Boston University, and Northeastern University. These days, it's an upset when BU doesn't win.

FITNESS CLUBS

Fitness clubs in Boston range from old-school gyms to the most modern of yoga and Pilates studios. It's fun to work out at the **Central YMCA of Boston** (316 Huntington Ave., 617/536-7800, www.ymca.net, day pass $10), the most affordable place to shoot hoops, swim laps, or lift weights. The gargantuan **Boston Athletic Club** (653 Summer St., 617/269-4300, www. bostonathleticclub.com, day pass $25) has indoor basketball, racquetball, squash, and tennis courts, along with nautilus and weight-training equipment. It's located in the Seaport District. Hands down, the most flexible man in Boston is Baron Baptiste, whose **Baptiste Power Yoga** (25 Harvard St., Brookline, 617/232-9642; 2000 Massachusetts Ave., Cambridge, 617/661-9642; www.baronbaptiste.com, classes $14) incorporates meditation, breathing, and nutrition consults into an energetic style of yoga. Personal trainers are available for drop-in classes or longer regimens. Bodies are sculpted through a variety of methods at **Boston Body** (8 Newbury St., 617/262-3333, www.bostonbody.com, one-time visit $20), which offers classes in yoga and pilates, as well as Thai massage and acupuncture.

RUNNING AND BIKING

As befitting the town where a marathon is one of the year's most anticipated events, Boston is

---

WHAT A RUSH: THE BOSTON MARATHON

The world's oldest annual marathon and one of its most prestigious, the Boston Marathon nearly swallows the city whole year after year, drawing runners from all over the world and spectators from every corner of the region. The race, which starts in the suburb of Hopkinton and ends in Boston's Back Bay, happens every year on Patriot's Day (the third Monday in April), and is by far New England's most-watched sports event. The size of the race itself is noteworthy, too; it boasts an average of 20,000 official runners (many other participants, called "bandits," run unregistered) – remarkable since the race's qualification requirements are unusually high (simply qualifying has become a bragging point in its own right). The exacting standards for entrance aside, the marathon is also famous for its tough course – the difficulty of which literally peaks at Heartbreak Hill. One of a series of hills in Newton, Heartbreak is feared not so much for its height, but because runners reach it between the 20th and 21st miles of the race – a time when they're likely to be already low on energy. Challenging as running the race is, viewing it can be tricky, too, given the crowds of spectators that average 500,000 every year. Sidewalks outside the city tend to have more viewing space, but if you're determined to get as close to the finish line as possible, the best way is to go early in the day to one of the restaurants or bars close to the finish line in Copley Square. By late afternoon, they become loud, boisterous parties full of revelers. But then again, by the end of the race, so have all the blocks surrounding the finish line.

crazy about running. Numerous runners' shops and paths exist to accommodate them. Biking is another story. A few years back, Boston was declared the worst city in the country for biking by *Bicycling* magazine, and despite some stabs at creating a more cohesive network of bike paths, it has yet to live down the reputation.

Sailboats spice up the view along the **Charles River Esplanade** (www.mass.gov/dcr/ parks/metroboston/charlesR.htm), the park of choice for runners, bikers, and inline skaters. A long strip of green along both sides of the river, the park runs 17 miles in a loop from the Charles River Dam to Watertown. More out of the way, but less traveled, is the **Southwest Corridor** (www.mass.gov/dcr/parks/metro-boston/southwestCorr.htm), a five-mile bicycling and running path that starts in the South End. After crossing Massachusetts Avenue, the path provides a mostly uninterrupted stretch of parkland all the way down to Forest Hills and the Arnold Arboretum. Landscape designer Frederick Law Olmstead envisioned an **"Emerald Necklace"** (www.emeraldnecklace. org) of parks that would encircle Boston, beginning at the Back Bay Fens and including the Arnold Arboretum and Franklin Park. The bulk of the necklace is still intact, especially along the Fens, where running paths trace leafy brooks and brackish fens that seem like they have left the city far behind. For more hardcore cyclists, the **Minuteman Bikeway** (www. minutemanbikeway.org) offers 11 miles of graded terrain along an old rail bed, beginning behind Davis Square in Somerville, and running all the way out to the suburb of Bedford, passing historic Arlington and Lexington along the way. If you start early enough, you can stop to see the Revolutionary War sights and still be back in plenty of time for dinner.

HIKING AND CAMPING

Surprisingly, there are many places to camp within and around Boston—and we're not talking about pitching a tent on the Common.

Boston Harbor Islands

Cradled within the arms of Boston Harbor are dozens of islands, ranging from a little dollop of land barely big enough for a seagull to land to the 188-acre **Peddock's Island,** which has a network of roads and trails as well as a campsite for overnight stays. Other islands within the harbor that allow camping include **Grape Island,** with quiet wooded trails and wild blackberries; **Lovell's Island,** which has paths among the sand dunes and rocky tidal pools; and **Bumpkin Island,** with fields of wildflowers and the remains of an old stone farmhouse to explore. All of the islands offer an enviable solitude in full view of the twinkling lights of the city skyline. While camping is not allowed on **Georges Island,** the island has a Civil War–era fort with ranger-led tours, as well as plenty of hiking trails along the beaches. Ferries leave from Long Wharf to Georges Island, where boats are available to other islands. Campers must bring all water and other supplies with them to the islands (617/223-8666, www.bostonislands.org, June–Oct., ferry: $14 adults, $10 seniors, $8 children 3–11, free children under 3; camping reservations: 877/422-6762, www.reserveamerica.com, group sites $25, individual sites $8), which are jointly managed by the National Park Service and the State Department of Conservation and Recreation.

Blue Hills Reservation

On the southern edge of Boston, the protected green space of the Blue Hills rises 600 feet into the sky. The reservation, which is popular with families in the summer, offers a full slate of recreational activities year-round. For hikers, 125 miles of trails wind their way through bottomland forests, swamps, and meadows. If you are lucky, you might spot a coyote or turkey vulture along the way; you are sure to see the delicate lady slipper, a beautiful but endangered Massachusetts flower. Trail maps are available at **Blue Hills Reservation Headquarters** (695 Hillside St., Milton, 617/698-1802, www.mass. gov/dcr/parks/metroboston/blue.htm).

BOATING
Canoeing

There are few better ways to spend an afternoon

than canoeing the Charles River and taking in the waterside views of the State House and Back Bay brownstones. **Charles River Canoe & Kayak** (1071 Soldiers Field Rd., Allston, 617/462-2513, www.ski-paddle.com, 12–8 P.M. Fri. and 10 A.M.–6:30 P.M. Sat.–Sun. May– early Oct.; 12–8 P.M. Mon.–Thurs. June–Aug., Rentals $7–24/hour, $28–96/day) rents a range of canoes and kayaks from its boathouse in Allston. On Friday nights, the company also offers "BBQ Tours" ($63) that include kayak instruction and a post-paddling grill-out.

Sailing

The sailboats picturesquely dotting the Charles in all those postcards belong to **Community Boating** (21 Mugar Way, 617/523-1038, www. community-boating.org, 1 P.M.–sunset Mon.– Fri. and 9 A.M.–sunset Sat.–Sun. Apr.–Oct.), an institution on the Charles River Esplanade for

70 years. It offers unlimited sailing instruction and boat privileges for a $190 flat fee for the season, as well as two-day sailboat rentals for experienced mariners for $100. To ply the waves of the harbor, **Courageous Sailing Center** (1 First Ave., Charlestown Navy Yard, Charlestown, 617/268-7243, www.courageoussailing.org, noon–sunset Mon.–Fri., 10 A.M.–sunset Sat.– Sun. May–Oct.) offers a range of lessons (three beginner sessions $250, three advanced sessions $299, private lessons $95–150/hour).

ROCK CLIMBING

For the weekend warrior who just can't wait for the weekend, the **Granite Railway Quarry** (Ricciuti Dr., off Willard St., West Quincy, 617/727-4573 or 617/698-1802, www.mass. gov/dcr/parks/metroboston/quincyquarries. htm) has some precipices nearly as challenging as those found in the White Mountains.

Accommodations

As with most major cities, hotels in Boston aren't cheap. The amenities offered at the upper end, however, rival any city on the planet—especially after a recent spate of new luxury hotels. For the budget-conscious, however, there is no need to go the fleabag route. Bed-and-breakfasts and furnished apartments scattered throughout the city offer excellent value, especially if you plan on staying a week or longer. A good place to check for listings is the **Bay Colony Bed & Breakfast Associates** (888/486-6018, www.bnbboston. com). Additionally, several low-cost hostels offer clean and comfortable lodging right in the hottest neighborhoods downtown.

BEACON HILL/GOVERNMENT CENTER/NORTH END
$100-150

A quaint bed-and-breakfast on the back side of Beacon Hill, the ◖ **John Jeffries House** (14 Mugar Way, 617/367-1866, www.johnjeffrieshouse.com, $108–184) helps keep costs down

further with kitchenettes in all of the rooms. Originally quarters for nurses at the nearby Massachusetts Eye & Ear Infirmary, the turn-of-the-century Victorian house has spartan but comfortable rooms.

Located in an addition built above a one-story chapel, **La Cappella Suites** (290 North St., 617/523-9020, www.lacappellasuites. com, $95–225) is the North End's only bed-and-breakfast. For an affordable rate, you get a balcony with a view of downtown Boston and complimentary Wi-Fi. Bathrooms are shared, and breakfast consists of frozen waffles, but who cares when you have the pastries of Hanover Street just three blocks away?

$150-250

Ho Chi Minh was a bellhop and Malcolm X a busboy at the historic **Omni Parker House** (60 School St., 617/227-8600, www.omnihotels. com, $159–239); still, the 150-year-old hotel is anything but revolutionary. It opts instead for polished, old-fashioned refinement in rooms with upholstered couches and heirloom antiques. The hotel was recently refurbished to add high-speed Internet and other technological gadgetry to the rooms.

$250 and Up

Before the TV show, CSI: Boston stood for the **Charles Street Inn** (94 Charles St., 617/314-8900, www.charlesstreetinn.com, $250–550), a luxury bed-and-breakfast that is the ultimate honeymoon hotel. Nine sumptuous rooms overflow with Victorian-era antiques, each channeling the personality of a different 19th-century luminary. All rooms feature four-poster beds with high-thread-count sheets, original marble fireplaces, whirlpool tubs, and other amenities.

The sleek design of boutique hotel **(Nine Zero** (90 Tremont St., 617/772-5800, www.ninezero.com, $240–369) is as stylish and modern as its high-powered clientele. In-room features include high-speed Internet access, printer, and OnDemand games. The stylish eye of the city's newfound fashion and celebrity storm, the cool-but-laid-back **(Liberty Hotel** (215 Charles St., 617/224-4004, www.libertyhotel.com, $290–760) is a magnet for fashion shows, local luminary's hosting parties in the lobby, and A-listers looking to crash while filming movies in the city.

DOWNTOWN
$150-250

Oriental rugs and sleigh beds deck out every room of the **(Harborside Inn of Boston** (185 State St., 617/723-7500, www.harborsideinnboston.com, $119–169), a converted 19th-century mercantile building that is one of the most affordable hotels downtown. Exposed brick walls hung with reproductions from the Museum of Fine Arts give a unique Boston feel to large rooms that overlook a central sky-lit atrium.

Unlike most of the cookie-cutter Courtyard by Marriott hotels, the Theater District's **Courtyard Boston Tremont Hotel** (275 Tremont St., 617/426-1400, www.marriott.com, $149–269) is located within a historic

1925 brick building with thoughtful touches like granite countertops in the bathrooms.

$250 and Up

One of the most unique hotels in Boston is located in the landmark 500-foot-tall Custom House Building, which for decades was the highest point in Boston. **Marriott's Custom House** (3 McKinley Sq., 617/310-6300, www.marriott.com, $189–329) has guest rooms elegantly decorated in navy and taupe, as well as kitchenettes and drop-dead views of downtown and the North End.

Located right on the park, the **Ritz-Carlton Boston Common** (10 Avery St., 617/574-7100, www.ritzcarlton.com/en/Properties/BostonCommon/Default.htm, $395–645) eschews its chain's stuffy reputation in favor of a towering building of glass and steel, filled with contemporary art and a stylish ambience. All of the luxury you'd expect is still there, however, including overnight shoeshine and laundry service, and a "bath butler" who will draw you one of a selection of aromatic baths. Packages include access to the on-site Sports Club/LA.

BACK BAY AND SOUTH END
Under $100

The minimalist style sense of the **YWCA Berkeley Residences** (40 Berkeley St., 617/375-2524, www.ywcaboston.org/berkeley, single $65, double $80, triple $99) makes this hostel seem cool rather than spartan. Friendly staff and ideal location combine to create the best budget option in the city. (Men are welcome as well as women.)

A short walk from Newbury Street, the **463 Beacon Street Guest House** (463 Beacon St., 617/536-1302, www.463beacon.com, $79–169) offers a range of rooms in a restored Back Bay brownstone. While small, the rooms are cheerily decorated with an eye toward period detail. The house also has furnished apartments for longer stays.

$100-150

You can't find closer accommodations to Newbury Street shopping than the **Newbury**

Guest House (261 Newbury St., 617/670-6000, www.newburyguesthouse.com, $120–219), which offers simple rooms with white bedspreads and pastel walls, as well as a full breakfast with trademark freshly baked muffins.

$150-250

The South End has many charming bed-and-breakfasts in its historic district. One of the best, the **Herbst Haus** (Appleton St., 617/266-0235, www.herbsthaus.com, $150–225) is located in an 1870s townhouse with two simple but comfortable suites, a parlor with a marble fireplace, and a friendly hostess.

$250 and Up

You might be forgiven if you think for a moment you are in Paris during a stay at the **Eliot Hotel** (370 Commonwealth Ave., 617/267-1607, www.eliothotel.com, $195–335). Everything here is made to conjure up the Continent, including marble bathrooms, French doors in the rooms, plush linens, and a refined, multilingual staff. Even its location on the Commonwealth Mall seems a nod to the Champs Elysées.

When it comes to the **◖ Jewel of Newbury** (254 Newbury St., 617/536-5523, www.jewel-boston.com, $175–295), the name says it all. One-of-a-kind suites blend a personal collection of North African, Indian, and Western antiques to create a sophisticated guesthouse right out of the world of Phineas Fogg. The art deco bar area is a jewel within a jewel.

FENWAY
Under $100

One of Boston University's most modern dorms is converted during the summer into the **Fenway Summer Hostel** (610 Beacon St., 617/267-8599, www.bostonhostel.org, single $100, quad $34.45–45), one of the nicest hostels you are likely to find anywhere. Basic rooms each contain just three beds, as well as a writing desk.

$150-250

French wallpaper, tasseled lampshades, and marble mantels are just some of the details

that make **◖ Gryphon House** (9 Bay State Rd., 617/375-9003, www.gryphonhouseboston.com, $189–365) a favorite place for returning visitors. A Victorian townhouse tucked into the back of Kenmore Square, the hotel has eight rooms, each with a different personality, including the sunny garden room and neo-Gothic sanctuary.

CAMBRIDGE
$100-150

Located behind Harvard University, **◖ A Bed & Breakfast in Cambridge** (1657 Cambridge St., Cambridge, 617/868-7082, www.cambridgebnb.com, $95–200) has three rooms decked out with antique writing desks, canopy beds, and down comforters. The owners clearly delight in hospitality, with freshly baked breads and homemade jams served for breakfast, and a library of books on Boston and Cambridge for guests to peruse. The three guest rooms share a common bath.

$150-250

Jaws often drop when their owners pass beneath the unassuming brick facade of the **Inn at Harvard** (1201 Massachusetts Ave., Cambridge, 617/491-2222, www.theinnatharvard.com, $1950–1700) and enter the spectacular four-story Italianate courtyard inside. Merely ten years old, the inn has worked hard to create an atmosphere befitting its namesake 400-year-old university. Rooms are luxuriously appointed with plush bedding and sheer curtains. Perks for guests include free calls to the Harvard telephone system and passes to the Harvard Faculty Club.

Located within a renovated 1894 Queen Anne–style brick firehouse, the **Kendall Hotel** (350 Main St., Cambridge, 866/566-1300, www.kendallhotel.com, $130–240) bills itself as a "historic boutique hotel" within the MIT campus. Rooms have been lovingly constructed to evoke the era, with country quilts, reproduction furniture, and period antiques. Rates include a breakfast buffet served at an in-house restaurant.

The **◖ Hotel Marlowe** (25 Edwin Land

Blvd., Cambridge, 800/825-7140, www.hotelmarlowe.com, $180–600) might not have the best location, situated above a mall in a no-man's-land between Boston and Cambridge. For style and ambience, however, there is no competition on either side of the river. Every inch has been designed to evoke a mind-blowing pastiche of Buck Rogers and Alice in Wonderland. Bold colors and plush fabrics combine with technological touches like in-room PlayStations and CD players to make this the boutique hotel of choice for the visiting urban sophisticate. Did we mention the complimentary evening wine hour and 24-hour room service?

$250 and Up

When the literati come to Cambridge, there is only place for them to stay. **(The Charles Hotel** (1 Bennett St., Cambridge, 617/864-1200, www.charleshotel.com, $300–480) is filled with every modern luxury, including down comforters, handmade quilts, Bose Wave radios, and DVD players in every room. At the same time, the hotel is quintessentially Cambridge, with an in-house lending library filled with autographed literary bestsellers and a health spa and restaurants frequented by resident academes and visiting celebrities alike.

Food

BEACON HILL AND GOVERNMENT CENTER
Classic New England
Daniel Webster used to polish off a glass of brandy with every dozen oysters he scarfed down at the raw bar of the **Union Oyster House** (41 Union St., 617/227-2750, 11 A.M.–9:30 P.M. Sun.–Thurs.; 11 A.M.–10 P.M. Fri.–Sat., www.unionoysterhouse.com, $22–34), the oldest operating restaurant in the United States. Entrées including baked scrod and filet mignon are a bit overpriced, but worth it for the Olde New England ambience.

French
In stark contrast to many of Charles Street's stuffier addresses, **Beacon Hill Bistro** (25 Charles St., 617/723-7575, 7 A.M.–10 P.M. daily, www.beaconhillhotel.com/bistro, $24–29) is an easygoing (but still upscale, mind you) bistro serving French stalwarts like steak *frites* alongside creative constructions such as skate with spinach and sunchokes.

Italian
The owner of **(Ristorante Toscano** (47 Charles St., 617/723-4090, 11:30 A.M.–10 P.M. Tues.–Fri.; 11:30 A.M.–11 P.M. Sat.–Sun., www.

toscanoboston.com, $13–36), Vinicio Paoli, is Tuscan to his core—and so is his eatery. No daredevil renderings here: The kitchen keeps it real with simple dishes of carpaccio and penne *arrabbiata*.

Middle Eastern
Who knew that one of New England's most Yankee neighborhoods was a prime place to experience the charms of Persian (that's Iranian to you) cuisine? Grab a table at refined, pretty **Lala Rokh** (97 Mt. Vernon St., 617/720-5511, 12 P.M.–3 P.M. daily; 5:30 P.M.–10 P.M. daily, www.lalarokh.com, $14–19) to dig into a menu loaded with rose petal–scented dishes, kabobs, and fruit-laden sauces. And don't miss the saffron ice cream.

Sandwiches
One of the area's most affordable lunches is found at **Panificio** (144 Charles St., 617/227-4340, 8 A.M.–10 P.M. daily., www.panificio-boston.com, $7–23), where you can snag an overstuffed sandwich—on, as the name suggests, great bread—and salad for under $15. At night, the bakery turns more posh: Candles are lit, prices go up, and dishes get more elaborate—à la lobster penne and gnocchi marinara.

BOSTON

DOWNTOWN AND CHINATOWN
American

Years before retro became so very this-minute, ◖ **Silvertone Bar & Grill** (69 Bromfield St., 617/338-7887, 12 P.M.–1 A.M. daily, silvertone-downtown.com, $10–20) had a lock on hip, vaguely 1950s style with homey dishes (the mac 'n' cheese is out of this world) and oversized cocktails.

Reserve (far ahead) at the very upscale ◖ **Radius** (8 High St., 617/426-1234, 11:30 A.M.–10 P.M. Mon.–Sat.; 11 A.M.–9 P.M. Sun., www.radiusrestaurant.com, $32–42) for a cutting-edge meal that might include tuna with radish and *yuzu*, for example. Not for nothing has chef Michael Schlow become the darling of rock stars and Hollywood bigwigs alike; his food is tremendous.

The North End may be Boston's Italian center, but **Teatro** (177 Tremont St., 617/778-6841, 5 P.M.–10:30 P.M. Fri.–Sat.; 4 P.M.–10 P.M. Sun.; closed Mon., www.teatroboston.com, $10–25) is a like-minded little enclave of its own. From the dramatic mosaic ceiling and blue lighting to the high-energy bar, the sleek trattoria hums with a well-heeled crowd eagerly digging into freshly made pastas.

Classic New England

Once upon a time, **Locke Ober** (3 Winter Pl., 617/542-1340, 5 P.M.–10 P.M. Mon.–Fri.; 5 P.M.–11 P.M. Sat.; closed Mon., www.locke-ober.com, $28–44) was literally the only place around for fine dining. Its venerable dark wood interior is still the place to come for lobster Savannah, *finnan haddie*, and other New England classics, updated by chef-owner Lydia Shire.

Chinese

Go with what the name suggests at ◖ **Jumbo Seafood** (7 Hudson St., 617/542-2823, 11:30 A.M.–10 P.M. Mon.–Sat.; noon–9 P.M. Sun., www.jumboseafoodrestaurant.com, $5–18), where the fish specials—served right from the tanks up front—are flapping-fresh. Plump, steamed oysters in

black-bean sauce are a specialty, as is the whole steamed sea bass with ginger.

Dim sum is the name of the game at **Chow Chau City** (83 Essex St., 617/338-8158, 8 A.M.–1 A.M. Mon.–Sat.; 11 A.M.–11 P.M. Sun., $7–15), where it's served every day, 8 A.M. to 1 P.M. The emporium caters to big groups with dishes both staid (scallion pancakes) and daring (shark-fin dumplings).

French

Fresh from a multimillion-dollar renovation, The Four Season's tony ◖ **Bristol Lounge** (Four Seasons Hotel, 200 Boylston St., 617/351-2037, 6:30 A.M.–2 A.M. Mon.–Sat.; 7 P.M.–midnight Sun., $35–45) has resumed its place among the city's most refined Big Deal restaurants. France rules the day here, from the china (Bernardaud) to the specialties (soufflés are a tradition)—-though the burgers are equally as popular.

Sandwiches

Line up with everyone else at **Chacarero** (101 Arch St., 617/542-0392, 11 A.M.–7 P.M. Mon.–Fri.; closed Sat.–Sun., www.chacarero.com, $2–8), a Chilean sandwich shop consisting of two windows serving piping-hot sandwiches. The secret ingredient: green beans.

Sushi

Not too many people head to Chinatown looking for good Japanese, but those who do are fed happily at **Ginza** (16 Hudson St., 617/338-2261, 11 A.M.–2 A.M. Mon.–Sat.; 11 A.M.–1 P.M. Sun., $11–46), the always-busy sushi spot. Easily one of the best sources for raw fish in town, it's home to creations such as Boston *maki* (lobster with roe and lettuce) plus good cooked Japanese staples.

NORTH END AND CHARLESTOWN
Italian

Reservations aren't accepted at the small, one-roomed **Pomodoro** (319 Hanover St., 617/367-4348, www.pomodoroboston.com, 11:45 A.M.–10 P.M. Mon.–Sat.; closed Sun.,

$15–24), but diners who arrive before the crowds are rewarded with a table immediately, and a much shorter wait for the fresh and authentic Italian specials. **Mamma Maria** (3 North Sq., 617/523-0077, 5 P.M.–11 P.M. Tues.–Sun.; closed Mon., www.mammamaria.com, $26–38) may sound like a cheap pizza joint, but it's in fact a refined spot full of tapestries and serving the likes of oysters Florentine with *prosecco zabaglione*. Before the North End became a Disneyland-style jumble of Italian-American ristorantes and caffes, there was the Old World likes of **Caffe Vittoria** (290-296 Hanover St., 617/227-7606, 7 A.M.–midnight daily, www.vittoriacaffe.com, $2–6). Lined with wooden pastry cases and filled with students and couples scarfing down everything from tiramisu to grappa, Vittoria could as easily be a neighborhood hangout in Milan. One of the first restaurants to put Boston on the national culinary map, **Olives** (10 City Sq., Charlestown, 617/242-1999, 5 P.M.–11 P.M. daily, www.toddenglish.com, $19–39)—the original prototype for celebrity chef Todd English's now national chain—is still going strong in historic Charlestown. The dramatic, loud dining room serves bold dishes like chargrilled squid with chickpeas and pistachio-crusted lamb loin.

BACK BAY AND SOUTH END
American

When celebration is in order (or money simply isn't an object), Bostonians reserve at **C Clio** (370 Commonwealth Ave., 617/536-7200, 6:30 A.M.–10:30 A.M., 5:30 P.M.–10 P.M. Mon.–Sat.; 5:30 P.M.–10 P.M. Sun., www.cliorestaurant.com, $34–44). With one of the most elegant menus in town, chef Ken Oringer pulls out all the stops on both flavor (butter-basted Maine lobster and California squab with truffles) and adventure (red shrimp sashimi with caviar).

Grab a seat at cheeky **C Delux Café** (100 Chandler St., 617/338-5258, 5 P.M.–1 A.M. daily, $7–13) and prepare for the unexpected. The clientele is a mix of seemingly every kind, as is the decor—which includes an Elvis shrine and a miniature Christmas tree that stays up all year. The menu makes the lowly grilled cheese sandwich into a work of art.

One of the first restaurants to help transform the South End into a restaurant mecca, **Hamersley's Bistro** (553 Tremont St., 617/423-2700, 5:30 P.M.–9:30 P.M. Mon.–Fri.; 5:30 P.M.–10 P.M. Sat.; 11 A.M.–2 P.M. and 5:30 P.M.–9:30 P.M. Sun., www.hamersleysbistro.com, $25–38) evokes a slice of French countryside. The buzzing, airy dining room fills with the smell of roasted chicken with garlic and the sound of conversation and food being enjoyed.

Ask most chefs where they go to unwind after hours and they'll tell you **C Franklin Café** (278 Shawmut Ave., 617/350-0010, 5:30 P.M.–2 A.M. daily, www.franklincafe.com, $16–19). There they can slip into the wooden booths and sup on rosemary-grilled shrimp and just chill out.

Short of hang gliding, the best view of the city is from the windows of the **Top of the Hub** (800 Boylston St., 617/536-1775, 11:30 A.M.–1 A.M. Mon.–Sat.; 11 A.M.–midnight Sun, www.topofthehub.net, $27–48), on the top floor of the Prudential Center. Go for the vista rather than the victuals; dinners are mostly perfunctory continental cuisine.

Cafés

Bumped up against the upscale world of Newbury Street, **The Other Side Café** (407 Newbury St., 617/536-9477, 11:30 A.M.–1 A.M. Mon.–Wed.; 11:30 A.M.–2 A.M.; Thurs.–Fri.; 10 A.M.–2 A.M. Sat.; 10 A.M.–1 A.M. Sun., www.theothersidecafe.com, $6–10) is a refreshing enclave of funky, alternative café culture and cheap vegetarian sandwiches and salads.

Gelati, sandwiches, and pastries fly from the counter to tables at **L'Aroma** (85 Newbury St., 617/412-4001, 7 A.M.–7 P.M. Mon.–Fri.; 7:30 A.M.–7 P.M. Sat.; 8 A.M.–7 P.M. Sun., www.laromacafe.com, $6–7).

Italian

On the bang-for-your-buck front, don't miss the eclectically decorated **Anchovies** (433 Columbus Ave., 617/266-5088, 5 P.M.–11 P.M.

Mon.–Sat.; 5:30 P.M.–11 P.M. Sun., $7–14). None of the pasta prices rise much above $10, and pizzas start at $5.

Meaning "crazy way" in Italian, **Via Matta** (79 Park Plaza, 617/422-0008, 11:30 A.M.–1 A.M. Mon.–Sat.; 11 A.M.–midnight Sun., www.viamattarestaurant.com, $16–38) is one of the hottest restaurants in a culinary ghetto known as Park Square. The loud dining room jumps with a crew of regulars downing perfectly made pasta and simple Italian classics.

Seafood

One of the hottest new tables in Back Bay is **City Table** (61 Exeter St., 617/933-4800, 11:30 A.M.–1 A.M. Mon.–Sat.; 11 A.M.–midnight Sun., $24–34), the big-ticket seafood restaurant that takes the whole ocean as its inspiration. Chef Robert Fathman has concocted witty takes like "oysters in bondage" (that is, encrusted in smoked salmon and potato, and daubed with sour cream and caviar). Now a national chain found in eight states, **Legal Sea Foods** (26 Park Plaza and other area locations, 617/426-4444, 10:30 A.M.–midnight daily, www.legalseafoods.com, $16–37) still sets the standard for creamy New England clam chowder and other classics like steamed cod and boiled lobster. Its latest menu twist is "ayurvedic" cuisine loaded with fiery South Indian spices.

Steakhouse

In most cases, a steakhouse is a steakhouse. But **Grill 23 Bar & Grill** (161 Berkeley St., 617/542-2255, 11:30 A.M.–2 A.M. Mon.–Fri.; 11 A.M.–2 A.M. Sat.; 11 A.M.–midnight Sun., www.grill23.com, $27–49) moves beyond the usual formulaic clubby decor and menu to include big bouquets of flowers in its airy space and tilapia on its specialty board. The usual suspects (prime rib to lobster) are there, too—as are desserts like rhubarb cobbler and an epic wine list.

Sandwiches

A café with counter service, **Flour Bakery** (1595 Washington St., 617/267-4300, 7 A.M.–9 P.M. Mon.–Fri.; 8 A.M.–6 P.M. Sat.; 9 A.M.–5 P.M. Sun., www.flourbakery.com, $8–13) does a swift business in both take-out and eat-in. The biggest draw is the baked goods—fruit tarts, sandwiches, and cookies.

At ◀ **Charlie's Sandwich Shoppe** (429 Columbus Ave., 617/536-7669, noon–10 P.M. Mon.–Sat.; 5 P.M.–10 P.M. Sun., $4–9), you go for the excellent turkey hash and breakfast specials, and stay for the communal tables, loud diner atmosphere, and funny wait staff.

Odds are you won't find a juicier burger in town than those at **Tim's Tavern** (329 Columbus Ave., 617/437-6898, 11 A.M.–11 P.M. Mon.–Sat.; 5 P.M.–10 P.M. Sun., $7–14), and if you do, you certainly won't find one any cheaper. The people-watching, meanwhile, is equally good: Cops gab with artists, barflies drink with students, and everyone plays tunes on the jukebox.

Southern

The eclectic **Tremont 647** (647 Tremont St., 617/266-4600, 10:30 A.M.–2 P.M. and 5:30 P.M.–10:30 P.M. Sun.–Thurs.; 10:30 A.M.–3 P.M. and 5:30 P.M.–10:30 P.M. Fri.–Sat., www.tremont647.com, $13–25), with its lively staff and even livelier dining room, has one of the most loyal clienteles in town. They come back for fixings like lamb sirloin with pomegranate glaze and "two stinky cheeses" with black truffle honey.

Tapas

The multi-floored **Tapeo** (266 Newbury St., 617/267-4799, 5 P.M.–midnight Mon.–Sat.; noon–10 P.M. Sun., www.tapeo.com, $24–25) is as popular for its al fresco patio as for its tiny plates of tapas (the roast duck with blackberry sauce is a knockout) and citrusy pitchers of sangria.

Picture the quintessential tapas hangout in Spain, and you've got **Toro** (1704 Washington St., 617/536-4000, noon–midnight Mon.–Sat.; 10:30 A.M.–2 P.M. and 4:30 P.M.–midnight Sun., $4–15), a paragon of the genre.

FENWAY
Cambodian

One of the more elegant ethnic restaurants around Boston, **Elephant Walk** (900 Beacon St., Cambridge, 617/247-1500, 11 A.M.–10 P.M.Mon.–Sat.; 10 A.M.–9 P.M. Sun., www.elephantwalk.com, $14–20) feels like a night in a well-appointed Phnom Penh hotel, between the swaying palm fronds and dark woods. But the menu is more Cambodia-meets-Cannes, split between classic French dishes and Southeast Asian dishes like banana leaf–wrapped scallops in coconut milk.

SEAPORT
Seafood

Overlooking Fort Point Channel, **The Barking Crab** (88 Sleeper St., 617/426-2722, 11:30 A.M.–1 A.M. daily, www.barkingcrab.com, $9–25) serves seafood the way it was meant to be eaten, with the smell of sea air and cackling of gulls. Loaded with salty decor, the joint serves platters of fried clams at long picnic tables.

Since 1963, **Anthony's Pier 4** (140 Northern Ave., 617/482-6262, 11 A.M.–9 P.M. Sun.–Thurs.; 11 A.M.–11 P.M. Fri.–Sat., www.pier4.com, $19–36) has served the classic seafood you came to Boston for, and offered an impressive wine list and sea view to boot.

Cult seafood favorite and hole-in-the-wall (**No-Name Restaurant** (15 Fish Pier, Northern Ave., 617/338-7539, noon–7 P.M. Mon.–Sat.; closed Sun., $5–23) is acclaimed for its seafood literally right off the boat. The menu changes depending on what's in season, but always includes some variation on a tummy-warming fisherman's stew. Other entrées are simply fried or baked, offering unadulterated seafood at half the price of more celebrated restaurants.

CAMBRIDGE AND SOMERVILLE
American

Playing the part of both cozy neighborhood restaurant and urban sophisticate, (**Central Kitchen** (567 Massachusetts Ave., Cambridge, 617/491-5599, 5 P.M.–1 A.M.Tues.–Thurs.; 5 P.M.–2 A.M. Sat.; closed Sun. and Mon., www.enormous.tv/central/index1.html, $20–28) hosts a nightly scene of regulars in for squid salad and grilled flank steak.

Rialto (1 Bennett St., Cambridge, 617/661-5050, 5 P.M.–11:30 P.M. daily, www.rialto-restaurant.com, $27–39) chef-owner Jody Adams has rightfully earned a following for her Mediterranean-inspired cuisine. Her spring pea soup is electric with both color and flavor, and her gnocchi is a marvel.

Few restaurants could pull off being so unabashedly glamorous in fusty Harvard Square, but **Upstairs on the Square** (91 Winthrop St., Cambridge, 617/864-1933, 5 P.M.–11 P.M. daily, www.upstairsonthesquare.com, $13–34) does so with huge fireplaces and walls of gold leaf and animal prints. Don't miss the buttermilk panna cotta with basil.

Caribbean

The fun and boisterous **Green Street Grill** (280 Green St., Cambridge, 617/876-1655, 5 P.M.–1 A.M. Mon.–Sat; 5:30 P.M.–1 A.M. Sun., www.greenstreetgrill.com, $11–24) is as loved for its spicy tropical menu as it is the well-mixed and potent drinks.

France and Cuba may be far apart on a map, but at sultry (**Chez Henri** (1 Shepard St., Cambridge, 617/354-8980,6 P.M.–10:30 P.M. Mon.–Sat; 5:30 P.M.–9:30 P.M. Sun., www.chezhenri.com, $26–30) they mingle seamlessly. The steak tartar with cumin and chile-cocoa sauce shouldn't be missed; ditto on the Cuban sandwich.

Cafés

The living room of Davis Square's lesbian community, **Diesel Cafe** (257 Elm St., Somerville, 617/629-8717, 7 A.M.–8 P.M. daily, www.diesel-cafe.com, $5–6) has crossover appeal for everyone, with a photo booth tucked by the pool table in the back, and a menu of creative coffee drinks and vegetarian sandwiches. High-octane coffee and a decidedly cool vibe are what have Central Square hipsters addicted to **1369 Coffeehouse** (1369 Cambridge St., Cambridge, 617/576-1369, www.1369coffeehouse.com,

6:30 A.M.–11 P.M. Mon.–Fri; 7 A.M.–11:30 P.M. Sat.; 7:30 A.M.–10 P.M. Sun., $3–6). The regulars come in as much to hang out as they do to nosh on freshly baked scones.

Eastern European
Good old-fashioned hospitality and simplicity of dining are in the spotlight at **Salts** (798 Main St., Cambridge, 617/876-8444, 5 P.M.–10 P.M. Tues.–Sun.; closed Mon., www.saltsrestaurant. com, $28–36). The humble bistro's homemade bread, lavender crème caramel, and thoughtful service are all reasons to keep coming back.

French
The spirit of simple French bistro cooking is found at **Ten Tables** (5 Craigie Circle, Cambridge, 617/576-5454, www.tentables.net, 5:30–10 P.M. Mon.–Thurs., 5:30–10:30 P.M. Fri.–Sat., 5–9 P.M., $19–25), an offshoot of the popular restaurant in Jamaica Plain. Chef David Punch assembles beautiful plates of locally sourced, intensely flavored, and always seasonal dishes—the likes of Atlantic cod with brussels sprouts in winter, garlicky roasted lamb in spring, and sumptuous freshly made tomato tarts in summer. Regulars come for the laid-back but romantic atmosphere as much as the food—and know to make reservations well ahead of time.

Sandwiches
It's hard to argue with a burger so big and juicy you can barely manage it with two hands. Said patty is the reason for the line outside **Mr. Bartley's Burger Cottage** (1246 Massachusetts Ave., Cambridge, 617/354-6559, 11 A.M.–9 P.M. Mon.–Sat; closed Sun., bartleysburgers.com, $10–13)—though accompaniments like sweet-potato fries and raspberry-lime rickeys have also earned fans.

Tapas
Surrealism meets romance—usually over sangria—at ◖ **Dalí** (415 Washington St., Somerville, 617/661-3254, 11 A.M.–10 P.M. Tues.–Sat; closed Sun. and Mon., www.dalirestaurant.com, $6–16), the brightly tiled

den serving excellent Spanish food with an emphasis on tapas. Share a few plates of potatoes, spicy baked cod, and a bottle of rioja in the dark bordello-like setting to experience the whole effect.

BROOKLINE
American
Those searching for a model of a modern New England restaurant should look no further than **The Fireplace** (1634 Beacon St., Brookline, 617/975-1900, 5 P.M.–10 P.M. Tues.–Sat.; 10 A.M.–10 P.M. Sun.; closed Mon., www.fireplacerest.com, $22–33), home to sublime dishes with fresh, local ingredients: maple-glazed pork ribs with green-apple slaw, for example. The restaurant itself is refined but comfy, full of linen-covered tables and (of course) a fireplace.

Kosher
Imagine your favorite Jewish deli. Now picture it with a pop-art makeover. That's **Zaftigs** (335 Harvard St., Brookline, 617/975-0775, 8 A.M.–10 P.M., www.zaftigs.com, $8–17), a longtime favorite for its killer potato pancakes, overstuffed corned-beef sandwiches, and rich kugel.

Thai
There's above-average Thai food to be found at ◖ **Khao Sarn** (250 Harvard St., Brookline, 617/566-7200, 11:30 A.M.–11 P.M. daily, $11–21), starting with standards like pad thai and culminating with specials like sautéed lobster with mango. The attractive, streamlined dining room is blessed with Thai textiles on the walls, and a friendly staff happy to answer any questions about the menu.

Sushi
First-rate sushi can be tough to find in Boston, so it's often in droves that locals head to **Fugakyu** (1280 Beacon St., Brookline, 617/734-1268, 11:30 A.M.–1:30 A.M. Mon.–Sat.; noon–1:30 A.M. Sun., www.fugakyu.net, $19–54). Beyond the long lines, though, await platters of extremely fresh, high-quality raw fish artfully arranged to impressive effect. (There's high-quality cooked Japanese food as well.) The two-

floored room, with its blonde wood and running fountains, is equally appealing.

OTHER NEIGHBORHOODS
Cuban

Loved for its casual Cuban fare, **Miami Restaurant** (381 Centre St., Jamaica Plain, 617/522-4644, 11:30 A.M.–10:30 P.M. Mon.–Fri; 11 A.M.–9 P.M. Sun., $3–8) is worth a visit if only for its Cubano—a savory pressed sandwich filled with pork, ham, and pickles. The cheap, quick meals are served to customers in a handful of booths beneath news clips and posters about baseball and Cuba.

Tapas

For sumptuous and authentic Spanish, **Tasca** (1612 Commonwealth Ave., Brighton, 617/730-8002, 5 P.M.–10 P.M. Mon.–Fri; 5 P.M.–9 P.M. Sun., www.tascarestaurant.com, $14.95–19.95) shouldn't be missed. From the charming brick facade to the savory paella and pitchers of sweet sangria, the dark restaurant is as cushy a setting for dates as it is for groups.

Information and Services

INFORMATION

A good place to get oriented is the **Boston Common Visitor Information Center** (148 Tremont St., 888/733-2678, www.bostonusa.com, 8:30 A.M.–5 P.M. Mon.–Sat., 9 A.M.–5 P.M. Sun.), located in the park halfway between the Park Street and Boylston Street T stops. There you can pick up maps and guides, along with discount museum coupons and brochures for major attractions. It's also the starting place for the Freedom Trail and several trolley tours around the city. Another information center is the **Prudential Center Visitor Information Center** (Prudential Center, 9 A.M.–5 P.M. Mon.–Fri.; 10 A.M.–6 P.M. Sat.–Sun.), located inside the mall. The National Park Service runs its own **Downtown Visitor Center** (15 State St., 617/242-5642, www.nps.gov/bost, 9 A.M.–5 P.M. daily), which includes a good collection of books on Boston and Massachusetts. If you are planning ahead, you can contact the **Greater Boston Convention and Visitors Bureau** (800/733-2678, www.bostonusa.com) for additional publications with the latest tourist information.

SERVICES
Emergencies

For medical emergencies, call 911. Boston has many hospitals with 24-hour emergency rooms, including **Massachusetts General Hospital** (55 Fruit St., off Cambridge St., 617/726-2000, www.massgeneral.org) and **Beth Israel Deaconess Medical Center** (330 Brookline Ave. at Longwood Ave., 617/667-7000, www.bidmc.org).

Internet

If you brought your laptop, you can access free wireless Internet in the Bates Reading Room at the **Boston Public Library** (700 Boylston St., 617/536-5400, www.bpl.org, 9 A.M.–9 P.M. Mon.–Thurs.; 9 A.M.–5 P.M. Fri.–Sat.). A guest library pass is required. You can also access the Internet through **Newbury Open.Net** (252 Newbury St., www.techsuperpowers.com/newburyopen.net, 9 A.M.–8 P.M. Mon.–Fri.; noon–7 P.M. Sat.–Sun., $5/hr), which runs a cyber café and also provides free wireless to many cafés on Newbury Street.

Discounts

If you plan on seeing a lot of attractions while in town, the **Go Boston Card** (85 Merrimac St., 800/887-9103, www.gobostoncard.com) provides good value. Cards are sold in one-day ($54 adult, $38 children 3–12), two-day ($80/$50), three-day ($110/$66), five-day ($158/$98), and seven-day ($196/$120) increments, and offer free admission to most area attractions, including many in Concord, Salem,

TROLLEY TOURS

In 1898, Boston produced the first subway in America. Since then, the city's tourism industry has done seemingly everything in its power to twist that form of transportation into as many silly (albeit often quite fun) ways to see the town as possible. Here are the most popular:

- **Boston Upper Deck Trolley Tours:** If it looks like there's a party going on inside these trolleys as they roll down the street, it's probably because there is. They come equipped with everything from strobe lights and disco balls to plasma TVs, bubble machines, and wireless microphones (departing from Long Wharf, 617/742-1440, www. discoverbostontours.com).

- **Duck Tours:** A full fleet of authentic WWI amphibious vehicles have been converted into "ducks" that take passengers on a narrated tour of the city's streets and the Charles River, encouraging them to "quack" throughout the tour (departing from the Prudential Center and the Museum of Science, 617/267-3825, www.bostonducktours. com).

- **Beantown Trolley:** These trackless trolleys stop at upwards of 20 major Boston museums and attractions, and allow passengers to take as many round-trips in a day as they like (800/343-1328, www.brushhilltours. com/tours/beantown.html).

- **Silver Trolley Tours:** The one-hour, narrated tour aboard silver trolleys made in Maine come complete with DVD players, air-ride suspension for comfort, and free tickets to either the Sports Museum (year-round) or a Boston Harbor Cruise (in summer). Children under 12 ride free (departing from various locations, 617/363-7899, www. cityviewtrolleys.com).

and surrounding areas. In addition, many guesthouses and hotels have discount museum passes for guest use.

Guided Tours

Taking advantage of Boston's reputation as a "walking city," **Boston By Foot** (77 North Washington St., 617/367-2345 or 617/367-3766 for recorded information, www. bostonbyfoot.com, $12 adults, $8 children 6–12) offers architectural and history tours of several Boston neighborhoods, including Beacon Hill, the Back Bay, and the North End. The organization also offers tours of the Freedom Trail for children, and a unique Boston Underground tour that explores closed-off subway tunnels and the construction of the Big Dig.

Getting There and Around

GETTING THERE
By Air

Flights to Boston's **Logan International Airport** (www.massport.com/logan) are available from almost all major cities. From Logan, ground transportation can be arranged from the information desk at baggage claim. The most efficient way to get into the city is via taxi, though expect to pay a minimum of $25 for downtown locations. A cheaper option is to take shared van service, which runs to hotels downtown and in the Back Bay for $10–12 per person. Water taxis also cross Boston Harbor to downtown and Seaport District locations, as well as Quincy and Hull, year-round, for about $10 per person.

A much cheaper option is to take a $1.70 subway ride; the airport station is on the Blue

Line, and accessible by taking the #22 or #33 bus from any terminal. All told, expect it to take 30–45 minutes to get downtown. Even easier is the Silver Line, which runs express bus service to South Station and picks up directly in front of terminals A and E. It takes 15–30 minutes.

By Rail

From most destinations, **Amtrak** (South Station, Summer St. & Atlantic Ave., 800/872-7245, www.amtrak.com) runs service to both South Station and Back Bay Station. Trains from New York and Washington take about four and seven hours respectively. Note that Amtrak trains from all destinations in Maine run to North Station, not South. The **Massachusetts Bay Transportation Authority** (617/222-5000, www.mbta.com) also runs commuter rail service from locations in Greater Boston for fares of up to $6. Trains from the North Shore, Lowell, and Fitchburg arrive at North Station, while those coming from the South Shore, Providence, and Worcester arrive at South Station.

By Bus

Bus service arrives at South Station. Most U.S. destinations are served by **Greyhound** (800/231-2222, www.greyhound.com). However, smaller bus companies also run from various locations around the region.

GETTING AROUND

Boston drivers are justly famous for the temporary insanity they acquire when they get behind the wheel. Don't expect much help from street signs downtown either; they have a habit of jumping out right before a needed turn. Pay close attention to the lane you are in, lest you find yourself routed up onto the Expressway unawares.

A smart alternative to a car is taking the "T," which is short for MBTA, itself an acronym for the **Massachusetts Bay Transportation Authority** (617/222-5000, www.mbta.com). Subway fares are $2 with a ticket—or $1.70 with a reloadable Charlie Card you can pick up at major stations (definitely worth seeking out if you are going to be in town for more than a dayS). More out-of-the-way locations require taking one of the MBTA buses, which are often slow but give good coverage across the city. Fare is currently $1.50, or $1.25 with a Charlie Card. Often overlooked as a means of transportation are the ferries that ply Boston Harbor. A trip from Charlestown Navy Yard to Long Wharf (perfect after completing the Freedom Trail) costs $1.70.

Keep in mind that the MBTA doesn't run between 12:30 A.M. and 5:30 A.M. The only option at that time is to take a taxi cab, which isn't cheap. Fares start at $2.60 for the first one-seventh mile, and add 40 cents for each additional one-seventh mile, with $24 for each hour of waiting time. Got that? Flat rates to certain communities around Boston are also available at $3.20 per mile. Also note that trips to Logan are saddled with an additional $2.75 for tolls, while trips from Logan cost an extra $6. There is no charge, however, for baggage or extra passengers. In some areas—notably downtown and the Back Bay—bicycle-driven "pedi-cabs" are available (617/266-2005, www.bostonpedicab.com). You can't beat the price, which is an enigmatic "pay as you please."

EASTERN MASSACHUSETTS

Traveling through the towns surrounding Boston is like leafing through the different eras of a history book. The area is filled with legends of resolute minutemen, grizzled sea-captains, dour Pilgrims, and unfortunate "witches," all of whom have left their mark on the forests and fields of Eastern Massachusetts. History books, however, don't allow you to smell the musket smoke on Patriot's day or the scent of corn cakes smoldering on the fire of a Native American encampment. Simply put, folks here know their past, and special-ize in bringing it alive for visitors better than anywhere.

The vast majority of the state's population lives within reach of I-495, which describes a lazy semicircle around Boston. Within that ring lie bedroom communities full of commuters to the city, crumbling old mill towns that once played a part in fomenting the Industrial Revolution, and small hamlets that have—so far—resisted the encroaching sprawl of the city. Recently, the Boston area was declared the most expensive place to live in the country, and it's easy to see why—there just simply isn't any-where to put new housing. Where open space does exist, it is jealously guarded by those resi-dents hoping to preserve the rural character that adds to the area's historic appeal.

For the most part, however, you won't see the density of the area manifest itself in strip malls or the runaway development that has ruined many an American city. Even though the resi-dents here are computer engineers and office drones, you can still imagine that stern-faced minuteman emerging from their doorways.

HIGHLIGHTS

◖ Witch Trials Sights: The original "witch city" is a fascinating journey back into a time of collective insanity (page 85).

◖ Hammond Castle: This authentic medieval castle has got to be one of the most elaborate wedding presents ever given (page 89).

◖ Minuteman National Historical Park: The larger-than-life events that shaped our nation are brought down to size at this park (page 98).

◖ Walden Pond State Reservation: Live deliberately (and take a dive) at the former home of America's first environmentalist (page 98).

◖ Worcester Art Museum: This little-visited gem specializes in genres missed by other art museums (page 104).

◖ Plimoth Plantation: It's virtually impossible to find a single anachronism at this meticulously re-created historic site (page 112).

LOOK FOR ◖ TO FIND RECOMMENDED SIGHTS, ACTIVITIES, DINING, AND LODGING.

PLANNING YOUR TIME

If you only have a few days to explore this area, you have a tough choice in choosing a direction to set out in. Do you go north, to explore the fishing and shipbuilding villages in and around the rocky shores of Cape Ann? If so, a must-see is the cultural mecca of Salem, which offers the **witch trials sights** and so much more. Another highlight of the region is the gritty fishing port of Gloucester, with its straight-out-of-Camelot **Hammond Castle** overlooking the harbor. Or do you go west, into the heartland of Boston's Revolutionary history? Here, you'll find the perfectly preserved battlefields of **Minuteman National Historical Park** and the literary monuments of Concord, which pay homage to literary legends Ralph Waldo

Emerson, Nathaniel Hawthorne, Louisa May Alcott, and Henry David Thoreau (including Thoreau's former stomping grounds at **Walden Pond**). Lesser known but equally fascinating attractions are the industrial center of Lowell, and the re-created hamlet of Old Sturbridge Village. Or should you go all the way back, and head south? Here, you can step on the same ground that the pilgrims did with a visit to **Plimoth Plantation,** and the whaling port of New Bedford.

Whichever direction you choose, you'll need a minimum of two or three days to really do any one of these areas justice; unless you are really a history buff, you probably shouldn't pick more than two of these areas to explore in one trip. In the fall, the country lanes around

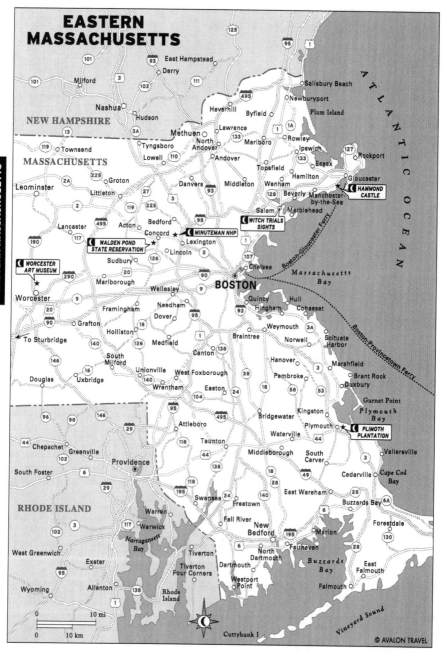

Concord and Lexington are bursting with fall foliage by October. At the same time, the cranberry bogs to the south are blooming with red berries. It goes without saying that if you are in the area in the weeks before Halloween, Salem is positively bewitching, while Plymouth pulls out all the stops in November leading up to Thanksgiving. During summertime, Bostonians here head to the shore. The coastlines both north and south of Boston have

devotees, and fistfights have broken out over whether Duxbury or Crane Beach is best. During wintertime, many of the attractions around Boston go into hibernation, but sitting by a roaring fire in a historic inn by the seacoast has its own charms to recommend. Even then, however, it pays to call ahead, as a handful of restaurants and hotels in the area are seasonal and either close or reduce their hours of operation in colder months.

The North Shore

The coastline north of Boston is smaller than the long curving seashore to the south. The ocean here, however, is arguably much more present in the towns that cling to the rocky coves and hidden beaches along the shoreline. The North Shore (that's "Noath Shoah" to locals) contains a mix of historic seaside villages like Essex and Ipswich; artists colonies like Rockport; and fishing communities like Gloucester. Newburyport's Plum Island and

Ipswich's Crane Beach are both known for bird-watching and sunbathing. The can't-miss destination of Salem is just as interesting for its museums and maritime history as for the witch trials that made it famous.

SALEM

On Valentine's Day, you go to Paris. For Mardi Gras, you head to New Orleans. For Halloween, there's only one place to go: 15

© MICHAEL BLANDING

the Witch House

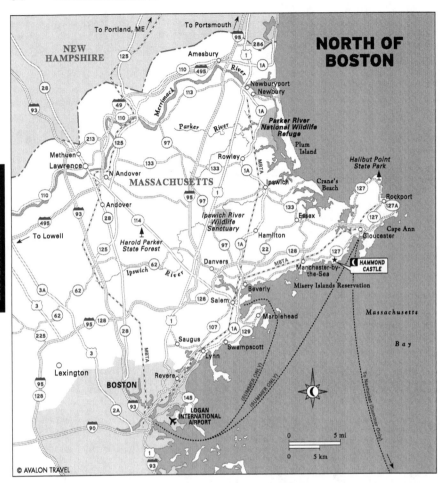

NORTH OF BOSTON

miles north of Boston to the original Witch City. Anyone who's seen or read Arthur Miller's *The Crucible* knows the story: In 1692, several young women took ill and cried out the names of alleged witches they claimed were causing their torments. The famous trials were convened, and from May to September of that year, 13 women and five men were tried, convicted, and hanged for vague crimes involving black magic.

Even now there's something about the historic seaport that curdles the blood after sundown. The country nights are inky dark, and the proximity of the ocean wafts spooky mists and fogs around the Gothic Victorian homes downtown. Witchcraft isn't the only thing that Salem has going for it, however. Settled in 1629 at the mouth of the Naumkeag River, the town got involved in the cod and West Indies trades early. By the start of the 19th century, its merchants and sea captains had made it the richest town in the *country,* second only to Boston in importance in the region. Among those who grew up here during

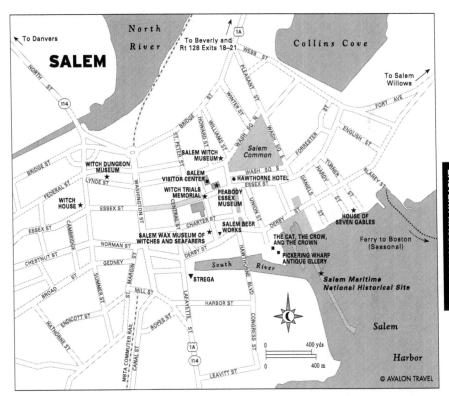

that time was Nathaniel Hawthorne, who was inspired by the town's history to weave some of the most haunting tales of American literature. Much of the history here is still very much in evidence, sharing cobblestone streets with cosmopolitan restaurants and occult bookshops.

◖ Witch Trials Sights

Looking back today, it's difficult to understand the collective madness that overtook the town here, leaving 18 people dead and making "witch trials" synonymous with unjust accusations. Many sights around Salem do their best to shed light on the tragedy, with results ranging from sobering to cheesy. The most affecting is the simple **Salem Witch Trials Memorial** (Liberty St., www.salemweb.com/memorial), which displays the names of the victims on stone benches next to the central

burying ground. Nearby, the **Witch House** (310½ Essex St., 978/744-8815, www.salemweb.com/witchhouse, 10 A.M.–5 P.M. May–early Nov., $8.25 adults, $6.25 seniors, $4.25 children 6–14, free children under 6) is the former home of magistrate Jonathan Corwin, who sentenced the guilty to death. Tours detail the restored interior, giving a sense of the time.

The most popular museum dedicated to the trials is the **Salem Witch Museum** (Washington Sq. North, 978/744-1692, www.salemwitchmuseum.com, 10 A.M.–5 P.M. daily Sept.–June, 10 A.M.–7 P.M. daily July–Aug., extended hours in Oct., $8 adults, $7 seniors, $5.50 children 6–14, free children under 6), which has an effective multimedia show that narrates the sequence of events in 1692. The museum also has an interesting exhibit about the perceptions of witches through the ages.

typical October visitors in Salem

© TIM GRAFFT/MOTT

A somewhat more hokey depiction of the trials is on display at the **Salem Wax Museum of Witches and Seafarers** (288 Derby St., 978/298-2929, www.salemwaxmuseum.com, 10 A.M.–6 P.M. daily Apr.–June, 10 A.M.–9 P.M. daily July–Aug., 10 A.M.–6 P.M. daily Sept., extended hours in Oct., 10 A.M.–5 P.M. Nov.–Dec., 11 A.M.–4 P.M. Jan.–Mar., $7 adults, $6 seniors, $5 children and students, free children under 5), which also purports to display the various pirates and rogue captains who colored the populace. A reenactment of the trials, using original transcripts, is performed at the **Witch Dungeon Museum** (16 Lynde St., 978/741-3570, www.witchdungeon.com, 10 A.M.–5 P.M. Apr.–Nov., extended hours in Oct., $8 adults, $7 seniors, $6 children 4–13), which has melodramatic exhibits on the affair.

Other Sights

With a collection originally culled from the private stores of merchant captains, the **Peabody Essex Museum** (East India Sq., 978/745-9500 or 866/745-1876, www.pem. org, 10 A.M.–5 P.M. Tue.–Sun., $15 adults, $13 seniors, $11 students, free youth 16 and under) should be on the short list of anyone visiting Salem. Exhibits include priceless antiques from Asia and Polynesia, as well as antique American furniture. The highlight is a 19th-century house imported post-and-beam from China. A new glass-enclosed wing provides even more space for top-notch temporary exhibitions. Exploring Salem's other claim to fame, the **Salem Maritime National Historical Park** (160 Derby St., 978/740-1650, www.nps.gov, 9 A.M.–5 P.M. daily, prices for tours vary), includes several authentic old sea-captain's homes, the Custom House featured in Hawthorne's *The Scarlet Letter*, and a replica of sloop from the Golden Age of Sail.

Speaking of Hawthorne, feel free to count the roofs at the **House of the Seven Gables** (115 Derby St., 978/744-0991, www.7gables. org, 10 A.M.–5 P.M. daily Nov.–June, 10 A.M.–7 P.M. daily July–Nov. 1, $12 adults, $11 seniors, $7.25 children 5–12, free children under 5)—they are all there. The 17th-century mansion is legendary for its role in the Nathaniel Hawthorne novel that probably tortured you in high school. Inside, costumed interpreters take guests through three centuries of Salem history, including the early years of its favorite native son.

Events

Three guesses for the biggest time of the year in Salem, and the first two don't count. Every October, **Haunted Happenings** (877/725-3662, www.hauntedhappenings.org) takes over the whole city with a month of spooktastic events. All of the historic sites get into the act with extended hours and special programs (such as the "Spirit of the Gables," when the Hawthorne house is open for tours by candlelight). The event culminates in a huge costume party on the Common that draws some 50,000 revelers from around the region to dance the monster mash until the wee hours.

Shopping

Unless you want to chance a hex, you'll visit Salem's "official" witchcraft shop, **The Cat, the Crow, and the Crown** (63R Wharf St., 978/744-6274, www.lauriecabot.com), where proprietrix Laurie Cabot hooks up amateur occultists with everything they need to cook up a spell. Showcasing the mercantile side of Salem, **Pickering Wharf Antique Gallery** (69 Wharf St., 978/741-3113) has 30 dealers with a range of American furniture and nautical souvenirs.

Food

More than a dozen hand-crafted brews are on tap at **Salem Beer Works** (278 Derby St., 978/745-2337, www.beerworks.net, 11 A.M.–10 P.M., Mon.–Sat.; 11 A.M.–8 P.M., Sun., $8–17), including the honey-scented Seven Gables Golden, the spicy Pumpkinhead Ale, and the hoppy Witch City Red. To pair with the suds is a creative menu of burgers, sandwiches, and bar food. Specials include New York strip steak or a full rack of ribs. Named after the Italian word for "witch," ◖ **Strega** (94 Lafayette St., 978/741-0004, www.stregasalem.com, 5 P.M.–10 P.M., Tues.–Sat.; closed Sun. and Mon., $17–20) goes beyond pasta to serve Italian-influenced meat and fish dishes. Befitting the

name, the dining room is decked out in over-the-top plush red fabrics and swooping blood-red curtains.

Information and Services

Information about all aspects of the town is available at the **National Park Visitor Center** (2 New Liberty St., 978/740-1650, www.nps.gov/sama).

MARBLEHEAD

Few towns in Massachusetts have as delightful a location as Marblehead. Situated on a rocky outcropping 17 miles north of Boston, the town is divided into two parts—the headland known as Marblehead Neck is populated with old-money mansions that are as stunning as the vantage they command; across the harbor, the town center is a pedestrian-friendly collection of old colonial homes and brick buildings shot through with clothing boutiques and eateries.

Like many towns on the North Shore, Marblehead earned its living early from the sea. Founded a year before Boston, it was recognized early as one of the best fishing harbors around. As the Revolution approached, it became a strategic location on the coast, and the British landed there in 1775 to capture ammunition, a year before a similar attempt at Concord (they were turned back without a battle). Residents also proudly proclaim the town the "birthplace of the American navy" for its role in outfitting and basing the small fleet of schooners that General Washington procured the same year to harass British shipping. The town is now better known as a yachting capital, with thick forest of white masts covering its sheltered harbor year-round.

Sights

The jaunty fife-and-drum squad depicted in the painting *The Spirit of '76* is one of the most iconic images in American history—so much so that you might expect it to be hanging in a museum in Washington. Actually, the massive 8-by-10-foot painting hangs on the wall of Marblehead's town hall, **Abbot Hall** (188 Washington St., 617/631-0000, 8 A.M.–5 P.M.

Mon., Tues., and Thurs.; 7:30 A.M.–7:30 P.M. Wed.; 8 A.M.–1 P.M. Fri., free). Painted in 1876 for the country's centennial by a native of the town (who used his father as one of the models), it was donated in honor of Marblehead's role in Revolutionary naval battles.

George Washington slept at the **Jeremiah Lee Mansion** (161 Washington St., 781/631-1768, www.marbleheadmuseum.org, 10 A.M.–4 P.M. Tues.–Sat., $5)—as did James Monroe, Andrew Jackson, and the Marquis de Lafayette. The three-story 1768 mansion was home to a shipping magnate who was once the wealthiest in Massachusetts. It is a rare New England example of Georgian architecture, with highlights including the only surviving example of hand-painted English wallpaper.

Entertainment and Events

The Tex-Mex **Rio Grande Cafe** (12 School St., 781/639-1828, 5:30 P.M.–10:30 P.M. Sun.–Wed.; 5:30 P.M.–12:30 A.M., Thurs.–Sat.) presents live blues and rock on the weekends.

The highlight of the social calendar, however, is **Race Week** (www.mheadrace.org, late July), when some 200 boats descend on the area for regattas in the harbor and parties on shore.

Shopping

The independent-minded **Spirit of '76 Bookstore** (107 Pleasant St., 781/631-7199, 10 A.M.–7 P.M., Mon.–Fri.; 10 A.M.–5 P.M. Sat.; 12 P.M.–5 P.M., Sun.; www.spiritof76bookstore.com) has been a mainstay of Marblehead for more than 40 years. In addition to the regular fiction and nonfiction selections, it boasts a strong section on sailing and nautical history. Try and resist uttering the words "Oh, how cute" when you enter **Lester Harry's** (140 Washington St., 781/631-4343, 10 A.M.–5 P.M., Mon.–Sat.; 12 P.M.–5 P.M. Sun., www.lesterharrys.com), a high-end baby and kid's clothing store chock-full of signature designs as well as to-die-for luxury American and European labels. In nearby Beverly Farms you'll find **Glee** (29 West St., Beverly Farms, 978/922-4777, www.glee.us), a favorite among the area's style-conscious

(though not overly trendy) females. Find embroidered coats by Biya, slouchy pants by Trina Turk, and unimaginably soft hand-knit sweater coats. Men needn't feel left out, either; there's plenty of high-quality haberdashery for them at **Giblees** (85 Andover St., Danvers, 978/774-4080, 10 A.M.–7:30 P.M., Mon.–Sat.; 12 P.M.–6 P.M., Sun., www.giblees.com), from Pelham slip-ons and button-down Oxfords to houndstooth Magli jackets and Nat Nast polos.

Food

A catering operation with an attached café, **Foodie's Feast** (114 Washington St., Marblehead, 781/639-1104, www.foodiesfeast.com, $3–7) is where the locals go for gourmet sandwiches (try the lavender-roasted chicken breast), soups, and salads. Located just a block from the harbor, the café is also acclaimed for its weekend brunch, which features eggs benedict, breakfast burritos, and super-addictive scones, served at *al fresco* tables with the smell of salt in the air. The views are as fine as the eating at **Red Rock Bistro** (141 Humphrey St., Swampscott, 781/595-1414, www.redrockbistro.com, $19–34), the little harborside boîte serving up seafood like pan-seared fluke with turnip mash, wood-grilled pizzas, and a brunch that has the whole of Swampscott addicted.

Information

In addition to providing a wealth of information about the town, the **Marblehead Chamber of Commerce** (62 Pleasant St., 781/631-2868, www.marbleheadchamber.org) sponsors historic walking tours of downtown.

CAPE ANN

Unlike the sandy barrier beach that makes up Cape Cod, its sister Cape Ann is a rocky headland jutting forcibly out into the rough waters of the Atlantic. Because of that, the cape has a dramatically different character than the rest of the Massachusetts coast, with rocky shores more reminiscent of Maine. The topography has drawn two very different types of people to the area—fishermen, who have used the vantage point for quick access to the prime

MOTIF NO. 1

If the little red fish shack perched on Rockport's Bradley Wharf looks familiar, that's because you've probably seen it in a painting somewhere. The picturesque shack was a favorite subject for the artists who came to Cape Ann every summer in the 1920s and '30s to paint the buildings and denizens of the harbor. One day after a student brought in yet another treatment of the building, Paris-trained illustrator and art teacher Lester Hornby is said to have shouted, "What, Motif Number One, again?" The name stuck, and to this day, "Motif No. 1" is known as one of the most frequently painted buildings in the world, turning up in paintings from South America to the Czech Republic. Rockport's "dirty little secret," however, is that the original building actually collapsed and washed out to sea during the swells of the great Blizzard of '78. Within a year, the town fathers had built and painted an exact replica to replace it. Perhaps it should be called "Motif No. 2"?

Rockport's Motif No. 1

© TIM GRAFFT/MOTT

fishing grounds of Georges Bank; and artists, who have delighted in the changing dance of sunlight and surf on the granite rock faces.

Roughly, the two groups are divided into the two towns that hug the point. On the north side, **Rockport** has been home to artists colonies for more than a century. A dry town until just a year ago, it has a quaint atmosphere full of art galleries and boutiques. By contrast, **Gloucester** is a rough-and-tumble fishing village. While it has gentrified somewhat over the years, the fishing tradition is very much alive in the working harbor and bars that line the waterfront. The town's 15 minutes of fame came a few years ago with the book and film *The Perfect Storm,* which told of the harrowing disaster of the fishing boat *Andrea Gail,* and gave what residents generally agree to be an accurate, if sentimentalized, view of their trade.

◖ Hammond Castle

No buts about it—Dr. John Hays Hammond Jr. was a singular individual. An energetic

psychologist who produced the patents for over 400 inventions (including the remote control and the stereo), Hammond was also a voracious collector of all things Roman, medieval, and Renaissance. In 1926, Hammond decided the perfect venue for displaying his treasures was a castle of his own, and over the next three years set about building an authentic medieval edifice on the shores of Gloucester harbor as a present for his wife, Irene. The two opened the castle (80 Hesperus Ave., Gloucester, 978/283-2080, www. hammondcastle.org, 10 A.M.–4 P.M. Sat.–Sun., $10 adults, $8 seniors, $6 children 4–12, free children under 4) as a museum in 1930, since which time it has left visitors agog at the rich collection of antiques. Highlights include the Gothic bedroom, Renaissance dining room, and the largest pipe organ in a private residence, a behemoth with 183 pipes. Every year at Halloween, ghosts and ghouls fill the halls for a scary hauntfest.

Other Sights

All aspects of the working waterfront are

covered at the **Gloucester Maritime Heritage Center** (23 Harbor Loop, Gloucester, 978/281-0470, www.gloucestermaritimecenter.org, 10 A.M.–5 P.M. daily late May–Oct.), which includes an ocean aquarium, boatbuilding demonstrations, and a flotilla of watercraft moored in the harbor, including working fishing boats and a replica of one of the Boston Tea Party ships. As might be expected with a rocky headland, Cape Ann has a half dozen lighthouses scattered around its rocky shores. Perhaps the most picturesque is **Annisquam Light** (Wigwam Point, Lighthouse Rd., Gloucester, www.lighthouse.cc), a 41-foot white tower ringed with a black railing, with a walkway over the rocks to the front door.

By far the most unusual sight in Gloucester is an abandoned village in the center of the peninsula. Once called the Commons Settlement, it was abandoned in the 1700s, when wild dogs took it over and it earned a new name: Dogtown. Now one of the country's oldest ghost towns, it comes alive again in **Walk the Words Tours** (978/546-8122, www.walkthewords.com, $15 adults, $7 children), guided hikes given by two local women who regale visitors with tales of some of its most colorful former residents. The highlight of the three mile hike is the Babson Word Rocks—23 huge boulders carved with motivational phrases commissioned to employ out-of-work Finnish stonecutters during the Great Depression. At the time, mottos like "Never Try, Never Win" and "Prosperity Follows Service" must have seemed inspirational, but now lost amidst the forest and cellar holes they seem downright ironic.

Entertainment

Made famous by *The Perfect Storm,* the **Crow's Nest** (334 Main St., Gloucester, 978/281-2965) is just as rough-and-tumble as you'd expect. Be forewarned, no one as cute as Mark Wahlberg or George Clooney warms the barstools.

Events

The highlight of the year in Gloucester is the **St. Peter's Fiesta** (www.stpetersfiesta.org, late June), a five-day Italian festival that celebrates Gloucester's fishing community with boat races, the annual "blessing of the fleet," and the always-entertaining greasy pole contest.

Shopping

The art galleries in Rockport are concentrated in the area known as **Bearskin Neck,** an artists colony jutting out into the working harbor. Studios are clustered around the picturesque red fish shack known as "Motif No. 1"—held up alternately as the most painted and most photographed building in the country (see the sidebar *Motif No. 1*). A good place to start is the **Rockport Art Association** (12 Main St., Rockport, 978/546-6604, www.rockportartassn.org). Though not as large, Gloucester has an artists colony called **Rocky Neck,** which features galleries of its own.

Food

Grab a true taste of this seaside community—literally and otherwise—at **Portside Chowder House** (7 Tuna Wharf, Rockport, 978/546-7045, 11:30 A.M.–9:30 P.M., daily, $8–16), where diners nosh casual seafood on a porch overlooking the water. Don't come expecting four-star fare, however; meals here are as straightforward as fried fish sandwiches, lobster rolls, and salmon salad. By contrast, the urbane, sleekly designed (**Franklin Cafe** (118 Main St., Gloucester, 978/283-7888, www.franklincafe.com, 5 P.M.–10:30 P.M., Sun.–Thurs.; 5 P.M.–12 A.M., Fri.–Sat., $15–22) is an echo of its popular Boston sister restaurant, though with slightly lower prices and a menu sporting more seafood. The kitchen does right by its fresh catches, too, with dishes like split-grilled lobster with lemon sauce and garlic-grilled calamari with pesto and white beans.

Despite its Rocky Neck location, the intimate **Duckworth's Bistrot** (197 East Main St., Gloucester, 978/282-4426. www.duckworthsbistrot.com, 5 P.M.–10 P.M., Tues.–Sat.; 5 P.M.–9 P.M., Sun., $12–30) conspicuously lacks a harbor view. That's a clue to the emphasis of Boston expat chef Ken Duckworth, which is all on the food. His menu includes such lovelies as sautéed filet of sole with caramelized corn and lemon-parsley brown butter, and Muscovy duck breast over couscous with a plum and red-onion relish. All of the entrées are available as half-portions.

Information

Info on the area can be found at the **Cape Ann Chamber of Commerce** (33 Commercial St., Gloucester, 978/283-1601, www.capeannvacations.com).

NORTH OF CAPE ANN

Hugging a shallow bay in the lee of Cape Ann, the town of Essex was once renowned around the world for its shipbuilding prowess, having launched some 4,000 wooden ships into harbors all over the world. These days, however, it's more known as the birthplace of the fried clam. Bostonians still make pilgrimages to this part of the North Shore simply to taste the buttery goodness of fried food on a summer day. Two towns that share the stretch of waterfront above Essex each have their own unique charms—Ipswich has dozens of 17th-century homes and miles of beautiful conservation land framing its harbor; while the brick downtown of Newburyport has been renovated into a pedestrian paradise of restaurants, shops, and fine restaurants.

Sights

It's difficult to understate the impact that the little town of Essex had on establishing American commercial supremacy in the period after the Revolution. The **Essex Shipbuilding Museum** (66 Main St., Essex, 978/768-7541, www.essexshipbuildingmuseum.org, 10 A.M.–5 P.M. Wed.–Sun. June–Oct. and Sat.–Sun. Nov.–May, $7 adults, $6 seniors, $5 children 6 and over, free children under 6) traces almost 350 years of framing, rigging, and outfitting the craft that carried on our country's trade before the advent of the steam engine. Twenty models on loan from the Smithsonian present the range of wooden vessels built here. Kids love trying their own hands at boring holes and caulking seams.

Children of all ages are fascinated by the animals at **Wolf Hollow** (114 Essex Rd., Ipswich, 978/356-0216, www.wolfhollowipswich.com, tours at 1:30 Sat.–Sun., by appointment only Mon.–Fri., $7.50 adults, $5 seniors and children 3–17), a wildlife sanctuary where 10 British Colombian timber wolves wander around the grounds.

Decidedly more civilized, the 1926 manor known as the **Great House at Castle Hill** (290 Argilla Rd., 978/356-4351, www.thetrustees.org, tours 10 A.M.–3 P.M. Wed.–Thurs., 10 A.M.–1 P.M. Fri.–Sat. June–Oct., $10 adults, $5 children minimum age 8) is the centerpiece of the Crane Estate, a Victorian expanse of buildings and grounds located overlooking scenic Crane Beach. The home, which is full of period antiques, is open for tours in the summer.

Entertainment

Located in a former fire station, **Firehouse Center for the Arts** (1 Market Sq., Newburyport, 978/462-7336, www.firehousecenter.org) is one-stop shopping for culture. Among its offerings are theater productions, folk singers, indie films, and even step-dancing workshops. In the same complex, **The Grog** (13 Middle St., Newburyport, 978/465-8008, www.thegrog.com, 5 P.M.–11:30 P.M. daily) is a restaurant and bar that features live rock, folk, and jazz.

Shopping

Ipswich may have the historic homes, but Essex specializes in filling them. Known as the "antiques capital of the Northeast," the little town is acclaimed as much for the quality as the quantity of stores. Any antiquing trek starts at the **White Elephant Shop** (32 Main St., 978/768-6901, www.whiteelephantshop.com, 10 A.M.–5 P.M., Mon.–Fri.; 11 A.M.–5 P.M., Sat. and Sun.), where owners Rick and Jene Grobe scour attics and estate sales to find the finest pieces, along with art from local artists. Another good bet is **Americana Antiques** (48 Main St., 978/768-6006, www.americanaantiques.com, 10:30 A.M.–5 P.M. daily), which specializes in Victorian and early 20th-century furniture.

Food

This is where it all began, folks. One summer day in 1916 on Massachusetts' North Shore, Lawrence "Chubby" Woodman dunked a littleneck clam into the deep-frier he used to cook potato chips, and *voila!*—the fried clam was born. Many have imitated the recipe in the century since, but few with the same success. Now a dining-and-catering empire, **Woodman's of Essex** (Main St./Rte. 133, Essex, 978/768-2559, www.woodmans.com, 11:30 A.M.–9:30 P.M., Mon.–Sat.; 12 P.M.–8 P.M. Sun.; $9–25) can get chaotic on weekends—but in these parts, it still sets the standard. To skip the lines, head to **The Clam Box** (246 High St., Ipswich, 978/356-9707, www.ipswichma.com/clambox/index.htm, 11 A.M.–8 P.M., Mon.–Fri.; 11:30 P.M.–7 P.M., Sun., $7–23), a no less venerable institution that has been serving up fresh bivalves for 60 years. (The creation is even kicked up a notch here, with special homemade tartar sauce.)

Sample a creatively tweaked menu of New England staples at the brick-walled **Scandia** (37 Main St., Amesbury, 978/834-0444, 5:30 P.M.–10:30 P.M. daily;, $15–23), where the steamed mussels are tossed with andouille sausage and the crab cakes come daubed with aioli. A tad more casual, the sunny, lively dining room of **BluWater Cafe** (140 High St., Newburyport, 978/462-1088, www.thebluwatercafe.com, 12 P.M.–11 P.M., Tues.–Sat.; 12 P.M.–10 P.M., Sun.; closed Mon., $15–25) focuses on daily deliveries of locally caught fish, prepared simply (as is the blackened swordfish) or with flair (like the yellowfin tuna, served with sesame, sticky rice, wasabi, and ginger). If the weather's cooperating, there's no beating the al fresco eating at the friendly **Black Cow Tap & Grill** (54R Merrimac St., Newburyport, 978/499-8811, www.blackcowrestaurants.com, 11 A.M.–11:30 P.M., Mon.–Sat.; 10:30 A.M.–9:30 P.M. Sun., $15–32). Otherwise—or if the deck (which boasts a fantastic water view) is full—then grab a seat in the tavern indoors and dig into simple, unpretentious fare like pan-roasted halibut with braised fennel.

Information and Services

Brochures and information can be found at **Essex National Heritage Area Visitors Centers** (221 Essex St., Salem, 978/740-0444, www.essexheritage.org).

SPORTS AND RECREATION

Beaches

The North Shore abounds in gorgeous beachfront. One of the very best in New England is **Crane Beach** (Argilla Rd., Ipswich, 978/356-4354, www.thetrustees.org), a four-mile stretch of white sands and crashing white surf. The only time it isn't idyllic is the brief period of greenhead fly season (usually late July or early August—call ahead to check). The half-mile **Good Harbor Beach** (Thatcher Rd./Rte. 127A, Gloucester) offers a range of terrain, including sandy barrier beach, salt marsh, and rocky headland for tidepooling. The more secluded **Singing Beach** (Masconomo St., Manchester) is named for an interesting phenomenon wherein under certain conditions the sand seems to sing—or more accurately, squeak—when you walk on it.

Hiking and Biking

The wilderness jewel of the North Shore is Plum Island, a barrier island extending for 11 miles along the entrance of Newburyport Harbor. The bulk of the island is taken up by **Parker River National Wildlife Refuge** (6 Plum Island Tpke., 978/465-5753, www.fws.gov), a stopover for migratory birds on the Atlantic Flyway. A two-mile trail wends its way through sand dunes and swamps, providing excellent opportunities for bird sightings. It's also possible to surf-fish from the beach. The five-mile **Marblehead Rail Trail** offers beautiful vantages of the ocean and oceanfront mansions, with a two-mile spur into Salem. Rent bikes from **Marblehead Cycle** (25 Bessom St., 781/631-1570, www.marbleheadcycle.com).

Boating

Sea-kayak tours of the tidal estuaries in and around the Essex River are offered by **Essex River Basin Adventures** (1 Main St., Essex,

978/768-3722, www.erba.com), which boasts sightings of osprey, heron, and egrets.

Whale Watches

Cape Ann is ideally suited for access to the humpbacks and finbacks that patrol Stellwagen Bank. The oldest company in the business, **Cape Ann Whale Watch** (415 Main St., Gloucester, 800/877-5110, www.seethewhales.com), boasts the speeds of its flagship *Hurricane,* which jets out to the fishing grounds at 30 knots.

ACCOMMODATIONS
Under $100

Located in a colonial home in the center of historic Marblehead, the 1721 **Brimblecomb Hill B&B** (33 Mechanic St., Marblehead, 781/631-3172 or 781/631-6366, www.brimblecomb.com, $95–125) was once owned by a close friend of Ben Franklin. The two less expensive rooms share a bath, while the pricier room has a private bath, four-poster queen-sized bed, and a wall full of books. Depending on the season, a continental breakfast is served by the fireplace or out in a small garden.

$100-150

Rockport abounds with bed-and-breakfasts situated in captain's houses and colonial homes. One of the most welcoming is (**Inn on Cove Hill** (37 Mount Pleasant St., Rockport, 978/546-2701, www.innoncovehill.com, $120–235), a lovingly restored Federal-style home crowded with antiques and original architectural flourishes. The rooms are named after members of the family of the original resident, Caleb Norwood, and feature a range of antique beds, including an iron trundle bed and Shaker low beds for children. The sense of humor of the current owner, Betsy Eck, is evidenced by her own line of "Inn Sane" clothing. Situated smack dab on Salem's common, the **Hawthorne Hotel** (18 Washington Square West, Salem, 978/744-4080, www.hawthornehotel.com, $114–315) is a miniature grand European hotel, with a marble lobby and ballroom. Rooms are individually furnished

with a rich, gender-neutral palette. Rates at Halloween include coveted tickets to the hotel's annual costume ball. You can't get any closer to the water than at the **Cape Ann Motor Inn** (33 Rockport Rd., Gloucester, 978/281-2900, www.capeannmotorinn.com, $80–275), a three-story family-style resort located right on the curving sands of Long Beach, on the Gloucester-Rockport line. All 31 rooms offer views of the water, and include mini-fridges and breakfast in the rates; kitchenettes are only slightly more expensive.

$150-250

Newburyport's premier lodging, the **Clark Currier Inn** (45 Green St., Newburyport, 978/465-8363, www.clarkcurrierinn.com, $125–195) is a grand Federal-style mansion once owned by a shipbuilder and silversmith. The eight rooms contain individual flourishes, including lace canopies, antique Victorian couches, and mahogany furniture. Several also offer separate entries for privacy. Offering a chance to stay on the historic Crane Estate, the **Inn at Castle Hill** (280 Argilla Rd., Ipswich, 978/412-2555, www.theinnatcastlehill.com, $115–385) brings alive the Victorian era with grand dimensions and a wraparound verandah. The overriding atmosphere, however, is one of pristine quiet, with elegant all-white and pastel furnishings, and an absence of televisions or radios on the grounds. Add a walk under the stars with the sound of the surf, and you could be miles from civilization.

GETTING THERE AND AROUND

From Boston, drive North on Route 1A to get to Marblehead (15 mi., 30 min.) or Salem (15 mi., 35 min.) For Cape Ann, take I-93 North to Route 128. Take exit 14 and head north on Route 133 for Essex (35 mi., 50 min.) and Ipswich (45 mi., 1 hr.). Follow 128 to the end for Gloucester (40 mi., 50 min.) and Rockport (45 mi., 1 hr.). The **Massachusetts Bay Transportation Authority** (617/222-3200, www.mbta.com) runs commuter trains to Salem, Manchester, Gloucester, Rockport,

Ipswich, and Newburyport. The MBTA also runs buses to Marblehead and Salem. The New Hampshire–based **Coach Company** (800/874-3377, www.coachco.com) runs daily buses to Newburyport. In addition, the **Cape Ann Transportation Authority** (800/874-3377, www.coachco.com) runs buses between Rockport and Gloucester.

West of Boston

It was an accident of geography that put Concord at the center of the American Revolution. The Sons of Liberty needed a place to store their guns and ammunition close enough to Boston to allow easy communication, but far enough away that the Minutemen would have time to rally in the event of attack. On the morning of April 19, 1775, the alarm was sounded that the British were marching to capture the weapons cache at Concord, and the rest, as they say, is history. Today, the twin towns of Concord and Lexington are among the wealthy suburbs west of Boston, where doctors, lawyers, and businessmen commute daily into the city, then return to bed down in old colonial homes. History is still very much in evidence in both towns, which have taken no small amount of pride in labeling themselves the birthplace of America. History isn't the *only* reason to visit, however. The cosmopolitan and educated populace of the area has built an infrastructure of fine restaurants, bookshops, and boutiques in and among the historic buildings.

A dozen miles north of Concord and Lexington, meanwhile, the old mill town of Lowell has a decidedly different feel, as poor as the other towns are rich, and as funky as they are patrician. Lowell, along with a dozen other cities in a ring of rivers around Boston, was instrumental in the Industrial Revolution that established New England as the nation's first manufacturing powerhouse. Now variously reincarnated as a home for artists and refugees from around the world, the city has done an excellent job of preserving the industrial past in a series of museums and exhibits.

LEXINGTON

Historians may debate where the famous "shot heard 'round the world" was actually fired, but there can be no doubt that the first armed combat of the Revolutionary War took place in the town of Lexington, 11 miles west of Boston. By all accounts, it was a tentative and slapdash affair, in stark contrast to the American victory at Concord Bridge that would take place a few hours later. Even so, it marks the first time that the rebellious colonists fired on their own country's troops, outnumbered and outgunned though they were. For that reason, the town now stands as monument to the patriot's courage.

Orientation

Because of the nature of the Battles of Lexington and Concord—which moved back and forth between the towns as the day went on—a visit here can be a confusing mishmash of history. The best way to tour them is to follow the chronology of the battle itself, starting at the visitors centers in Lexington and seeing the Battle Green and the historic sights there; then heading into Concord to see the Old North Bridge; and then retracing your steps by foot or car down the Battle Road to end up again in Lexington.

Historic Houses

Paul Revere arrived in Lexington on the night of April 18, 1775, on a mission—to get word to John Hancock and Samuel Adams. "The regulars are out," he told the two rebel leaders, who were staying as guests in a parsonage now known as the **Hancock-Clarke House** (35 Hancock St., 781/862-1703, 10 A.M.–4 P.M. Sat.–Sun. April to mid-June and daily mid–June–Oct., $6). Today, the home retains much of its original 18th-century character, as well as several artifacts from the day of the battle.

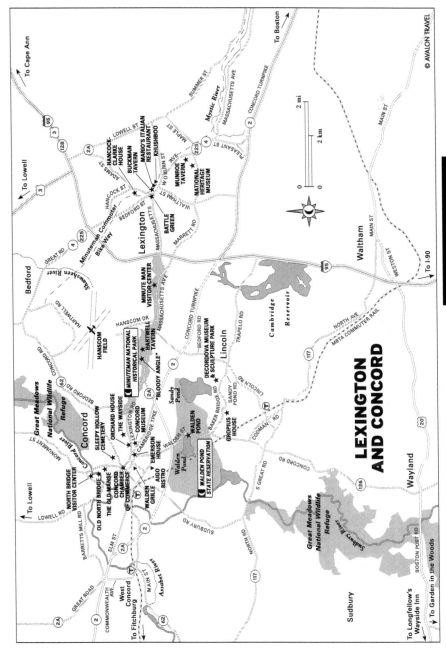

© AVALON TRAVEL

To Boston

To Cape Ann

To Lowell

SUMMER ST

Mystic River

MASSACHUSETTS AVE

CONCORD TURNPIKE

MAIN ST

95

3

128

2A

MAPLE ST

LOWELL ST

W OBURN ST

WALTHAM ST

HANCOCK CLARKE HOUSE

BUCKMAN TAVERN

MARIO'S ITALIAN RESTAURANT

KHUSHBOO

225

4

PLEASANT ST

MUNROE TAVERN

NATIONAL HERITAGE MUSEUM

ADAMS ST

HANCOCK ST

Lexington

BEDFORD ST

BATTLE GREEN

MASSACHUSETTS

MARRETT RD

2 mi

2 km

0

0

Waltham

MAIN ST

WESTON ST

To I-90

225

4

GREAT RD

Bedford

Shawsheen River

Minuteman Commuter Bike Way

HARTWELL RD

HANSCOM DR

HANSCOM FIELD

MINUTE MAN VISITOR CENTER

MINUTEMAN NATIONAL HISTORICAL PARK

HARTWELL TAVERN

"BLOODY ANGLE"

MASSACHUSETTS AVE

CONCORD TURNPIKE

BEDFORD RD

95

Cambridge Reservoir

NORTH AVE

MBTA COMMUTER RAIL

117

20

DECORDOVA MUSEUM SCULPTURE PARK

Lincoln

TRAPELO RD

SANDY POND RD

BAKER BRIDGE RD

LINCOLN RD

GROPIUS HOUSE

CODMAN RD

S GREAT RD

CONCORD RD

126

Wayland

Sandy Pond

2

CONCORD RD

BEDFORD RD

Great Meadows National Wildlife Refuge

Concord

MONUMENT ST

Concord River

NORTH BRIDGE VISITOR CENTER

OLD NORTH BRIDGE

THE OLD MANSE

CONCORD CHAMBER OF COMMERCE

SLEEPY HOLLOW CEMETERY

ORCHARD HOUSE

THE WAYSIDE

CONCORD MUSEUM

LEXINGTON RD

EMERSON HOUSE

WALDEN GRILLE

ADO BISTRO

CAMBRIDGE TPKE

WALDEN ST

Walden Pond

WALDEN POND STATE RESERVATION

WALDEN POND

BARRETTS MILL RD

LOWELL RD

To Lowell

ELM ST

2A

2

GREAT RD

COMMONWEALTH AVE

MAIN ST

West Concord

Assabet River

SUDBURY RD

NORTH RD

117

Sudbury

Sudbury River

Great Meadows National Wildlife Refuge

BOSTON POST RD

To Garden in the Woods

To Longfellow's Wayside Inn

2A

2

62

To Fitchburg

LEXINGTON AND CONCORD

After debating their course of action, Hancock and Adams decided to flee back to Boston to evade capture, while other rebels took up arms. During the long night, they gathered at **Buckman Tavern** (1 Bedford St., 781/862-5598, 10 A.M.–4 P.M. daily Apr.–Oct., $6) under the leadership of Captain Jonas Parker to steel themselves for the confrontation. The interior of the tavern has been meticulously restored to its original state, down to its old front door that still bears a bullet hole from a British musket ball.

Later in the afternoon of April 19, the retreating British again stopped in Lexington under much different circumstances to regroup and treat their wounded. They set up their headquarters at **Munroe Tavern** (1332 Massachusetts Ave., 781/674-9238, 12–4 P.M. Sat.–Sun. Apr.–mid-June and daily mid-June–Oct., $6), a 17th-century barroom where George Washington also later dined; the table where he sat is marked to prove it. All three of these historic homes are now owned by the **Lexington Historical Society** (www.

lexingtonhistory.org), which offers regular guided tours of their interiors. A combination ticket for all three houses is $10.

Lexington Battle Green

By order of Congress, an American flag flies 24 hours a day on the green in the center of Lexington, marking the place where colonists first took up arms against the Redcoats. Unless you have the good fortune of arriving for Patriot's Day celebrations, you'll now have to imagine the fateful battle that kicked off the fight for Independence, which as battles go was somewhat anti-climatic. Captain Parker lined his 77 men in a ragtag formation behind a meeting house at the western side of the green. Outnumbered by the 300-some British who marched into town (with another 400 behind them), they were ordered by British Major John Pitcairn to disarm. Somewhere a shot rang out, and in the ensuing melee eight Americans were killed and 10 wounded before Parker beat a hasty retreat.

Several monuments on the green bear testimony to the fracas. At the eastern end, the

The Minuteman **stands over Lexington Green.**

callipygous statue of *The Minuteman,* which represents Parker, was placed there in 1900. A rock halfway down the green shows the location of the original battle line. At the far end, where the minutemen actually fell, is an older monument placed over their graves in 1799 with an inscription capturing the passion of the events only 20 years earlier.

Other Sights

If you haven't already had enough of the battles, you can drink your fill at the **National Heritage Museum** (33 Marrett Rd., 781/861-6559, www.monh.org, 10 A.M.–4:30 P.M. Tue.–Sat., 12–4:30 P.M. Sun.), a free museum with an ongoing exhibit on the Revolution as well as other aspects of American history.

Events

The events of the battle are commemorated on the third Monday of every April in a statewide Massachusetts holiday called **Patriot's Day,** when costumed interpreters reenact the events of that long-ago April morning. You'll have to get up pretty early to see them—the first shots on Lexington Green are fired, in keeping with history, at 6 in the morning, with events transpiring along the Battle Road for the rest of the day.

Shopping

Artisans around the world have found a home at **Muse's Window** (The Concord Depot, 84 Thoreau St., Concord, 978/287-5500, www.themuseswindow.com), an *Alice in Wonderland*–type shop featuring eclectic crafts in glass, wood, and more. More-traditional New England handicrafts and souvenirs can be found at the **Crafty Yankee** (1838 Massachusetts Ave., 781/863-1219, www.craftyyankee.com), which counts ties with a Minuteman motif among its offerings.

Food

In addition to the usual curries and Tandoori dishes, the fine Indian restaurant **Khushboo** (1709 Massachusetts Ave., 781/863-2900, www.khushboorestaurant.com, $13–16) has

some more unusual offerings on the menu, including South Indian *dosas,* pan-roasted shrimp curry, and many vegetarian selections like Punjabi black lentils. Hearty (but not heavy) Italian takes center stage at **Mario's** (1733 Massachusetts Ave., 781/861-1182, $17–24), known most for its rich pastas and jovial atmosphere. Note: Arrive early at lunchtime—-the place fills up quickly for its daily specials. Also in the successful Italian category is **Bertucci's** (1777 Massachusetts Ave., 781/860-9000, www.bertuccis.com, $15–21), a brick-oven-pizza joint that began in Massachusetts and can now be found around the country. Ask for extra rolls, you won't be sorry. Meanwhile, the menu at nearby **C Catch** (34 Church St., Winchester, 781/729-1040, www.catchrestaurant.com, $21–28) is far from "the usual." The cushy bistro wows diners nightly with presentation of salt-roasted Wellfleet clams and grilled lemon, scallops with celery root and roasted pineapple, and oysters with *yuzu* sauce.

Information and Services

Just off the Battle Green, the **Lexington Chamber of Commerce** (1875 Massachusetts Ave., 781/862-2480, www.lexingtonchamber.org) has an office with information and brochures, as well as patriot-themed gifts and an excellent diorama of the battle. Located within the national historic park it shares with Concord (see next section), the **Minute Man Visitor Center** (250 North Great Rd., 978/369-6993, www.nps.gov/mima) has exhibits detailing the events (Boston Tea Party, Paul Revere's Ride, etc.) leading up to the first battles; it also has a posted schedule of ranger-led talks and activities happening that day.

Most medical centers closest to Lexington are specialty clinics, so for general **emergency services,** it may be wisest to contact one of the excellent hospitals in Boston. For outpatient services, **Beth Israel Deaconess** does have a Lexington Center (482 Bedford St., Lexington, 781/672-2000) for adults and children. Fill prescriptions or satisfy other pharmacy needs at **CVS Pharmacy** (1735 Massachusetts Ave., Lexington, 781/862-4080).

Paid **wireless Internet** access is offered at Starbucks (1729 Massachusetts Ave., Lexington, 781/863-8485), and faxing and shipping services are available at **The UPS Store** (405 Waltham St., Lexington, 781/861-7770).

CONCORD

"I think I could write a poem to be called Concord," wrote writer and philosopher Henry David Thoreau. "For argument I should have the River, the Woods, the Ponds, the Hills, the Fields, the Swamps and Meadows, the Streets and Buildings, and the Villagers." The town has changed little since Thoreau's day, with the same distinguishing features surrounding a quaint downtown of shops and historic sights.

In addition to its role in the Revolution, Concord played another significant part in history some 60 years later, when it became the home base for a 19th-century literary and religious movement known as transcendentalism. Its proponents, among them Thoreau, Ralph Waldo Emerson, and Bronson Alcott, believed in a new philosophy inspired by nature, replacing the formalistic theology they'd inherited from Europe. Their writings helped inspire the flowering of a truly American form of literature, as well as the modern environmental movement.

◖ Minuteman National Historical Park

After their easy victory in Lexington, British soldiers marched on to Concord, where they found the pickings not quite so easy. There, about 500 minutemen from surrounding towns had converged by the Old North Bridge to protect the weapons cache beyond it. When a British soldier fired at them, the colonists fired volley after volley, scattering the regulars back to town. The **Old North Bridge** is now one of the highlights of the national historical park, which has kept alive much of the original infrastructure of the route the British took back to town. While the current bridge, built in 1969, is the fourth on the site, the location gives a good idea of what the minutemen faced. A statue by Daniel Chester French depicts Captain Isaac Davis, head of the Acton militia, who was killed in the battle.

Located by the bridge, the **North Bridge Visitor Center** (174 Liberty St., 978/369-6993, www.nps.gov/mima) has an informative film and ranger talks as well as guides to the rest of the park. Although it's possible to drive along the highway or take a shuttle to major sites, try and walk some of the trail to really understand the claustrophobia felt by the panicked retreating British. Along the way, highlights include the **"bloody angle,"** where 30 British soldiers were ambushed and killed by colonists, and **Hartwell Tavern,** an authentic colonial public house that hosts military and domestic demonstrations daily.

◖ Walden Pond State Reservation

"I went to the woods because I wished to live deliberately…" As his famous words explain, Henry David Thoreau retired for two years to the shores of Walden Pond to seek a simpler mode of living closer to nature. The book he wrote about the experience, *Walden,* has since inspired generations of philosophers, environmentalists, and other readers, who now come regularly to pay homage to the site of **Thoreau's cabin** (915 Walden St., 978/369-3254, www.mass.gov). While the home itself is no longer there, the hearthstone from his chimney was uncovered years later. Nearby, a huge cairn of rocks grows yearly with the offerings of pilgrims. (If you'd like to add one, bring one with you, as the woods around the site have been picked clean.)

Sights

A wealth of artifacts bringing alive both the military and literary history of Concord are on display at the **Concord Museum** (200 Lexington Rd., 978/369-9763, www.concordmuseum.org, 11 A.M.–4 P.M. Mon.–Sat., 1–4 P.M. Sun. Jan.–Mar.; 9 A.M.–5 P.M. Mon.–Sat., 12–5 P.M. Sun. Apr.–Dec., $10 adults, $8 seniors and students, $5 children 6–17, free children under 6), a small museum with an enviable collection. Among the highlights are the simple bed, writing desk, and snowshoes that Thoreau used at Walden; the red-carpeted study of Ralph Waldo Emerson; and one of the two extant signal lanterns that warned Paul Revere of British attack—a simple iron lamp whose plainness belies its place in history. Unlike Thoreau, who died in poverty, his compatriot Ralph Waldo Emerson was recognized as the preeminent philosopher of his time, traveling around the world to deliver his essays. The **Emerson House** (28 Cambridge Turnpike, 978/369-2236, www. rwe.org/emersonhouse, 10 A.M.–4:30 P.M. Thurs.–Sat., 1–4:30 P.M. Sun. mid-Apr.–Oct., $7 adults, $5 seniors and students, free children under 7) remains furnished much as it was during his time—except for the furniture in his study (which is now in the museum across the street).

Other literary landmarks in the area include **Orchard House** (399 Lexington Rd., 978/369-4118, www.louisamayalcott.org, 10 A.M.–4:30 P.M. Mon.–Sat., 1–4:30 P.M. Sun. Apr.–Oct.; 11 A.M.–3 P.M. Mon.–Fri., 10 A.M.–4:30 P.M. Sat., 1–4:30 P.M. Sun. Nov.–Mar., $9 adults, $8 seniors and students, $5 children 6–17, free children under 6), where Louisa May Alcott penned *Little Women*. Fans of that book will swoon over the rooms, which contain original furniture owned by the family, including the writing desk made by Louisa's father, Bronson. Next door, **The Wayside** (455 Lexington Rd., 978/318-7826, www.nps. gov/archive/mima/wayside/index.htm) was Alcott's earlier home, where she and her sisters performed the childhood plays famously recreated in her book. It was also home in later years to novelist Nathaniel Hawthorne, whose study is largely intact. Several of the incestuous transcendentalists also inhabited **The Old Manse** (269 Monument St., 978/369-3909, www.thetrustees.org, 10 A.M.–5 P.M. Mon.–Fri., 12–5 P.M. Sun. mid-Apr.–Oct., $8 adults, $7 seniors and students, $5 children 6–12, free children under 6), by the Old North Bridge. They include Emerson, Hawthorne, and Emerson's

grandfather, Rev. William Emerson, who witnessed the battle there. The final resting place of many of the Concord authors can be found at **Sleepy Hollow Cemetery** (Bedford St., 978/318-3233, 7 A.M.–dusk daily), which contains the graves of Thoreau, Emerson, Hawthorne, and Alcott in an area poetically named Author's Ridge.

Tours

If you don't have a car of your own, a good way to see the sights in both Lexington and Concord is aboard the **Liberty Ride** (33 Marrett Rd., Lexington, 781/862-0500, www.libertyride.us, 10:30 A.M.–3 P.M. daily, $25 adults, $10 students 5–17, free children under 5), a shuttle that makes regular 90-minute trips from one end of the Battle Road to the other. You can get off and on as much as you'd like. In Concord proper, **Concord Guides** (48 Monument Sq., Concord, 978/287-0897, www.concordguides.com, 2–4 P.M. Sat.–Sun. Apr. 15–Nov. 1, $19 adults, $15 seniors and students, $12 youth 11–18, $7 children 6–10, free children under 6) offers two-hour walking tours with various themes, including history, literature, and architecture.

Entertainment and Events

In the center of Concord, the **Colonial Inn** (48 Monument Sq., 978/369-9200, www.concordscolonialinn.com, no cover) features nightly live music, including jazz, rock, and acoustic folk.

The **Festival of Authors** (late Oct.–early Nov.) keeps Concord's literary traditions alive with big-name authors in a two-week-long festival every year. In addition to book readings, the festival usually includes sessions on literary history and how-to advice for writers.

Shopping

The best independent bookstore in the area, **The Concord Bookshop** (65 Main St., 978/369-2405, 10 A.M.–5 P.M. Mon.–Fri.; 11 A.M.–5 P.M. Sat and Sun., www.concordbookshop.com) has an attractively arranged selection of bestsellers, books by all of the Concord authors, and an extensive kids' section. Across from an old fishing spot, **Many Nations Trading Post** (19 Main St., 978/369-0668, 10 A.M.–5 P.M. Mon.–Sat.; closed Sun., www.manynationstradingpost.com) has crafts made by local Native Americans, including peace pipes and turquoise jewelry, presented in an authentic setting. In addition to selling gourmet cheeses and foodstuffs from around the world, **The Cheese Shop** (29 Walden St., 978/369-5778, www.concordcheeseshop.com) regularly hosts events such as wine-and-cheese tastings and mozzarella-making demonstrations.

Food

A popular spot with locals, **Helen's** (17 Main St., 978/369-9885, $6–10) is a cute lunch spot with comfy booths and a retro feel. The menu contains 50 different kinds of burgers, sandwiches, and wraps for both meat-eaters and vegetarians alike, as well as a few dinner plates. Concord's old fire station has been reincarnated as **Walden Grille** (24 Walden St., 978/371-2233, www.waldengrille.com, $14–23), a casual yet sophisticated eatery that draws a regular crowd of young professionals. The menu runs toward simply prepared comfort cuisine, such as hanger steak with rosemary parmesan polenta or steamed cod loin wrapped in a banana leaf. The homey, rich flavors of Southern France are the draw at **La Provence** (105 Thoreau St., Concord, 978/371-7428, www.laprovence.us), a sweet little spot with a welcoming staff and addictive menu. Specialties like coq au vin and bouillabaisse come out at dinnertime, while simple-but-delicious sandwiches filled with pate, cheese, and ham are the focus at lunchtime.

Information

The **Concord Chamber of Commerce** (15 Walden St., 978/369-3120, www.concordchamberofcommerce.org) runs an informative visitors center.

LINCOLN AND SUDBURY

Just south of Lexington, the sleepy town of Lincoln is a mostly residential community

home to some of the richest people in the state. While it lacks the history of its neighbors, however, it does have several sites worth visiting. Sudbury, meanwhile, is a rural town whose namesake river meanders through fields of grass and purple heather.

Sights

The best Boston-area museum consistently missed by visitors is the **DeCordova Museum** (51 Sandy Pond Rd., Lincoln, 781/259-8355, www.decordova.org, 10 A.M.–5 P.M. Tues.–Sun., $12 adults, $8 seniors, students, and children 6–18, free children under 6), a contemporary art museum and sculpture garden with a heavy emphasis on New England artists. Every spring, the museum highlights the best art of the area in its annual exhibition. The adjoining sculpture garden is a 35-acre preserve of walking trails interspersed with some 75 works that both harmonize and clash with the native environment. Another modern work situated in a natural environment is the **Gropius House** (68 Baker Bridge Rd., Lincoln, 781/259-8098, www.spnea.org, 11 A.M.–4 P.M. Wed.–Sun. June–Oct. 15 and Sat.–Sun. Oct. 16–May 31, $10), which was designed by architect Walter Gropius, founder of the Bauhaus movement. Daily tours show off the home's pleasing minimalist design.

It's difficult to get more "Ye Olde New Englande" than **Longfellow's Wayside Inn** (72 Wayside Inn Rd., Sudbury, 978/443-1776, www.wayside.org), a historic tavern mentioned in *Tales from a Wayside Inn* by Henry Wadsworth Longfellow. In 1923, the property was bought by auto-titan Henry Ford and restored into a historic tourist attraction, with an old grist mill, and even the schoolhouse to which Mary's little lamb allegedly followed her each day. A few miles away over the border in Framingham, the **Garden in the Woods** (180 Hemenway Rd., Framingham, 508/877-7630, www.newfs.org, 9 A.M.–5 P.M. Tues.–Wed. and Sun., 9 A.M.–7 P.M. Thu.–Fri. Apr. 15–July 3; 9 A.M.–5 P.M. Tues.–Sun. July 4–Oct. 31, $8 adults, $6 seniors and students, $4 children 6–18, free children under 6) is a must-visit for any plant- or flower-lover. The acres of trails are planted with some 1,600 different species, including such lovelies as Trout Lilies, Wood Phlox, and Calopogon orchids.

Food

While you are visiting the **Wayside Inn** (72 Wayside Inn Rd., Sudbury, 978/443-1776, www.wayside.org, 11:30 A.M.–9:30 P.M. Mon.–Sat.; 12 P.M.–8:30 P.M. Sun., $19–33), you can stop in for a bite. The inn specializes in hearty New England classics, from prime rib to lobster pie. As might be expected, the dining room is decorated with authentic colonial antiques, and attended by families and seniors who have been dining here for decades.

LOWELL

The Industrial Revolution wasn't invented in Lowell, but it was perhaps perfected here. No other city in the Northeast poured more of its heart into the project of industrial production. Blessed by the natural turbines of the Merrimack River, the city became the center of cloth and textile manufacturing in the region

in the middle half of the 19th century. In fact, European visitors raved over the city as a miracle of modern ingenuity. As one Scottish visitor of the time said: "Niagara and Lowell are the two objects I will longest remember in my American journey—the one the glory of American scenery, the other of American industry."

Much of the success of the story, of course, was based on the exploitation of the workforce, mostly immigrant women from French Canada, Ireland, Italy, and other countries. Because of that, Lowell and the neighboring city of Lawrence could also be said to be the beginning of the modern labor movement, as these women risked their lives to strike for better working conditions. Lowell today is still a melting pot of immigrants from different countries, including a strong Cambodian community that settled here after the Vietnam War. Now that the mills have shut down, the city is one of the poorest in the state. It has seen new life in the past decade, however, as a haven for artists priced out of Boston, as well as a proud multicultural city—making it one of the most dynamic destinations in New England.

EASTERN MASSACHUSETTS

HEY, JACK KEROUAC

Beat Generation writer Jack Kerouac is most often associated with the frenetic city life of New York or San Francisco, but it's in the quiet backstreets of his native Lowell that you'll find the writer's soul. It's here that Kerouac grew up, and it's here he set much of his early fiction, including *Visions of Gerard, Doctor Sax, Maggie Cassidy, Vanity of Duluoz,* and his first published novel, *The Town and the City.* And it's also here that he came to die – when disillusioned with the acid tests and love-ins of the later beatniks, he returned to embrace his native Catholicism and live out his last years with his mother as a lonely alcoholic. Lowell honors its wayward son with the **Kerouac Commemorative** (Eastern Canal Park, Bridge St.), a series of stone monoliths inscribed with passages from his writings and arranged in a Buddhist mandala on the riverfront. Another

popular pilgrimage site for beat-idolaters is his grave in Edson Cemetery (375 Gorham St.), where a simple headstone is engraved with a three-word epigraph chosen by his third wife: "He Honored Life." Like Jim Morrison's grave in Paris, it is often surrounded by flowers, scraps of poetry, and even bottles of cheap booze left by fans. For information on more sites where Kerouac hung out in Lowell, stop by the **Lowell National Historic Park Visitors Center** (246 Market St., 978/970-5000, www. nps.gov/lowe, 9 A.M.–5 P.M. daily, free parking available), which has a guided-tour pamphlet, as well as a short film about Kerouac's life shown daily at 4 P.M. Or visit during October, when latter-day beats fill the streets for **Lowell Celebrates Kerouac!** (877/537-6822, http:// lckorg.tripod.com), an annual homage to the writer that includes readings of his works.

EASTERN MASSACHUSETTS

Sights

The industrial past of Lowell is celebrated at the **Lowell National Historical Park** (246 Market St., 978/970-5000, www.nps.gov/lowe, visitors center 9 A.M.–5:30 P.M. daily Aug. 24–Sep. 7; 9 A.M.–5 P.M. daily Sept. 8–Oct. 12), which centers around the most prosperous mills of the 19th century. The centerpiece of the park is the Bootts Cotton Mill Museum, which includes a working weave room of 88 power looms, along with the squalid boarding houses of the "mill girls." A more moving evocation of the lives of immigrant workers is displayed in the **Mill Girls and Immigrants Exhibit** (40 French St., 978/970-5000, www. nps.gov/lowe, 1–5 P.M. daily June 24–Sept. 7; 1:30–5 P.M. daily Sept. 8–Oct. 12, free), affiliated with the University of Massachusetts–Lowell, which explores the lives of immigrants over the years. Among the exhibits there, don't miss a small case that incongruously displays the backpack and typewriter of Beat writer Jack Kerouac, one of Lowell's native sons (see the sidebar *Hey, Jack Kerouac*).

Another native son, James McNeil Whistler, is honored by the **Whistler House Museum of Art** (243 Worthen St., 978/452-7641, www. whistlerhouse.org, 11 A.M.–4 P.M. Wed.–Sat., $5 adults, $4 seniors and students, free children). Located in the home where the painter was born, the collection does not, unfortunately, include the famous *Whistler's Mother* (which hangs in the Musee d'Orsay in Paris)—though it does contain a copy done by the artist's cousin. The galleries also contain etchings by Whistler, who was among the most celebrated American artists of the 19th century, alongside works of other artists of the period. The modern artistic community of Lowell can be found at the **Revolving Museum** (122 Western Ave., 978/937-2787, www.revolving-museum.org, 11 A.M.–4 P.M. Tues.–Sun., free), an art and performance space that relocated here from Boston several years ago. The city has actively encouraged the arts scene by helping build the **Ayer Lofts Art Gallery** (172 Middle St., 978/970-3556, www.ayerlofts.com), in a building inhabited by working artists.

Events

Celebrating the multicultural nature of the city, the **Lowell Folk Festival** (978/970-5200, www.lowellfolkfestival.org) is a cornucopia of culture, featuring hundreds of music and dance performers from around the world. In August, the **Lowell Southeast Asian Water Festival** (978/596-1013, www.lowellwaterfestival.org) celebrates Cambodian culture with traditional Khmer dance performances and the mesmerizing sight of hundreds of candles floating on the Merrimack River.

Food

Located in the center of town in a restored mill building, **Cobblestones** (91 Dutton St., 978/970-2282, www.cobblestonesoflowell. com, 11:30 A.M.–10 P.M. Mon.–Sat., closed Sun., $7–29) has something for everyone. A formal dining room serves grilled flatbreads, risotto, and fisherman's stew, while a casual bar area dishes out sandwiches, buffalo wings, and a variety of oysters on the half shell (including, we kid you not, Rocky Mountain oysters). The oldest Asian restaurant in Lowell, the **◖ Southeast Asian Restaurant** (343 Market St., 978/452-3182, www.foodventure.com, 11:30 A.M.–10 P.M. daily, $4–13) was started by an Italian man and his Laotian wife, who set about trying to re-create the food served in open-air stalls across the subcontinent. Twenty-five years later, it is still one of the most popular eateries in the city, serving a range of authentic Cambodian, Laotian, Vietnamese, Thai, and even Mongolian cuisine in a large and festive dining room.

Information

The **Greater Merrimack Valley Convention and Visitors Bureau** (40 French St., 978/459-6150, www.merrimackvalley.org) runs an office stocked with information about Lowell and the surrounding region.

SPORTS AND RECREATION

Beaches

In addition to the connection with Thoreau, **Walden Pond State Reservation** (915 Walden

St., Concord, 978/369-3254, www.mass.gov) draws hordes of summer visitors every year to swim in its deep, cool waters. Be forewarned that the only parking available is in the official lot, which fills up quickly on hot summer mornings.

Hiking

Situated along the banks of the Concord and Sudbury Rivers, the **Great Meadows National Wildlife Refuge** (73 Weir Hill Rd., Sudbury, 978/443-4661, www.fws.gov/northeast/greatmeadows) contains almost 4,000 acres of meadow and marshland that teems with wildlife. Trails wind their way through both parts of the reservation, one located in Concord and the other in Sudbury. Among the wildlife that can be spotted are deer, red fox, and great blue herons.

Boating and Fishing

Before *Walden,* Thoreau wrote *A Week on the Concord and Merrimack Rivers.* You can follow in his paddle marks by renting a canoe at the **South Bridge Boathouse** (496 Main St., Concord, 978/369-9438, www.canoeconcord. com) for a trip down the heather-lined banks of the Concord River.

ACCOMMODATIONS
Under $100

A strange blend between a motel and a greenhouse, the **Battle Green Inn** (1720 Massachusetts Ave., Lexington, 781/862-6100, www.battlegreeninn.com, $89–109) has cute and affordable rooms arranged around a central indoor courtyard. Its location just steps from the Battle Green and other historic sites can't be beat. Your best bet for lodging in Lowell is the **Courtyard by Marriott** (30 Industrial Ave. East, Lowell, 978/458-7575, www.marriott.com, $74–174), which has pay-per-view movies and in-room coffee service.

$100-150

It may sound too cozy to be true, but **Fireside Bed and Breakfast** (24 Eldred St., Lexington, 781/862-2053, www.firesidebb.com, $90–140),

lives up to its name with modern bathrooms, beds laid with homemade quilts, and a location snug up against miles of conservation land. In colder seasons, the elaborate breakfasts are served in the formal dining room next to (where else?) the fireplace. Just off the highway on the north side of Lexington, the **Quality Inn & Suites** (440 Bedford St., Lexington, 781/861-0850, www.choicehotels.com, $70–120) offers complimentary Wi-Fi as well as sports-club passes, cable TV, and a free shuttle to nearby historic attractions.

$150-250

No lodging in Concord gets more into the spirit of the town than the 【 **Hawthorne Inn** (462 Lexington Rd., Concord, 978/369-5610, www. concordmass.com, $125–325), which trumpets its location on land once owned by Emerson, Hawthorne, and the Alcotts, and challenges its guests to "think an original thought" while they stay. The seven guest rooms are decked out with original artwork and handmade quilts, as well as copies of poetry and novels written by the Concord authors to provide the proper inspiration while you are there.

While it's not quite within walking distance of the Old North Bridge, the **North Bridge Inn** (21 Monument St., Concord, 978/371-0014, www.northbridgeinn.com, $165–275) is as close as you are likely to get to Concord historic sites. The unpretentious guesthouse features all-suite accommodations, from a "studio suite" with microwave alcove to a larger suite with separate room and kitchenette. Lithographs of Revolutionary battles on the walls and toile bedspreads on the beds give the inn a colonial feel without going overboard. A full breakfast is served at a sunny breakfast nook downstairs.

GETTING THERE
AND AROUND

To drive to Lexington from Boston, take Route 2 west to exit 55, then Route 4 north to Lexington center (15 mi., 30 min.). For Concord, take Route 2 west from Boston past I-95. When the road takes a sharp left, continue on straight down the Cambridge Turnpike to Concord Center (25 mi., 40 min.). From Lexington to Concord, take Route 2A west, parallel to the Battle Road (7 mi., 5 min.) To drive to Lowell from Boston, take I-93 north to I-95 south to US Route 3 north (30 mi., 40 min.).

The **Massachusetts Bay Transportation Authority** (MBTA, 617/222-3200, www.mbta.com) runs commuter trains to stations in Concord (90 Thoreau St.) and Lowell (Thorndike St.). Buses by **Yankee Line** (800/942-8890, www.yankeeline.us) run once daily from Boston to Concord, stopping at Concord Center.

It is difficult to get around Concord without the benefit of your own car, unless you plan on walking a lot around town. The major historical sites are all a mile's walk from the train station. In Lexington, a shuttle bus called **Lexpress** (781/861-1210, http://ci.lexington.ma.us) runs routes throughout the town. Lowell is also bus-rider friendly, with trips all over town run by the **Lowell Regional Transportation Authority** (978/452-6161, www.lrta.com).

Worcester and Vicinity

West of Concord, the area between I-495 and the Pioneer Valley is a transitional area of suburbs and farms, as the urban core of Boston gives way to the more rural western part of the state. Because of that, it's an area that is often passed over by travelers, on their way from one end of the state or the other. Those who stop, however, will find several attractions to catch their interest, including Worcester's underrated art museum and the historical village at Sturbridge.

WORCESTER

Though Worcester is the third-largest city in Massachusetts, it has had a troubled economic history. Named county seat in 1731, it suffered from lack of good transportation and waterpower, which prevented it from becoming an industrial powerhouse like other towns. Managing a good living as a manufacturing center instead, it drew waves of immigrants who flooded the city to produce tools and household items. Since the city's economy collapsed after World War II, however, it has yet to find a winning formula to rescue its downtown. On the upside, the city is notable for several fine museums and nine colleges and universities, including Clark and Holy Cross, which infuse a young energy into its nightlife.

◖ Worcester Art Museum

Given Worcester's reputation, many natives are surprised to discover the city even *has* an art museum, never mind that it's one of the very best in New England. Though it does have some paintings by top-name artists—such as Paul Gauguin's excellent *The Brooding Woman*—most of the collection (55 Salisbury St., 508/799-4406, www.worcesterart.org, 11 A.M.–5 P.M. Wed.–Fri., 11 A.M.–8 P.M. third Thurs. of every month, 10 A.M.–5 P.M. Sat., $10 adults, $8 seniors and students, free children under 18) focuses on areas rarely covered by other museums, making the halls of WAM (as it's known) a constant discovery. Among the museum's strengths are a wonderful collection of early American portraits, dozens of medieval paintings and sculptures, and a good cross-section of pre-Columbian Native American artwork. Weekly tours are given by docents on Saturday at 11 A.M. and Sunday at 1 P.M.

Other Sights

Founded by an eccentric millionaire with a taste for romantic sagas, the **Higgins Armory Museum** (100 Barber Ave., 508/853-6015, www.higgins.org, 10 A.M.–4 P.M. Tues.–Sat., 12–4 P.M. Sun., $10 adults, $7 seniors and children 4–16, free children under 4) draws fans of King Arthur to wow over a vast collection of weapons and armor. The museum has hundreds of suits of armor, including a rare Roman gladiator helmet, and features demonstrations on weapon-making and wielding. The Worcester Art Museum was founded by Stephen Salisbury, a leading industrialist whose home is now on display as **Salisbury Mansion** (40 Highland St., 508/753-8278, www.worcesterhistory.org, 1–4 P.M. Thurs.–Sat., $5 adults, free children under 18). Period 1830s furnishings and changing exhibits bring Worcester's manufacturing heyday to life. More than just a zoo, the **EcoTarium** (222 Harrington Way, 508/929-2700, www.ecotarium.org, 10 A.M.–5 P.M. Tues.–Sat., 12–5 P.M. Sun., $10 adults, $8 seniors and students, $8 children 3–18, free children under 3) bills itself as an indoor-outdoor nature center, with polar bears, foxes, and other wildlife on the grounds. Among its more unusual experiences is a tree-canopy walkway 40 feet above the ground.

Entertainment
The gorgeous 19th-century **Mechanics Hall** (321 Main St., 508/752-5608, www.mechanicshall.org) anchors the arts scene of the city with regular performances by classical orchestras from around the region. The young and the restless converge at **Palladium** (261 Main St., 508/797-9696, www.thepalladium.net), a dance club and concert hall that spotlights acts like The Mighty Mighty Bosstones and The Dropkick Murphys. Even bigger, national acts perform at the **DCU Center** (50 Foster St., 508/755-6800, www.centrumcentre.com), the largest concert hall in New England, which often draws performers that don't appear in Boston.

Shopping
Located at the Worcester Antiquarian Society, the **Ben Franklin Book Store** (21 Salem St., 508/753-8685, www.benfranklinbookstore.com) has dozens of cases full of rare, out-of-print, and first edition books. Among other subjects, the store specializes in history, music, and psychology. A browser's paradise of antiques and collectibles, the **Kelley Square Flea Market** (149 Washington St., 508/755-9040)

EASTERN MASSACHUSETTS

THE DINER CAPITAL OF THE WORLD

Worcester is virtually synonymous with diners. Tradition has it that the modern diner started out as a horse-drawn lunch carriage pioneered by Providence, Rhode Island, entrepreneur Walter Scott in 1872. But it was the commercial manufacturing of lunch wagons starting in Worcester in 1887 that ensured their popularity. Over the next few years, several companies set up shop in the city, but the most famous was the Worcester Lunch Car Company, which pioneered the railroad-diner-car look in the 1930s. The diner cars were designed for factory workers, who needed a good hearty meal served cheap and quickly, and frequently at odd hours to accommodate their schedules. Now genuine Worcester cars are prized by restaurant owners all over the Northeast. Of course, there are many fine examples of diners in the city that once created them. Known locally as "the Bully," the 24-hour **Boulevard Diner** (155 Shrewsbury St., 508/791-4535, $5-8) sets the mood with a neon exterior and dark wood interior. But it's the greasy-spoon menu of homemade meatloaf, leg of lamb, and chicken soup that really brings back yesteryear. Across from the former site of the Worcester Lunch Car Company itself, the **Miss Worcester Diner** (300 Southbridge St., 508/753-5600, 5 A.M.-2 P.M. Mon.-Fri., 6 A.M.-2 P.M. Sat.-Sun., $4-8) has been reopened after being shuttered for several years. Otherwise known as the "Miss Woo," it is located inside the original Worcester Lunch Car No. 812, which once served the factory workers who made the cars themselves; now it may be the only surviving Worcester car in the city that gave them their name.

is an indoor emporium with booths operated by some 150 members.

Food

An enthusiastic favorite among locals, **O'Connor's Restaurant & Bar** (1160 W. Boylston St., 508/853-0789, www.oconnorsrestaurant.com, 11:30 A.M.–11 P.M. Mon.–Sat.; 11:30 A.M.–10 P.M. Sun., $11–21) is a family-style Irish restaurant that draws a cross-section of city residents. The maze of dining rooms is covered floor-to-ceiling with Irish beer and liquor advertisements. The menu includes authentic Auld Sod dishes like shepherd's pie and bangers 'n' mash. The upper crust from around Central Massachusetts converges on **111 Chop House** (111 Shrewsbury St., 508/799-4111, www.111chophouse.com, 4 P.M.–10 P.M. Mon.–Thurs.; 4 P.M.–11 P.M. Fri.–Sat.; 4 P.M.–9:30 P.M. Sun., $19–36) for high-quality steaks and other meat dishes such as Dijon-encrusted rack of lamb. The swank dining room is a welcome change for Worcester; a cheaper tapas-and-pizza menu is served at the bar.

Information and Services

The **Central Massachusetts Convention and Visitors Bureau** (30 Elm St., 508/755-7400, www.worcester.org) runs a visitors center downtown with information on Worcester and the surrounding area.

The area's biggest hospital is **Umass Memorial Hospital** (119 Belmont St., Worcester, 508/334-1000, www.umassmemorial.org), which provides emergency and various other services. Chains such as **CVS Pharmacy** (283 Park Ave., Worcester, 508/792-3866, www.cvs.com) and **Walgreens** (320 Park Ave., Worcester, 508/767-1732, walgreens.com) fill prescriptions and sell other medicines.

Free **Internet access** on terminals is offered at **Worcester Public Library** (3 Salem Sq., Worcester, 508/799-1655, www.worcpublib.org) and free wireless access is offered (with purchase) at cafes such as **Java Hut Cafe** (1073-A Main St., Worcester, 508/752-1678). Faxing and printing services are available

at **Staples** (541B Lincoln St., Worcester, 508/852-3771, www.staples.com).

STURBRIDGE

Arriving in the small town of Sturbridge expecting historic New England heaven, many visitors are surprised instead to find the worst kind of strip-mall purgatory. Push on past the town center, however, and you'll find what puts the town on all the tour-bus itineraries: Old Sturbridge Village, a living-history museum that completely immerses visitors in the spirit of the past.

Old Sturbridge Village

New England history is mostly associated with the Revolutionary War era, but it's the prosperous period just before the Industrial Revolution that most closely typifies the image of small-town life passed down to us from Burl Ives and Grandma Moses. That's the time period captured at this living-history museum (1 Old Sturbridge Village Rd., 508/347-3362, www.osv.org, 9:30 A.M.–5 P.M. daily Apr.–Oct. 23; 9:30 A.M.–4 P.M. Wed.–Sun. Oct. 24–Nov.; Thu.–Sun. Dec.–Mar., $20 adults, $18 seniors, $7 children 3–17, free children under 3), a reconstructed 1830s New England village. It dates back to the 1920s, when several local industrialists, overwhelmed with a fast-moving society of motion pictures, automobiles, and airplanes, set out to preserve a simpler past. They found buildings all over the region, moved them to the site of an old farm, and filled them with antiques gathered in decades of collecting.

The coup de grace—and what still makes the village so interesting today—was hiring dozens of costumed actors who assumed roles in the town and learned traditional country skills to demonstrate to visitors. Today, you can spend several hours going from building to building to see performers (who *never* break character) demonstrate blacksmithing, weaving, food storage, and animal husbandry. The museum has adjusted over the years to become a year-round destination, offering sleigh rides in the winter and old-time baseball games in summer. Whenever you visit, you'll leave more thankful for your dishwasher than ever.

Other Sights

Nurse Clara Barton is best known for founding the Red Cross in 1881. The Victorian Renaissance woman, however, was equally well known in her time as a suffragette and social reformer. Her accomplishments are on display at the **Clara Barton Birthplace Museum** (66 Clara Barton Rd., North Oxford, 508/987-2056, www.clarabartonbirthplace. org, 11 A.M.–5 P.M. Wed.–Sun. June–Aug.; 11 A.M.–5 P.M. Sat. Sept., $6 adults, $3 children 6–12, free children under 6), which contains exhibits on her life.

Events

The best-known antiques fair in the country, the **Brimfield Antique Show** (www.brimfield-show.com), occurs yearly in Brimfield, the town next door to Sturbridge. Every September, the small town of 3,000 people explodes in population, as 30,000 visitors and 5,000 dealers descend upon it to barter over their wares.

Shopping

If you are intrigued by the craftsmen demonstrations at Old Sturbridge Village, you can pick up some of their handiwork at the **Shops at Old Sturbridge Village** (1 Old Sturbridge Village Rd., 508/347-0244, www.osv.org, 10 A.M.–5 P.M. daily), which features village-made tin and pottery items, along with heirloom seeds and books on New England history. A whirlwind of sampling and noshing, the snack emporium that is **Cracker Barrel Old Country Store** (215 Charlton Rd., 508/347-8925, 6 A.M.–10 P.M. Sun.–Thurs.; 6 A.M.–11 P.M. Fri.–Sat., www.crackerbarrel.com) peddles everything from candied popcorn tins and cheddar cheese to peanut brittle and relish. Many a holiday gift basket is born here——as are equally many "homemade" creations, by way of the shop's corn muffin mix and cherry cobbler filling.

Food

Sturbridge has two types of restaurants—fast food and colonial-style taverns. In the latter category, costumed interpreters provide music and circulate among diners at **Wight Tavern** (1 Old Sturbridge Village Road, 508/347-3362, 10 A.M.–5 P.M. daily, $9–14), a family-style tavern at the center of Old Sturbridge Village that serves up burgers, sandwiches, and affordable Yankee dinners. Four different rooms are each filled with antiques and exhibits drawn from the museum's collections. The best in the category is the **Whistling Swan** (502 Main St., 508/347-2321, www.thewhistlingswan.com, 11 A.M.–10 P.M. Sun.–Thurs.; 11 A.M.–11 P.M. Sat., $24–37), a formal dining room with quiet New England ambience that prides itself on the freshness of its ingredients. The menu includes hearty entrées of the likes of rack of lamb and lobster filet mignon. The less pretentious **Ugly Duckling Loft** ($14–37) offers up the same menu, along with lower-priced items, in a pub setting next door.

SPORTS AND RECREATION
Skiing and Hiking

Algonquin for "the great hill," **Wachusett Mountain Ski Area** (499 Mountain Rd., Princeton, 978/464-2300, www.wachusett. com, 9 A.M.–10 P.M. Mon.–Fri., 8 A.M.–10 P.M. Sat.–Sun., $29–54 adults, $20–40 seniors and children 6–12) is a magnet during winter months for skiers who can't make it up north to Vermont or New Hampshire. While the mountain can't compare, of course, to its northern cousins, its 22 trails provide enough terrain to occupy a range of skill levels, including some decent moguls and challenging vertical runs. In the summer months, the trails are open to hikers, who delight in the views from the highest mountain for miles around.

Camping

One of the prettiest campgrounds in the state, **Wells State Park** (Rte. 49, 508/347-9257, www.mass.gov) offers 60 sites in an attractive woodland setting within easy striking distance of Worcester and Sturbridge. A lake on the premises is for the exclusive use of campers.

ACCOMMODATIONS
Under $100
Directly across from Old Sturbridge Village, **Motel 6** (408 Main St., Sturbridge, 508/347-7327, $50–70) offers bare-bones accommodations for the cheapest price around. Rooms are polyester-chic, but the motel does include cable TV and a large pool in back.

$100-150
Don't let the canopy beds and Victorian flourishes fool you; **The Inn at Restful Paws** (70 Allen Hill Rd., Holland, 413/245-7792, $120–160, www.restfulpaws.com) welcomes as many four-legged guests as it does two-legged. ("The place where pooches bring their people to relax" is their motto.) From bean bag beds and special towels for pets, the place bends over backwards to make pets comfy—-and does the same for humans, with picturesque walking trails, not to mention healthy breakfasts and clothing steamers in rooms. The region also abounds with numerous chain hotels, including a **Hampton Inn** (800/426-7866, www.newenglandhampton-inns.com, $105–169) in both Worcester and Sturbridge.

$150-250
Catering to skiers at the nearby mountain, **Wachusett Village Inn** (9 Village Inn Rd., Westminster, 978/874-2000, www.wachu-settvillageinn.com, $109–189) is a full-service inn with simply designed rooms, but lots of perks. Some rooms have fireplaces, while the grounds have a pool, hot tub, and spa. Packages suited to families and couples also include

vouchers for dinner and massage treatments. While Worcester and luxury aren't often included in the same sentence, the **Beechwood Hotel** (363 Plantation St., Worcester 508/754-5789, www.beechwoodhotel.com, $179–340) provides beautiful boutique accommodations in the center of the city. Despite its lackluster exterior, the hotel's interior features dark woods and plush furniture, along with all of the amenities—printer, high-speed Internet, Frette linens, fitness center—a business traveler could ask for.

More casual and catering to business travelers, **The Crowne Plaza Hotel** (10 Lincoln Sq., Worcester, 508/791-1600, www.ichotelsgroup.com, $152–309) is part of the national chain offering guests services from valet and newspapers to complimentary breakfast.

GETTING THERE AND AROUND
To drive to Worcester from Boston, take the Mass Pike (I-90) West (45 mi.,55 min.) Continue along the Pike another 15 mi. (20 min.) for Sturbridge.

The **Worcester Train Station** (2 Washington Sq.) is serviced by both AMTRAK (800/872-7245, www.amtrak.com) and the Massachusetts Bay Transportation Authority (617/222-3200, www.mbta.com) commuter trains from Boston. **Peter Pan Bus Lines** (800/343-9999, www.peterpanbus.com) runs buses to Worcester Bus Terminal (2 Washington Sq.).

Buses throughout Worcester are run by the **Worcester Regional Transit Authority** (508/791-9782, www.therta.com).

South of Boston

Follow Route 3A from Boston down toward Cape Cod and you'll find yourself on what many argue was the state's oldest public highway—once called the "Mattachusetts Payth." It ran between Boston and Plymouth, where the Pilgrims had made their fateful arrival on the Mayflower in 1620 and soon thereafter established the Plymouth Colony. Farther south lie the waters of Buzzard's Bay, a sheltered arc between Long Island and Nantucket Sounds that is home to two great port cities: the former whaling port and fishing community of New Bedford, and the textile center and immigrant gateway of Fall River.

THE SOUTH SHORE

While the Plymouth Pilgrims may have been the first settlers of the area, they were followed in no short order by countless other Brits, who set up fishing and trading posts that would later become the cities of Weymouth and Quincy. From there, small waves of Pilgrims—with last names like Alden, Bradford, Weston, and Winslow—were granted land and built houses in areas now called Duxbury, Marshfield, Kingston, and Pembroke.

Thanks to the efforts of extremely active local conservation groups, many of those homes are well preserved today—as is much of the shore's natural beauty. Many of the towns maintain strict zoning laws mandating only specific paint colors for homes and stone walls instead of Jersey barriers, and barring chain stores in certain areas of town.

Of course, commerce still reigns supreme in much of the region. Cities like Hanover, Weymouth, and Braintree are home to plenty of shopping malls and commercial centers. But oftentimes just down the road a few miles is a town like Cohasset, with its pristine harbor, or Duxbury, with its quietly conserved meadows, scarlet cranberry bogs, and picturesque beaches. And scattered throughout all of it are homes built by those who first came over on the Mayflower, maintained by dedicated residents and descendants.

Sights

The **John Alden House** (105 Alden St., Duxbury, 781/934-9092, www.alden.org, noon–4 P.M. mid-May–mid-Oct., $5 adults, $3 children under 18) is remarkable not only as a piece of 17th-century architecture built by one of America's original settlers but as a family heirloom; it is still owned today by the Alden Kindred of America, Inc. Likewise the **Maritime and Irish Mossing Museum** (301 Driftway, Scituate, 781/545-1083, www.scituatehistoricalsociety.org, 1–4 P.M. Sat.–Sun. July–Aug., $4 adults, $3 seniors, free children under 18), housed in the 1739 residence of Capt. Benjamin James. The museum spotlights the South Shore's place in history as a seafaring center through an epic collection of photos, a history of original families, and a dramatic "Shipwreck Room," which, true to its name, relays the stories of some of the area's most historic storms. Pity that some of those storms' victims didn't find themselves closer to the heroes featured in the **Hull Lifesaving Museum** (1117 Nantasket Ave., Hull, 781/925-5433, www.lifesavingmuseum.org, 10 A.M.–4 P.M. Sat.–Thurs.; 10 A.M.–1 P.M. Fri., year-round, $5 adults, $3 seniors, free children 18 and under). Here find all kinds of tributes—exhibits on lifebuoys, tours, and collections of gear—to the local maritime culture and, in particular, 19th-century coastal lifesavers.

In Hingham, the bucolic **World's End** (250 Martin's Ln., 781/740-6665, www.thetrustees.org, 8 A.M.–sunset daily year-round, $5 adults, free children 12 and under) makes for a magnificent walk—the 251-acre property designed by Frederick Law Olmsted overlooks Hull and Boston Harbors, and is particularly stunning in the fall. Trees, however, hardly have a lock on fall foliage.

Entertainment and Nightlife

As a primarily residential community, the South Shore has only a small handful of noteworthy nightlife destinations. For concerts of

EASTERN MASSACHUSETTS

almost every stripe (from Julio Iglesias to Ani DiFranco), there's the **South Shore Music Center Circus** (130 Sohier St., Cohasset, 781/383-9850, www.themusiccircus.org, summer only). Year-round, **Eli's Pub in The Barker Tavern** (21 Barker Rd., Scituate, 781/545-6533, www.barkertavern.com,4 P.M.–10 P.M., Tues.–Fri.; 5 P.M.–10 P.M. Sat.; 1 P.M.–10 P.M., $12–15) is a cozy and convivial spot for a drink on weeknights and weekends. The historic harborside watering hole is full of local couples, boat lovers, and chatty singles.

Events

Autumn brings the South Shore's cranberry bogs to a brilliant red hue, and aside from sampling the tart little treasures, there's but one way to celebrate: at October's **National Cranberry Festival** held at **Edaville Railroad** (7 Eda Ave., South Carver, 877/332-8455, www.edaville.com, $18, free children under 2), where you can ride an antique steam train through a working berry bog.

Shopping

Apart from Braintree and Hanover's goliath shopping malls filled with chain stores, you'll find plenty of independent (often quaint) shops in the South Shore's smaller towns. Case in point: **Olivia Rose** (1945 Ocean St., Marshfield, 781/834-8851, http://oliviarosechildrensboutique.com/, 10 A.M.–5 P.M. Mon.–Sat.; 12–4 P.M. Sun.) is far from your run-of-the-mill children's clothing shop. Score everything from Baby Lulu capris and Mulberribush pinafores to Mustela baby beauty products.

The selection of home accessories and furnishings—both new and antique—at **Octavia's** (35 Depot St., Duxbury, 781/934-9553, www.octaviashomedecor.com, 10 A.M.–5 P.M. Mon.–Sat.; noon–5 P.M. Sun.) is interwoven with handmade jewelry, fine art paintings, colorful pottery, and hand-painted lamps.

Some of the most meticulously tailored men's clothing around the Boston area can be found at **Natale's** (2001 Washington St.,

Hanover, 781/982-8080, natalesofhanover. com, 9 A.M.–9 P.M. Mon.–Fri.; 9 A.M.–5:30 P.M. Sat.; 12–5 P.M. Sun.)—whether you're in the market for bespoke suits or windbreakers.

One of New England's finest selections of hard-to-find beauty supplies is at **Zona** (65 South St., Hingham, 781/749-4500, 2–8 P.M. Mon.; 9 A.M.–8 P.M. Tues.–Thurs.; 9 A.M.–6 P.M. Fri.–Sat.)—everything from the chic Japanese line Shu Uemura and Kerastase to Kiehl's and Red Flower.

Adults and kids can get their literary fill at the quaint **Westwinds Bookshop** (45 Depot St., Duxbury, 781/934-2128, www.westwindsbookshop.com, 10 A.M.–5 P.M. Mon.–Fri.; closed Sun.), stocked with a slew of titles (covering everything from taxidermy to taxes), cards, toys, and gifts made around the area.

Food

Dining on the South Shore was once an unfortunate chore, with only baked-stuffed everything, a few inauthentic Italian joints, and poor-quality Chinese food as typical options. But the past decade has pushed the area to new heights, to a point where plenty of food lovers from all over New England—including Boston—are making the drive for a great meal. One major draw is █ **Tosca** (14 North St., Hingham, 781/740-0080, 4 P.M.–10 P.M. Tues.–Sun.; closed Mon., www.eatwellinc. com, $23–30), named for Puccini's famed opera, and almost as dramatic. From the bustling open kitchen the staff serves authentic, creative Italian in the high-ceilinged, white-linen dining room—specialties like wild-boar Bolognese and lavender-brined pork chop. But enough with the turf; in an area with this many ties to the water, seafood's the thing. Find it in one of its freshest forms at **Jake's Seafood** (250 Nantasket Rd., Hull, 781/925-1024, www.jakesseafoods.com, 11:30 A.M.–9:30 P.M. Mon.–Sat.; 12 P.M.–9:30 P.M. Sun., $14–24), the quintessential fish shack perched between a little bay and Nantasket Beach. From the fine specimens of simple boiled lobster to fried clams and scallops and linguine, the casual atmosphere is a nice balance between formality and net-and-buoy kitsch. Equally delicious and fun is the brunch at the funky seaside **Arthur & Pat's** (239 Ocean St., Brant Rock, 781/834-9755, $6–12), which serves a killer lobster omelet, fried oyster roll, and fresh crab eggs Benedict. The morning lines (quelled by the complimentary mimosas passed out) can get long but are always worth the wait. Speaking of something worth waiting for, the Danish ice cream parlor **Farfar's** (272 Saint George St., Duxbury, 781/934-5152, 11 A.M.–6 P.M. daily) churns out cold stuff that's so rich and exquisite it's considered a local tourist attraction in its own right.

Information and Services

Because the South Shore is an expansive area of many towns of various sizes, the information and types of services offered from town to town varies widely. Start by gathering general information, maps, and brochures on the area at **Plymouth Convention & Visitors Bureau** (170 Water St., Suite 24, Plymouth, 508/747-0100, www.seeplymouth.com). The area's biggest full-service hospital is **South Shore Hospital** (55 Fogg Rd., South Weymouth, 781/624-8000, www.

sshosp.org). Fill prescription needs at the 24-hour branches of **CVS Pharmacy** (474 Washington St., Weymouth, 781/335-0404; 600 Southern Artery, Quincy, 617/472-7534; or 1880 Ocean St., Marshfield, 781/837-5381, www.cvs.com).

Free **Internet access** on terminals is offered at nearly every town library, as well as by payment at office centers such as **FedEx Office Print & Ship Center** (44 Granite St., Braintree, 781/849-7737, www.fedex.com) and **The UPS Store** (300 Grove St., Braintree, 781/356-8771, www.theupsstore.com). The latter also offers faxing and shipping services as well.

PLYMOUTH

Here it is, the place where this experiment in democracy we call America first started. Named after the Mayflower's port of embarkation in England, Plymouth was the first permanent settlement in New England. Fleeing what they viewed as the Church of England's incomplete work of the Reformation, the Pilgrims (mostly poor farmers) bid adieu to what they considered Britain's lax morality, endured a grueling transatlantic voyage, hit land, and

---

BERRY IMPRESSIVE

Cranberries are an enormous industry in Southeastern Massachusetts and Cape Cod, employing thousands of workers. They also do their part to beautify the region: Every September and October, the wetlands on which they're grown become crimson with their ripened bounty. (Known as bogs, the spongy, low-lying wetlands retain enough water to provide an ideal habitat for the berries.) The fruits are native to the region (early settlers called them "crane-berries" because their blossoms reminded them of the heads of cranes), but today they are grown commercially in man-made bogs, created by planting small vines in sandy plots. The state requires that each acre of planted cranberries be surrounded by at least four acres of wetlands. Most cranberry

harvests are done in the late fall by flooding the bogs and using a machine to gently dislodge the berries from the vines. Employees then use tubing to collect the berries onto a conveyer belt. Family farmers Jack and Dot Angley fill in the missing links between berries and juice with free daily tours of their **Flax Pond Farm** (1 Robbins Path, Carver, 508/866-3654, www.flaxpondfarms.com, 1–5 P.M. daily mid-Sept.–Oct.). Tours include a trip to the old "screening house" where kids can try their hand at sorting berries on antique equipment. Or view one from above by booking with **Ryan Rotors'** aerial tours via helicopter (Plymouth, 508/746-3111).

You'll never taste cranapple juice the same way again.

EASTERN MASSACHUSETTS

quickly set about founding Plymouth Colony in 1620.

It's here that you'll find the famed Plymouth Rock (kept protected under a stone, miniature Parthenon-like canopy these days)—not to mention hordes of tourists snapping pictures of it. But of course, the rock itself tells extraordinarily little about the Pilgrims' history or how they lived their lives in the area. For that, visitors turn to **Plimoth Plantation,** a historically accurate working replica of their settlement, complete with actors playing the parts of real Pilgrims. In the real world beyond the plantation's gates, Plymouth is a modern fishing center popular for its boating areas, beaches, and other tourist sites.

(Plimoth Plantation

A living-history museum, the plantation is best known for replicating a 17th-century colonial village from top to bottom (an enclave known as the "1627 Village"). Virtually everything here is now as it was then—from the foods grown and eaten to the chores and social structure.

the *Mayflower II* at Plymouth

But the plantation also encompasses a Native American camp (called **Hobbamock's Homesite**) that houses Wampanoags—not actors, but real native New Englanders whose people have lived in the area for more than 12,000 years—in their traditional homes. Thanks to the combination of perspectives experienced through these two camps, Plimoth Plantation may be one of the best ways to teach kids about America's humble beginnings, with a slew of hands-on educational programs that teach about this slice of life through the eyes of both the Pilgrims and the area's indigenous people.

There's also an exact replica of the vessel that bore the first settlers here—*Mayflower II*—which (again, courtesy of actors playing historic characters) sheds some light on what they endured and how they lived on their journey. Rounding out the experience are the **Carriage House Craft Center** (where you can quiz modern craftspeople about historic trades like weaving, basket-weaving, and glass-blowing)

and the **Nye Barn,** a major conservation effort full of rare and heritage breeds of livestock.

Other Sights

To many, the sight of the literal **Plymouth Rock** (Pilgrim Memorial Park, Water St., 508/747-5360) is fairly underwhelming. It is, after all, merely an oversized glacial boulder. But lest we forget, the fuss is really over the New World that it symbolizes, and the story of those who first sighted it. Our concepts of guts and glory these days tend to be laid at the feet of sports teams. But the Pilgrims lacked nothing in the bravery department themselves. In fact, they were what you might call the original nation builders (take that reference with whatever positive or negative connotations you like) who felt strongly enough about their religious beliefs that they were willing to risk everything they had in England—their lives included—to find a land in which to practice it.

Unfortunately, theirs was an intolerant and extremist creed, and still more unfortunately,

Wampanoags at Hobbamock's Homesite

© KINDRA CLINEFF/MOTT

high **National Monument to the Forefathers** (Allerton St., one block from Plymouth Rock), a solid-granite statue erected in 1889. Two abutting tablets list the names of each original Mayflower passenger.

Bearing little if any connection at all to Plymouth's legitimate historic sites, but entirely fun regardless, are the **Lobster Tales Pirate Cruises** (Town Wharf, 508/746-5342, www. lobstertalesinc.com, May–Oct., call for times, $18). On these cruises little buccaneers are offered face paint and pirate hats as the ship sets sail to do battle and reclaim a treasure chest in the harbor. Gimmicky? Of course. But when the kids have gotten antsy from an overload of education, it's the ideal fix.

Witness the way corn was ground during the time of the Pilgrims at the rebuilt **Jenney Grist Mill** (6 Spring Ln., Plymouth, 508/747-4544, www.jenneygristmill.com, 9:30 A.M.–5 P.M. Mon.–Sat., noon–5 P.M. Sun., Apr.–Nov.; closed Dec.–Mar., $6 adults, free youth under 17); the original, owned by Pilgrim John Jenney, was destroyed by a fire in 1847. Today the mill makes for a fun family outing, with tours, a spring herring run in the abutting pond, and a general store peddling freshly ground corn and penny candy.

Events

Autumn puts Plymouth in its element, with foliage hitting its colorful peak, cranberry bogs alight with crimson berries, and Thanksgiving bringing a spotlight to the area. **Halloween Lantern Tours** hit in late October at Plimoth Plantation, offering guided nighttime walking tours of the historic village by punched-tin lanterns. Come November, there are few more appropriate places to be than Plymouth, site of the first Thanksgiving. The town pulls out all the stops, throwing **America's Hometown Thanksgiving Celebration** (508/746-1818, www.usathanksgiving.com) with a giant parade, marching bands, and floats galore down its center street; the Plantation rolls out scores of 17th-century family activities—from games and hands-on crafts to a full Victorian Thanksgiving Dinner.

they ran roughshod over many of the peoples who had already existed on their newfound continent for thousands of years. (Plimoth Plantation is to be commended for acknowledging the reality of this fact.) But history is history, and in a nation that to this day admires pluck as much as anything, it makes sense to learn about our chutzpah-based roots, if not necessarily admire each and every last one of them.

To that end, a visit to the **Pilgrim Hall Museum** (75 Court St., 508/746-1620, www. pilgrimhall.org, 9:30 A.M.–4:30 P.M. daily Feb.–Dec., $7 adults, $6 seniors, $4 children 5–17, free children under 5) can be as educational as one to Plimouth Plantation, if a tad bit less fun. Exhibits include displays of artifacts and possessions of the Pilgrims (aka Separatists) from both England and Holland, explanations detailing their transatlantic sojourn, the first contact with the Wampanoags, and accounts of the first Thanksgiving. In honor of Miles Standish, William Bradford, and the rest of the gang, stands the 81-foot-

Shopping

You'll find the requisite seaside and colonial-themed tourist traps in the center of town, but also a number of unique shops like the pretty, old-fashioned **Lily's Apothecary** (6 Main St. Ext., 508/747-7546, www.lilysapothecary.com, 10 A.M.–5 P.M. Mon.–Fri., 10 A.M.–3 P.M. Sat.). Its shelves are lined with imported cosmetics, tony fragrances like Payot Paris, plus skin and hair products by Mario Badescu and Bumble & Bumble. Souvenirs of a more concrete (literally) nature are found at **Sparrow House Pottery** (42 Summer St., 508/747-1240, www.sparrowhouse.com, 10 A.M.–5 P.M. daily). Score plenty of stoneware and handmade porcelain pottery made by local artists, not to mention contemporary gemstone jewelry, sculpture, glass and hand-inlaid boxes. Right next to Plimoth Plantation is the quaint **Bramhall's Country Store** (2 Sandwich Rd., 508/746-1844, 10 A.M.–8 P.M. daily in summer), a great stop for fresh fruits, smoothies, sweets, and sandwiches best devoured at the outdoor picnic tables.

Food

Fresh bounty from the nearby sea is the catch at **Lobster Hut** (25 Town Wharf, 508/746-2270, 11 A.M.–9 P.M. Tues.–Sat.; 11 A.M.–8 P.M. Sun.; $3–18), the ultra-casual takeout joint. (In nice weather, hit the outdoor deck for a water view.) Kick things off smoothly with the rich lobster bisque, or just dive right into an all-meat lobster roll. Breakfast is served all day at the **All-American Diner** (60 Court St., 508/747-4763, allamericandiner.biz, 7 A.M.–3 P.M. daily, $3–8), a wise choice for cheap and hearty (borderline overwhelming, in fact) omelets and decent chili burgers, served at a classic retro diner counter. With a striking view of Plymouth Harbor, **Mamma Mia's** (122 Water St., 508/747-4670, http://mammamiaspizzas.com, 11 A.M.–10 P.M. daily, $11–15) is a key spot for families in search of simple pastas and pizzas. Meanwhile, Mexican and Southwestern fixings get the spotlight at **Sam Diego's** (51 Main St., 508/747-0048, www.samdiegos.com, 11:30 A.M.–9 P.M. daily, $3–12), though the kids' menu of burgers and other such simple noshes gets quite a workout, too. It's also a favorite for its setting—just a few minutes from Plymouth Rock in an old historic fire station. Meanwhile, no one seems to pay much attention to the setting of **Peaceful Meadows Ice Cream** (170 Water St., Village Landing, 508/746-2362, 10 A.M.–10 P.M. daily, www.peacefulmeadows.com)—for the record, a friendly little waterfront creamery—because they're far too preoccupied lapping up homemade ice cream and creating their own sundaes from goodies like crushed Oreos, peanut butter sauce, hot apples, and chocolate-covered almonds.

NEW BEDFORD

On the very same expedition on which British explorer Bartholomew Gosnold settled Cuttyhunk Island in 1602 (note to Mayflower descendants: that was a full 18 years before anyone landed on Plymouth Rock), he and his troupe also set up camp in what is now New Bedford. Had they not left that same year to return to Mother England, New Bedford might well have been what Plymouth is today.

Instead, New Bedford has enjoyed a very different kind of fame: In the early 19th century, it was second only to Nantucket as the world's major whaling center—by the middle of the century, it had surpassed it. Unlike Nantucket, however, New Bedford had other sources of revenue in place when whale oil was made obsolete by the discovery of petroleum in 1859—namely cotton goods manufacturing and fisheries, both of which were in full swing by the mid-19th century. The city is still a center for the New England fishing industry, though to a much lesser extent, since overfishing has greatly affected the area's fish population. The human population, meanwhile, has risen to 100,000, with a citizenry that reflects its globally recognized past. The Portuguese population is of particular influence in and around New Bedford, and it shows in its restaurants and festivals.

Sights

Dedicated to the history of humanity's interaction with the great mammals of the sea, the

New Bedford Whaling Museum (18 Johnny Cake Hill, 508/997-0046, www.whalingmuseum.org) also houses 150,000 whaling artifacts and whale-related art, including the world's largest ship model. Built between 1831 and 1832 as a memorial to whalers who had lost their lives at sea, the **Seamen's Bethel** (15 Johnny Cake Hill, 508/992-3295)—the same one in Melville's *Moby-Dick*—is today used to honor fisherman whose fate has been the same. Search the main wall for three cenotaphs; you'll find a list of all of their names. On a cheerier note, it's well worth the short drive to **Westport Rivers Winery** (417 Hixbridge Rd., Westport, 508/636-3423, www.westportrivers.com). The working vineyards, which produce excellent reds, whites, and a lovely bubbly, are reminiscent of Provence.

Events

Every July, the folk- and arts-centric **Greater New Bedford Summerfest** (New Bedford Whaling National Historic Park, 508/979-1568, www.newbedfordsummerfest.com) takes over the city with its whaleboat races, fireworks, performances, and plentiful seafood. And during the first weekend in August, upwards of a hundred thousand pour into New Bedford for the Portuguese **Annual Feast of the Blessed Sacrament** (at the junction of Achushnet Ave. and Earle St., 508/992-6911, www.portuguesefeast.com). The massive celebration dates back to 1915 and is a frenzy of live entertainment, Portuguese food, music, and dance.

Shopping

Play 19th-century shopper at the **Bedford Merchant** (28 William St., 508/997-9194, 10 A.M.–7 P.M. Mon.–Sat.; 12 P.M.–5 P.M. Sun.), stocked with reproductions of old clocks, ship models, and lots of cast iron—in the form of everything from bird feeders to garden finials. And what's a former whaling capital without a little scrimshaw? Duck into **Whale's Tale Scrimshanders** (42 North Water St., 508/997-4233, 10 A.M.–5 P.M. daily) and pick up an intricately carved jewelry box or lightship basket.

Food

In a town so filled with delicious Portuguese food, it's tempting to eat nothing but linguica all day long. But other options abound, too—like the casual but tasty menu at **Freestones City Grill** (41 William St., 508/993-7477, www.freestones.com, 4 P.M.–10 P.M. Mon.–Sat.; 4 P.M.–9 P.M. Sun., $8–19)—an assembly of classically prepared stuffed quahogs, reggae chicken jerk sandwiches, and grilled meatloaf. Or just skip the kid's stuff and go for some of the town's best eats at ◖ **Antonio's** (267 Coggeshall St., 508/990-3636, 5 P.M.–10 P.M. daily, $14–25, cash only), where classic Portuguese foods meet the incredibly fresh fish of New Bedford. Sample *bacalhau* (salt cod), grilled sardines, and superb seafood stew.

CUTTYHUNK ISLAND

You won't hear it mentioned alongside Nantucket's yacht-filled wharfs or Martha's Vineyard's sophisticated restaurants anytime soon, but that may be precisely what makes this New England island so inviting. With just a small handful of businesses and restaurants (including a pizza joint, a casual hotel serving weekend brunch, a gift shop, and a post office), little-known Cuttyhunk is where to come when you don't just want to get away from it all, you want to get away from it *all*. That includes cars, too; golf carts and bikes are the preferred method of transport all over the island. (And a word of warning: Hit the ATM before boarding the ferry, as there aren't any on-island, and credit cards are rarely accepted.)

But what the island lacks in luxury it makes up for in history and heart-stopping natural beauty. Situated in the far southwestern corner of the Elizabeth Islands, the two-mile-long Cuttyhunk was actually one of the first pieces of America spotted by British explorer Bartholomew Gosnold (all of the Elizabeth Islands together comprise the town of Gosnold). And not terribly much about the island has changed since then, thanks to enormous conservation efforts that have kept the epic marshes clean, the woods intact, and the water views unsullied by McMansions or huge hotels.

Sights

Much of Cuttyhunk's allure is its distinct lack of things to do and see—that is, other than watch the sunset over grassy cliffs, pick wildflowers, and slurp oysters on the dock. However, a few sites do deserve a visit: foremost the **Navy Lookout Bunker** (Tower Rd.) that sits at the island's highest point, boasting breathtaking views of nearly the entire island and its surrounding waters. Another worthy jaunt: through the **Nature Preserve/Cliff Walk** (follow the road past the Fishing Club) conservation lands, which stretch through winding trails in flower-filled woods and windswept marshes.

Entertainment

In lieu of any actual bars or clubs, Cuttyhunk has found its own form of evening entertainment: bonfires. In this weekend ritual, locals bring their own wood to the spit connecting the dock at Capasit Point, add it to the fire, tell stories, and let the giant orange flames lick the inky black sky.

Shopping

It isn't tough deciding where to spend your cash on Cuttyhunk; there simply aren't many options. The best bets for souvenirs of any kind are the **General Store** (Broadway and Post Office Way), one of the only spots in town to find a deli and snacks, and film and pottery; and the **Cuttyhunk Corner Store** (at the Four Corners, 508/984-7167, 10 A.M.–5 P.M. Mon.–Sat.; 12 P.M.–5 P.M. Sun.) for handmade jewelry, pottery, clothing, and beach bags. You may feel more inclined to look than buy at the contemporary **Pea in Your Pants Gallery** (Bayview Dr., 603/321-6326,hours vary; call ahead), but its makeshift gallery-in-a-barn is worth a look, for certain.

Food

A word to the wise: Plan your meals carefully. Wait just a little too long, and you'll find yourself fresh out of options, as the few eateries available here close quite early. The most reliable is **Soprano's Pizza** (Broadway, 508/992-7530, 11:30 A.M.–7 P.M. Mon.–Sat.; closed Sun., $10–19), which is essentially a pizzeria run out of a local's garage. At the **Fish Market** (Town Dock), you place your orders for fresh seafood—shucked oysters or cooked lobster—early in the day and pick them up at 6 P.M. sharp. Catch dessert a few doors (literally) down at **The Ice Cream Stall.**

FALL RIVER

This former textile epicenter is best known not for the clothing it once produced, or for the diversity of immigrants that industry has attracted over the years. In fact, its biggest draw is its most notorious (ex)citizen—one Lizzie Borden, who murdered both her parents in 1892. Balancing out that unfortunate karma is the modern-day hometown boy, celebrity TV chef Emeril (Bam!) Lagasse.

Sights

Step into the fleet of naval ships known as **Battleship Cove** (5 Water St., 508/678-1100, www.battleshipcove.org, 9 A.M.–5 P.M. daily summer; 9 A.M.–4:30 P.M. daily spring, $15 adults, $13 seniors, $9 children 6–12, free children under 6) and you'll have free reign of all of the vessels, including the 46,000-ton **USS Massachusetts.** What used to be the **Lizzie Borden House** (92 Second St., 508/675-7333, www.lizzie-borden.com, tours 11 A.M.–3 P.M., $12.50 adults, $10 seniors and students, $5 children 6–15, free children under 6) where the infamous murders took place is now a bed-and-breakfast and tourist site, restored to look almost exactly as it did—from the couches to the pear trees outside—on that fateful day.

Events

Every summer, everyone anywhere near Fall River flocks into town for **Fall River Celebrates America** (Battleship Cove at Fall River Heritage State Park, 508/676-8226, www.fallrivercelebrates.com, Aug.). The four-day waterfront fiesta includes music performances, food fiestas, parades, rides, and fireworks.

Shopping

With a past so tied to textile manufacturing, it's little surprise to find lots of locally made clothing in Fall River. Opened in 1911, **Northeast Knitting Mills** (657 Quarry St., 508/678-7553, www.neknitting.com, 10 A.M.–6 P.M. Mon.–Fri.; 10 A.M.–5 P.M. Sat.; closed Sun.) sells sweaters made by the fourth generation of the family that founded it. Pick up a souvenir or two at **Desro Gift Shops** (638 Quequechan St., 508/646-9096, 9 A.M.–5 P.M. daily), chock-full of handmade candles, dried wreaths, and home accessories.

Food

Provincetown has its lobsters, Boston has its cream pies, and Fall River has its hot dogs. In fact, Fall River has a *lot* of hot dogs. One of the best is at **Tabacaria Acoriana Restaurant** (408 S Main St., 508/673-5890, 11 A.M.–4 P.M. Mon.–Fri.; closed Sat. and Sun.), though the kitchen's marinated grilled chicken is also a favorite. Just as casual, but with a few more ties to the city, is the pork pie. **Hartley's Original Pork Pies** (1729 South Main St., 508/676-8605, 11:30 A.M.–7 P.M. daily) serves them up piping hot and made with the traditional recipe, the way they have been in Fall River for decades.

SPORTS AND RECREATION
Beaches

As a residential community, the South Shore tends to fill its wide, sandy beaches with locals rather than tourists. That means that each beach tends to take on many of the characteristics of its town. **Duxbury Beach** (Duxbury Beach Park by Gurnet Rd., 781/934-1108, www.town.duxbury.ma.us) is the very picture of quaint coastal living. With its long wooden bridge spanning the abutting bay, the beach attracts hordes of preppy families (mostly to the area near the main parking lot and bathhouse, though in-the-know locals make the trek all the way down toward the lighthouse, where there's notably more space to stretch out). Likewise, the clean, long shoreline of **Horseneck Beach**

(Rte. 88, Westport Point, 508/636-8816, www.mass.gov) is a magnet for day-trippers in search of an easy-to-access pristine natural setting—but things can get crowded, so it's best to arrive early to claim a spot. Trading bucolic for breezy, cheesy charm, **Nantasket Beach** (Rte. 3A, Hull, 617/727-5290, www.mass.gov) is swarmed during summer months with a jumble of sun worshippers, from the trendy to the tattooed. The beach's boardwalk stretches from end to end, sporting everything from bingo rooms and sports bars to clam shacks. The buzz continues into autumn, too; families and packs of teens line up to ride the historic wooden **Paragon Carousel** (205 Nantasket Ave., Hull, 781/925-0472, www.paragoncarousel.com), one of the few remaining vestiges left from Nantasket's heyday as a 19th-century seaside theme park and resort.

Hiking and Biking

A handful of excellent land reservations around the South Shore make for great walks—many blessed with spectacular views of the ocean. **World's End** (250 Martin's Ln., Hingham, 781/740-6665, year-round, 8 A.M.–sunset daily, $5 adults, free children), for example, is upwards of 250 acres of rolling hills, wooded paths, and groves—with glimpses of Hingham Harbor and the Boston skyline throughout. Leashed dogs and mountain biking are permitted. At the smaller **Ellisville Harbor State Park** (Route 3A, Plymouth, 508/866-2580, year-round) there are 100 acres of well-tended hiking, fishing, and cross-country ski trails. Small but charming, the **Two Mile Farm** (Union St., Marshfield, 781/784-0567, year-round) abuts the winding North River—which it has beautiful views of. The park, which allows pets but no bikes, is considered a local gem for bird-watchers.

Boating and Fishing

Many of the premiere boating clubs on the South Shore are private clubs, but there are also marinas like **Onset Bay** (RFD #3, Green St., Buzzards Bay, 508/295-0338, www.onsetbay.com), which repairs and stores boats, and

Borden Light Marina (1 Ferry St., Fall River, 508/678-7547, www.bordenlight.com), which provides fueling and docking services.

ACCOMMODATIONS
$100-150

The one, the only place to lay your head on Cuttyhunk is the **Cuttyhunk Fishing Club** (One, Road to the Landing, Cuttyhunk Island, 508/992-5585, www.cuttyhunkfishingclub. com, $164–185). Perched above the roaring ocean surf, the breezy building is much like the island itself: quiet, humble, and a little rough at the edges. Still, there's a musty library filled with hurricane lamps and board games, and the hotel serves an extremely popular brunch on weekends. Touristy Plymouth, meanwhile, has the lion's share of the South Shore's hotels and inns. Named after the long-necked flocks at the nearby beaches, the **White Swan B&B** (146 Manomet Point Rd., Plymouth, 508/224-3759, www.whiteswan.com, $120–175) is a simply decorated 1800s home with a surprising number of amenities, including wireless Internet, a whirlpool tub, hair dryers, and in-room fridges. Overlooking the spot where the Mayflower hit dry land, **The Governor Bradford Inn** (98 Water St., Plymouth, 508/746-6200, www.governor-bradford.com, $79–129) is actually more of a hotel than inn—the rooms have all the personal charm of a Ramada—but for pure proximity to Plymouth Rock, it can't be beat. Small, friendly, and a stone's throw from working cranberry bogs, **Cranberry Cottage Bed & Breakfast** (10 Woodbine Dr., Plymouth, 508/747-1726) is home to four guest rooms (some with fireplaces), a pool, and outdoor games like horseshoes, badminton, and table tennis.

$150-250

More of a residential than resort community, Duxbury really has need for only one inn, but it's a lovely one. Surrounded by impeccably kept gardens, the 🕻 **1803 Winsor House Inn** (390 Washington St., Duxbury, 781/934-0991, www.winsorhouseinn.com, $110–210) houses an English-style pub and rooms with antiques, canopy beds, and an impressive homemade breakfast.

GETTING THERE AND AROUND

To drive from Boston to the South Shore, take I-93 South to US Route 3 South. For Hingham, take exit 15 (25 mi., 40 min.), for Duxbury, exit 11 (35 mi., 45 min.), and for Plymouth, exit 6A (40 mi., 50 min.) To drive from Boston to New Bedford, take I-93 South to Route 24 to Route 140 (60 mi., 1 hr. 10 min.).

From Boston, you can access the South Shore easily by public transportation on the Massachusetts Bay Transportation Authority (MBTA, 617/222-5000, www.mbta.com); the subway's Red Line runs from numerous in-city stations, including South Station, to Quincy, Wollaston, and Braintree stations. From there, and between a number of key South Shore points, you can access MBTA buses that run throughout most of the area's towns. Check the website for individual schedules.

To get to Cuttyhunk, take the **Cuttyhunk Ferry Co.** (66B State Pier, South Bulkhead, New Bedford, 508/992-0200, www.cutty-hunkferryco.com, $25/40 adult, $20/30 children 12 and under).

With careful planning and a schedule from the **Plymouth & Brockton** (8 Industrial Park Rd., Plymouth, 508/746-0378, www.p-b.com) bus line, you can get nearly anywhere on the South Shore—even all the way to Provincetown on the tip of Cape Cod, if need be. Call for schedules and route information.

CAPE COD AND THE ISLANDS

As President, John F. Kennedy didn't only create the Peace Corps and stare down Fidel Castro. He also signed a sweeping law in 1961 that protected 27,000 acres of some of the most beautiful beachfront in America. The Cape Cod National Seashore is one of the conservation jewels not only of Massachusetts, but of the entire region, drawing generations of beachgoers to the miles of sandy beach fronting the Atlantic. Perhaps because it lacks the development of, say, the Jersey Shore, the Cape has always had an old-time feel, with ice cream parlors and clam shacks dotted among the distinctive shingled cottages that gave their name to a style of house architecture. Then there is the conservation land itself, an expanse of dunes, grasslands, and scrub-pine forests, cut through with biking trails and anchorages.

It's fitting that Kennedy should have signed the bill that preserved all of this beauty. After all, he and his family summered in Hyannisport in the compound that still bears the family name. Outside the summer capital of Hyannis, the Cape has a striking diversity of landscapes, from the acclaimed oceanographic institute of Woods Hole to the Ye Olde Yankee ambience of the bayshore towns, and from the pristine beauty of the Outer Cape beaches to the flamboyant gay mecca of Provincetown. Along the way, of course, are all the mini-golf courses and tacky souvenir shops you can ask for.

Cape Cod, as might be imagined, is named for the rich fisheries that lay just off the coast in an oceanic rise known as Georges Bank. The rich ecosystem there has supported generations

© HYANNIS AREA CHAMBER OF COMMERCE

of fishing fleets, which still leave from the towns of the Outer Cape. Though over-fished almost to the point of extinction 50 years ago, the fishery has made a comeback through delicate environmental management, and cod is once again a staple of New England restaurant menus.

The Cape itself, with its sideways-L topography, was formed by the moraine of the last continental ice sheet, which stopped here some 20,000 years ago. The same ice sheet had previously retreated from its last gasp to the south, where it formed Massachusetts' two major islands—resort communities with characters as different as old and new money. On buttoned-up Nantucket, whale belts and lightship baskets are always in fashion, while trousers-rolled Martha's Vineyard is where the rich and famous come to kick back by the surf.

ORIENTATION

Residents often speak of Cape geography as resembling an arm, held up at 90 degrees and curved towards the face. The Cape's de facto capital, Hyannis, is just about tricep level, Chatham is at the elbow, and Provincetown at the furthest tip of the fingers. The area is further divided into three different regions—the Upper Cape, which runs from the canal to the Barnstable line; the Mid-Cape, which takes in Barnstable and Hyannis through to Brewster and Harwich; and the Lower Cape, which encompasses the National Seashore from Monomoy Island to the Province Lands. To confuse matters more, locals sometimes refer to the area from Chatham to Orleans as the Lower Cape, while calling the area from Eastham to Provincetown the Outer Cape. A more practical division is between the bayshore, which is typified by tidal flats and warmer water, and the oceanside, home to the colder and wilder beaches.

PLANNING YOUR TIME

Summertime is, of course, when the Cape comes into its glory, but it can also mean roads clogged with traffic, and beaches, especially in the Mid-Cape, insufferably crowded. It makes sense to base yourself in one area, since traffic

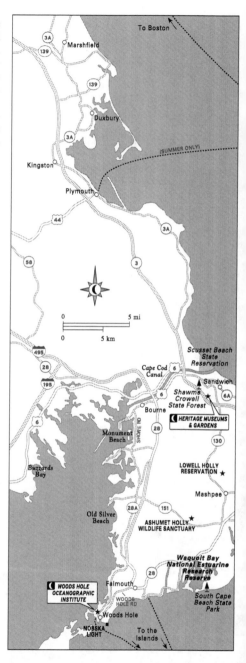

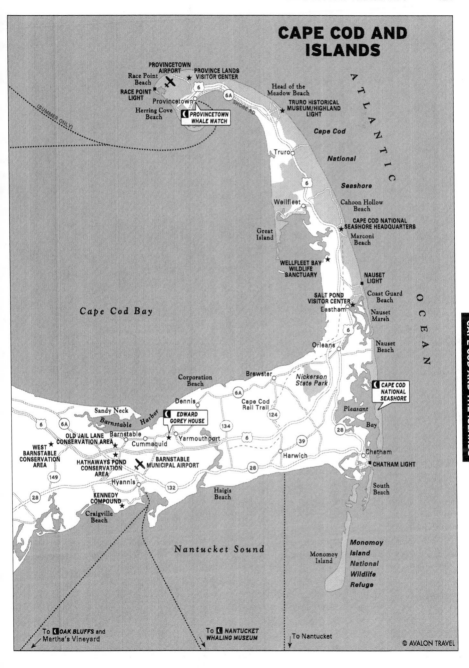

CAPE COD AND ISLANDS

PROVINCETOWN AIRPORT
PROVINCE LANDS VISITOR CENTER
Race Point Beach
RACE POINT LIGHT
Provincetown
Herring Cove Beach
PROVINCETOWN WHALE WATCH

Head of the Meadow Beach
TRURO HISTORICAL MUSEUM/HIGHLAND LIGHT

ATLANTIC

(SUMMER ONLY)

SHORE RD.

Cape Cod

Truro

National

6

Seashore

Wellfleet

Cahoon Hollow Beach

CAPE COD NATIONAL SEASHORE HEADQUARTERS

Great Island

Marconi Beach

WELLFLEET BAY WILDLIFE SANCTUARY

NAUSET LIGHT

SALT POND VISITOR CENTER

Coast Guard Beach

Eastham

Nauset Marsh

Cape Cod Bay

6

Nauset Beach

Orleans

O C E A N

Corporation Beach

Brewster

Nickerson State Park

CAPE COD NATIONAL SEASHORE

6A

Dennis

Cape Cod Rail Trail

124

Pleasant

Sandy Neck

Barnstable Harbor

EDWARD GOREY HOUSE

Barnstable

Bay

6

6A

OLD JAIL LANE CONSERVATION AREA

Yarmouthport

Cummaquid

134

6

39

Chatham

CHATHAM LIGHT

WEST BARNSTABLE CONSERVATION AREA

HATHAWAYS POND CONSERVATION AREA

BARNSTABLE MUNICIPAL AIRPORT

28

Harwich

149

Hyannis

132

South Beach

28

KENNEDY COMPOUND

Haigis Beach

Craigville Beach

Nantucket Sound

Monomoy Island

Monomoy Island National Wildlife Refuge

To **OAK BLUFFS** and Martha's Vineyard

To **NANTUCKET WHALING MUSEUM**

To Nantucket

© AVALON TRAVEL

HIGHLIGHTS

◖ **Heritage Museums & Gardens:** Two centuries of Americana live on at this palatial garden estate (page 124).

◖ **Woods Hole Oceanographic Institute:** Deep-sea explorers reveal the mysteries of the real "final frontier" (page 124).

◖ **Edward Gorey House:** Stephen King, move over for the true "master of macabre" (page 126).

◖ **Cape Cod National Seashore:** Stroll miles of sandy beaches with nothing between you and Portugal but waves (page 132).

◖ **Provincetown Whale Watch:** Seeing these leviathans in their natural habitat is anything but a fluke (page 133).

◖ **Oak Bluffs:** This Vineyard town is on permanent vacation (page 140).

◖ **Nantucket Whaling Museum:** Scrimshaw, harpoons, and a giant skeleton bring *Moby-Dick* to life (page 150).

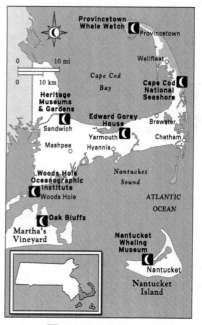

LOOK FOR ◖ TO FIND RECOMMENDED SIGHTS, ACTIVITIES, DINING, AND LODGING.

can make driving difficult and quickly spoil a good vacation. The Upper Cape is the easiest to get to and least crowded. It's also home to several popular family attractions, including the eclectic **Heritage Museums & Gardens** and the educational **Woods Hole Oceanographic Institute.** The Mid-Cape is home to historic attractions and the best restaurants and nightlife. One can't-miss attraction in this area is Yarmouthport's **Edward Gorey House,** dedicated to the late great creepy kids' book author. The Lower Cape, meanwhile, is your destination for beaches and the natural beauty of **Cape Cod National Seashore.**

You can easily spend a week based in any one of these areas, relaxing at the beach and taking a few day trips to other attractions on the Cape. No

Cape vacation is complete, however, without at least a day trip to one of the islands of Nantucket or Martha's Vineyard. In fact, either one of these islands has plenty to offer for a longer visit of a few days to a week. (Though don't expect to beat the crowds by taking the ferry; half of Boston goes to the islands every summer weekend.) Choosing which island to visit is largely a matter of temperament: Nantucket is old New England, buttoned-down and traditional, with plenty of historical sites that pay homage to its one-time whaling industry (starting with the excellent and recently renovated **Nantucket Whaling Museum**). The Vineyard, meanwhile, is where the jet-set comes to play; the larger of the two islands, it also has more varied scenery and more secret hideaways to reward a longer visit.

Cape Cod has a year-round population of about 230,000, but every year between Memorial and Labor Days it groans under the weight of thousands upon thousands of tourists. Though summer is undoubtedly the warmest time of year to visit, its crowds can make true relaxation a challenge, which is why many opt instead to go during shoulder season (mid- to late spring and again in early to mid-fall). Hotel prices are lower, stores are still open, and the weather, while not sunbathing-friendly, is warm enough for beach visits and outdoor activities ranging from hiking to biking.

In the winter, many tourist-driven businesses close for the season, though a handful of hotels and shops in every town often do stay open. Restaurants tend to greatly reduce their hours of operation, and some even close completely. So be sure to call ahead. And these days, holiday events and festivities often attract enough visitors in December to keep them open as well. January through March is extremely chilly in Cape Cod—usually too cold for most outdoor activities or extended strolls—but early spring, while brisk, can also be surprisingly pleasant.

Upper and Mid-Cape

Summer tourists frequently rush past the first part of the Cape on their way to the outer beaches. Because of that, the Upper Cape is sleepier and more residential than the rest of the peninsula. It's worth visiting, however, for two very different towns—historic Sandwich and the bustling research center of Woods Hole. The Mid-Cape is traversed by three parallel highways. On the bayside, Route 6A is known as the Old King's Highway, and it retains the colonial feel of some of the oldest towns in the state, crawling with quiet bed-and-breakfasts and antiques stores. Along Nantucket Sound, meanwhile, Route 28 is the bustling beachfront terrain of mini-golf courses and sticky fried seafood, anchored by the relative metropolis of Hyannis. In between the two routes, US Route 6 is the featureless but efficient express route to the Lower Cape.

SANDWICH AND FALMOUTH

Though it has nothing to do with the famous lunch item, Sandwich *was* named after the same earl who invented it. Founded just 17 years after the Pilgrims landed, the village was a haven for Quakers and others who disagreed with the powers-that-be in Plymouth. Later, it became one of the first tourist communities for hunters and beachgoers from Boston. Both qualities are retained in a village that is one of the most quaint in Massachusetts.

Despite its location below where the Cape's proverbial arm attaches to the body, Falmouth

THE CAPE'S FORMATION

The existence of Cape Cod as we know it is owed largely to the advance and retreat of the most recent continental ice sheet that resulted in changes of sea level.

About 23,000 years ago, in the late Pleistocene geological era, the sheet reached its greatest southward extent, then eventually retreated back from the Cape. When it melted, it pushed the sea level to rise roughly 11 feet per millennium between 6,000 and 2,000 years ago, then slowed down to about three feet per millennium.

Eventually the sea level was high enough to start eroding the glacial deposits that the melted ice sheet had left behind, and carry them along the shoreline all the way out to the tip of the Cape. As a result, the Provincetown Spit today is made up primarily of marine deposits transported from farther up the shore.

is anything but the armpit of the Cape. Its downtown is pure Americana—befitting the town where Katherine Lee Bates first penned "America the Beautiful"—and its coastline is spotted with nature preserves and forested beaches. At the far end of Falmouth, Woods Hole has been a center of science since 1927, when the eponymous oceanographic center was founded. The town is now a delightful confluence of scientists, fishermen, and tourists passing through to the Vineyard.

(Heritage Museums & Gardens

When he was a child, pharmaceutical giant J. K. Lilly collected ticket stubs and coins; as he grew older, fascination became an addiction, leading to collections of classic cars and folk art. Now more than 200 years of American history are breathlessly encapsulated on Lilly's former 100-acre estate (67 Grove St., Sandwich, 508/888-3300, www.heritagemuseumsandgardens.org, 10 A.M.–5 P.M. daily Apr.–Oct, $12 adults, $11 seniors, $6 children 4–16, free children under 4). Various exhibits include an antique-car museum, a windmill, a carousel, and the Hall of Fame for the Cape Cod Baseball League. If that isn't enough, the grounds are filled with bed after bed of hybrid flowers created by the estate's previous owner.

(Woods Hole Oceanographic Institute

How many of us once harbored dreams of swimming with the dolphins? At WHOI (locally pronounced as "hooey"), visitors can fulfill their marine biology fantasies at the country's most prominent oceanographic research institution. The institute is home to the famous Alvin submersible, which famously discovered the wreck of the *Titanic,* as well as the new five-foot-long REMUS, which can explore 98 percent of the ocean floor. A good exhibit center (15 School St., 508/289-2663, www.whoi.edu, by appointment April; 10 A.M.–4:30 P.M. Mon.–Sat. May–Oct. and Tues.–Fri. Nov.–Dec., donation requested) details the institute's past, including an exhibit on the *Titanic* and a life-size replica of Alvin. During the summer, scientists lead a more hands-on view of the facility with tours (10:30 A.M. and 1:30 P.M. Mon.–Fri. July–Aug., free) of the labs and docks.

Other Sights

In the 19th century, entrepreneur Deming Jarves opened a glass factory in Sandwich, importing sand from Florida when the local stuff wouldn't work. His output is on display at the **Sandwich Glass Museum** (129 Main St., Sandwich, 508/888-0251, www.sandwichglassmuseum.org, 9:30 A.M.–5 P.M. daily Apr.–Dec.; closed Jan.; 9:30 A.M.–4 P.M. Wed.–Sun. Feb.–Mar., $5 adults, $1.25 children 6–14, free children 6 and under), a fascinating tour through the history and techniques of the art, including glassblowing demonstrations using a 2,000-degree furnace. The modest **Woods Hole Science Aquarium** (166 Water St., Woods Hole, 508/495-2001, http://aquarium.nefsc.noaa.gov, 11 A.M.–4 P.M. Tues.–Sat. June–Aug.; 11 A.M.–4 P.M. Mon.–Fri. Sept.–May, free) makes a good activity for kids and rainy days, complete with a seal pool and "touch tanks" where you can pick up crabs and other critters.

Shopping

The **Sandwich Antiques Center** (131 Route 6A, Sandwich, 508/833-3600, 10 A.M.–5 P.M. daily, www.sandwichantiquescenter.com) includes a good selection of Sandwich glass.

Food

There's nothing earth-shattering about the menu of steaks and seafood at **(** **The Captain Kidd** (77 Water St., Woods Hole, 508/548-8563, 5:30 P.M.–11 P.M. Mon.–Sat.; 5 P.M.–10 P.M. Sun., www.thecaptainkidd.com, $10–26), a cozy pub in the center of Woods Hole. The freshness of the ingredients and back patio overlooking Eel Pond, however, make it a favorite for both fishermen and scientists, who meet here nightly to talk over the day's catch. With cheeky menu divisions like "not so small" and "not small at all," **Roöbar** (285 Main St., Falmouth, 508/548-

8600, 5 P.M.–11 P.M. Tues.–Sat.; 5 P.M.–10 P.M. Sun.; closed Mon., www.theroobar.com, $18–33) adds a dash of high-spirited fun to the sometimes fusty Cape restaurant scene. High-concept dishes like Polynesian lobster spring rolls and wasabi oyster shooters introduce New England seafood to the world. Not to be confused with the foregoing, **The Raw Bar** (252 Shore Dr., Mashpee, 508/539-4858, www.therawbar.com, 11 A.M.–7 P.M. daily June–Oct.; 11 A.M.–5 P.M. daily Oct.–May, $4–23) has plenty of cheap eats like hot dogs—but why would you order them when the lobster rolls here are the best around? Atmosphere is somewhere between Spring Break and Mardi Gras.

Information

Information about Sandwich and surrounding towns is available at the **Sandwich Visitor Center** (Rte. 130, 508/833-1632, www.capecodcanalchamber.org). Info for Falmouth and Woods Hole is available from the **Falmouth Chamber of Commerce** (20 Academy Ln., 508/548-8500, www.falmouthchamber.com).

HYANNIS

Technically speaking, Hyannis is just one of the seven villages of the large town of Barnstable. Practically, it overshadows every other town on the cape as the hub of activity. The bars and restaurants are ground zero for the scores of teens and college students who descend upon the Cape each summer, while its streets throng with tourists awaiting the ferries or perusing souvenir shops for just one more Cape Cod sweatshirt.

Sights

Joseph P. Kennedy and his wife, Ethel, first rented a cottage on Marchant Avenue in Hyannisport in 1926. Three years later they bought it, ushering the lasting association with the Cape through their three children, John, Robert, and Ted. The so-called **Kennedy Compound** consists of six cottage-dotted acres behind a high fence, though only three of the houses within are owned by the Kennedys. It's

possible to do a quick drive-by in the off-season. During the summer, two police cars guard the turnoff onto the road (though rumor has it that the troopers in the front seat are just stuffed dummies).

In Hyannis proper, the modest and somewhat disappointing **John F. Kennedy Museum** (397 Main St., 508/775-2201, jfkhyannismuseum.org/, 9 A.M.–5 P.M. Mon.–Sat. and 12–5 P.M. Sun. late–May–mid-Oct.; 10 A.M.–4 P.M. Thurs.–Sat. and 12–4 P.M. Sun. mid-Oct.–Dec. and mid-Feb.–mid-May, $5 adults, $2.50 children 10–17, free children under 10) has a short video about the Kennedys' time here, along with a collection of black-and-white photographs of JFK sailing, playing ball, and relaxing with his family on the Cape.

Entertainment

Firmly planted on the Las Vegas circuit, the **Cape Cod Melody Tent** (21 W. Main St., 508/775-5630, www.melodytent.com) draws deathless crooners such as Tony Bennett and Engelbert Humperdinck, along with occasional more modern performers. Cheekily known as the BBC, the **British Beer Company** (412 Main St., 508/771-1776, www.britishbeer.com) draws a teen and twentysomething crowd for live rock, DJs, and karaoke.

Events

Calling chowder soup is like calling filet mignon steak. Lovers of New England's favorite appetizer flock to the **WCOD Chowder Festival** (Cape Cod Melody Tent, W. Main St., June) to sample the best offerings from local restaurants.

Shopping

The only shopping mall for miles, the **Cape Cod Mall** (Rte. 132, Hyannis, 508/771-0200, www.simon.com, 10 A.M.–9:30 P.M. Mon.–Sat.; 12 P.M.–7:30 P.M. Sun.) draws hordes of teens to shop at stores including Macy's, Sears, Best Buy, and Barnes & Noble. When you tire of the standard Cape Cod T-shirts, stop by **Vanilla & Chocolate** (497-503 Main St.,

508/778-4844, 10 A.M.–7:30 P.M. Mon.–Sat.; 12 P.M.–5 P.M. Sun.), which will put pop culture icons from Homer Simpson to Oscar the Grouch on your chest.

Food

Hyannis is one of the only options on the Cape for good ethnic cuisine. The hole-in-the-wall **Bangkok Thai Cuisine** (339 Barnstable Rd., 508/771-2333, entrées $9–19, 11 A.M.–9 P.M. Mon.–Sat.; closed Sun.) is a cut above most Thai places, with specials such as crispy duck with tamarind. Traditional *rodizio* is on the menu at **Brazilian Grill** (680 Main St., 508/771-0109, www.braziliangrill-capecod.com, 11:30 A.M.–9 P.M. Mon.–Thurs.; 11:30 A.M.–10 P.M. Fri and Sat; 5 P.M.–9 P.M. Sun., 13–26), where waiters carve skewer after skewer of beef, pork, and sausage at your table. One of the only places to check email on the Cape, the **Cape Cod Internet Cafe** (599 Main St. #13, 508/862-8025, $5 minimum for 30 min., 10 A.M.–8 P.M. daily) has Wi-Fi and printers, as well as pastries and cold bubble teas.

Information

The **Cape Cod Chamber of Commerce** (Rtes. 6 & 132, 508/362-3225, www.capecodchamber.org) runs a comprehensive center for the region. The **Hyannis Area Chamber of Commerce** (397 Main St., 508/775-2201, www.hyannis.com) focuses on the city.

The area's largest full-service hospital is **Cape Cod Hospital** (27 Park St., Hyannis, 508/771-1800, www.capecodhealth.org). Fill prescription needs at the 24-hour branches of **CVS Pharmacy** (176 North St., Hyannis, 508/775-8462 or 105 Davis Straights, Rte. 28, Falmouth, 508/540-4307, www.cvs.com). The commercial center of town is home to a handful of banks and ATMs.

Free **wireless Internet access** is offered to patrons with laptops at the **Hyannis Public Library** (401 Main St., Hyannis, 508/775-2280, www.hyannislibrary.org), and by payment on terminals at **FedEx Office Print & Ship Center** (297 North St., Hyannis,

508/778-9454, fedex.com/us/office). The latter also offers faxing and shipping services as well.

YARMOUTH TO BREWSTER
◖ Edward Gorey House

The name might not be immediately recognizable, but Edward Gorey's not-quite-children's books have a way of drilling themselves into the subconscious. His best-known book, the *Ghastlycrumb Tinies* ("A is for Amy who fell down the stairs; B is for Basil, assaulted by bears") serves as inspiration for this delightfully macabre home (8 Strawberry Ln., Yarmouth Port, 508/362-3909, www.edwardgoreyhouse.org, 11 A.M.–4 P.M. Thurs.–Sat. and 12–4 P.M. Sun. mid-Apr.–June; 11 A.M.–4 P.M. Wed.–Sat. and 12–4 P.M. Sun. June–early Oct., $5 adults, $3 students and seniors, $2 children 6–12, free children under 6) where the author lived for 25 years. Many of the docents are the late Gorey's friends, who are if anything just as eccentric as he was, and regale even casual visitors with tales of the bearded author.

Other Sights

The sophisticated **Cape Cod Museum of Natural History** (869 Route 6A, Brewster, 508/896-3867, www.ccmnh.org, 11 A.M.–3 P.M. Thurs.–Sun. Feb.–Mar. and Wed.–Sun. Apr.–May and Oct.–Dec.; 9:30 A.M.–4 P.M. daily June–Sept., $8 adults, $7 seniors, $3.50 children 3–12, free children under 3) uses wave tanks and computer screens to trace the effects of Cape Cod geography and landscape on its native wildlife. Behind the museum, a trail leads to flats perfect for tidepooling.

Twenty-five years ago, Cape residents frustrated with the amount of local artwork leaving for Paris and Washington founded the **Cape Cod Museum of Art** (Rte. 6A, Dennis, 508/385-4477, www.ccmoa.org, 10 A.M.–5 P.M. Mon.–Sat., until 8 P.M. Thurs., 12–5 P.M. Sun. late May–mid-Oct., $8 adults, free children), which showcases consistently high-quality work in a restored Victorian barn.

© HYANNIS AREA CHAMBER OF COMMERCE

Edward Gorey House

Shopping

An old-time country store modified for pre- or après-beach stop-offs, **The Brewster Store** (1935 Rte. 6A, Brewster, 508/896-3744, www. brewsterstore.com, 9:30 A.M.–6 P.M. daily May–Aug.; 10 A.M.–5 P.M. daily Sept.–April) is filled with penny candy, beach toys, house-wares, and antiques. The mother of the Cape's independent bookstores, the **Parnassus Book Service** (220 Rte. 6A, Yarmouthport, 508/362-6420, www.parnassusbooks.com, 10 A.M.–5 P.M. daily June–Aug.; hours vary in winter) stocks thousands of used tomes, along with new books on the Cape and a complete catalog of Edward Gorey. An outdoor exten-sion is open around the clock on the honor system.

Food

The best fried seafood on the Cape is doled out at ◖ **Kream N' Kone** (961 Rte. 28, W. Dennis, 508/394-0808, www.kreamnkone. com, 11 A.M.–10:30 P.M. daily July and August; 11 A.M.–9:30 P.M. Sept.–June, $11–19), a garish strip-mall shack known to spawn pilgrimages

from Boston—or farther—for its juicy fried clams and onion rings. Winner of countless chowder competitions, **Captain Parker's Pub** (668 Rte. 28, W. Yarmouth, 508/771-4266, www.captainparkers.com, 11 A.M.–10 P.M. daily July and August; 11 A.M.–9:30 P.M. Sept.–June, $12–27) is a family-style pub overlook-ing the scenic Parker's River that is a favored spot for locals. Fresh-cut flowers fill the manor house at ◖ **Chillingsworth** (2449 Rte. 6A, Brewster, 508/896-3640, www.chillingsworth. com, $60–70 prix fixe, $17–37 à la carte), the most romantic dining room on the Cape. The kitchen mixes the rich flavors of French truf-fles and foie gras with fresh local seafood for a gut-busting seven-course menu.

Another of those restaurants that is slowly dragging the Cape into the 21st century cu-linary light is ◖ **Gracie's Table** (800 Main St., Dennis, 508/385-5600, www.graciesta-blecapecod.com, 5:30 P.M.–9 P.M. Mon.–Sat.; 5 P.M.–9 P.M. Sun.; 5 P.M.–9:30 P.M. Wed.– Mon., May–Sept., call for hours in the off-sea-son, $18–30), an authentic Spanish restaurant featuring tapas and "petite entrées" from the

Basque region of Northwestern Spain and Southwestern France. It features both traditional tapas items such as *patatas bravas* and *bacalao,* with more unexpected offerings—pork adobo and frog's legs Provençal. Situated in Dennis' arts complex, a stone's throw from the Cape Cod Playhouse (see below), Cape Cod Cinema, and Cape Cod Art Museum (see above), it's the perfect place to catch a bite and a glass of Rioja before or after the show.

Entertainment

Humphrey Bogart, Gregory Peck, and Lana Turner are among those who got their start at the **Cape Playhouse** (820 Rte. 6A, Dennis Village, 877/385-3911, www.capeplayhouse. com), the nation's oldest summer theater, which has been drawing crowds for musicals, comedies, and dramatic premieres for more than 80 years.

Information

Each of the Mid-Cape towns has its own information center, as follows: **Yarmouth** (424 Rte. 28, W. Yarmouth, 508/778-1008, www. yarmouthcapecod.com), **Dennis** (238 Swan River Rd., 508/398-3568, www.dennischamber.com), **Brewster** (2198 Rte. 6A, 508/896-3500, www.brewstercapecod.com), and **Harwich** (Intersection of Schoolhouse Rd. and Rte. 28, Harwich Port, 508/432-1600, www. harwichcc.com).

SPORTS AND RECREATION
Beaches

The warmest beaches on the Cape are on Buzzard's Bay. The popular **Old Silver Beach** (Quaker Rd., N. Falmouth) features soft sand, gentle surf, and a snack shack and other amenities, while **Chapoquoit Island** is rockier and more secluded. Tidepooling is popular on **Brewster Flats,** so-called because the beach along Cape Cod Bay stretches out for a mile at low tide. Eight beaches line 6A in Brewster. On Nantucket Sound, the under-21 set flocks to **Craigville Beach** (Craigville Rd., Barnstable) for cruising and ice cream, while **Red River Beach**

BEACH FACTS

Most Cape Cod beaches have parking lots that charge a daily fee (usually between $5 and $15) from Memorial Day until Labor Day. Many have public bathrooms and concession stands as well; when the latter is not available, local grocery stores often cater to beachgoers' picnic needs.

The beaches on Cape Cod's north and west shores face Cape Cod Bay, and have mile-wide tides and the least surf. Thus, they're often the best for toddlers and babies. The southside beaches face Nantucket Sound, and tend to have small waves, so they're also relatively safe for toddlers. More wave action – and undertow – happens on the east-facing beaches of the Atlantic Ocean.

(Uncle Venies Rd., Harwich) is a quiet stretch ready-made for sunbathing.

Biking

The only bike path on the Cape that runs along the seashore, the aptly named **Shining Sea Bikeway** is a four-mile paved ride along former Native American paths. The highly scenic route takes in scrub forest, hidden bays, and swampland along the Falmouth coastline, from Woods Hole to Pin Oak Way. Bikes can be rented at **Woods Hole Cycle** (6 Luscombe Ave., 508/540-7718). The longer and more varied **Cape Cod Rail Trail** starts in South Dennis, off of Route 134, and runs almost 30 miles through wooded conservation land along a former railroad right-of-way to the salt marshes of Orleans. Bikes are available at **Barbara's Bike Shop** (430 Rte. 134, S. Dennis, 508/760-4723, www.barbsbikeshop.com), at the trailhead.

Boating and Fishing

The best way to see the Kennedy Compound without risking arrest is to take a tour of Hyannis harbor with **Hy-Line Cruises** (220 Ocean St., Hyannis, 800/492-8082, www.hy-linecruises. com), which runs one-hour jaunts as well as jazz and blues cruises. Harwichport is home to many deep-sea fishing boats, including the gargantuan **Yankee** (508/432-2520) and the more intimate **Tuna Eclipse** (508/737-0923, www.tunaeclipse.com). Romantic sails along the Falmouth coast and Vineyard Sound are offered on **The Liberté** (508/548-2626, www.theliberte.com) a 74-foot three-masted schooner. **Pirate Adventures** (Ocean St. Dock, Hyannis, 508/430-4693, www.pirateadventures.com) promises more spirited expeditions, complete with face paint, buried treasure, and sea shanties.

Camping

Situated among forested kettle hole ponds, **Nickerson State Park** (Rte. 6A, Brewster, 508/896-3491) has some 400 campsites, as well as eight miles of trails for hiking and mountain biking.

ACCOMMODATIONS
Under $100

Despite the high concentrations of tourists in the summer, the even higher concentrations of motels around Hyannis helps keep costs down. The **Seacoast Inn** (33 Ocean St., Hyannis, 508/775-3828, www.seacoastcapecod.com, $68–148) has the best rates downtown, along with free continental breakfast and microwaves in some rooms.

$100-150

Located within walking distance of downtown and beaches, **Woods Hole Passage** (186 Woods Hole Rd., 508/548-9575, www.woodsholepassage.com, $100–195) is a charming bed-and-breakfast in a renovated century-old carriage house. Rooms are decked out in bright colors and fish-themed artwork, with wireless Internet and private baths. Breakfast might include strawberry shortcake or crème brûlée French toast. Known as much for its excellent restaurant as for its accommodations, the **Bramble Inn** (Rte. 6A, Brewster, 508/896-7644, www.brambleinn.com, $140–170) offers small but cozy rooms featuring four-poster beds and skylights. Innkeeper Cliff Manchester is as free with local recommendations as his wife,

Ruth, is proficient in the kitchen. A path behind the bed-and-breakfast leads to the beaches of Brewster Flats.

$150-250

With that extra "e" on its name, you know that old-time ambience is key at the antiques-filled **◖ Belfry Inne** (8 Jarves St., Sandwich, 508/888-8550, www.belfryinn.com, $149–315), a complex of four historical buildings in the heart of Sandwich. Stained-glass windows and other architectural details are preserved in the Abbey, while whirlpool tubs and DVD players seduce guests in the renovated 1638 Meetinghouse.

$250 and Up

The spirit of the Great Gatsby lives at the sprawling 400-acre **Ocean Edge Resort** (2907 Rte. 6A, Brewster, 508/896-9000, www.oceanedge.com, $99–325), the Mid-Cape's premier resort. At its center is an 1890s mansion with marble fireplaces, brass sconces, and a grand staircase leading to function rooms

room at the Belfry Inne

© HYANNIS AREA CHAMBER OF COMMERCE

with sweeping views of the long forearm of the Cape. Guest rooms include kitchenette suites that range from large to humongous, along with beachside villas and family-friendly cottages. Other amenities include six pools, four restaurants, an 18-hole golf course, and front-lawn croquet.

GETTING THERE AND AROUND

Cape Air (800/352-0714, www.flycapeair.com) runs daily flights from Boston, Providence, and the Islands (Nantucket and Martha's Vineyard) to **Barnstable Municipal Airport** (480 Barnstable Rd., Hyannis, 508/775-2020, www.town.barnstable.ma.us). Buses by **Plymouth & Brockton Bus Lines** (508/746-0378, www.p-b.com) run from Boston and Plymouth to the **Hyannis Transportation Center** (215 Iyannough Rd., Hyannis, 508/775-8504).

The **Cape Cod Regional Transit Authority** (800/352-7155, www.capecodtransit.org) runs the Breeze shuttle throughout Hyannis and along Route 28 from Woods Hole to Orleans.

Lower Cape

The stable of seaside communities in this region prides itself on comprising the "less touristed" area of the Cape. With an increasing number discovering its pretty (and often public) beaches, that claim may become more and more dubious with the years. But for now, the little artists communities of Wellfleet, the year-round residents of Orleans, and the preservationists of Truro can be content in knowing that the area's biggest draw remains the beautiful Cape Cod National Seashore. When travelers envision the sandy shores and soft dunes of New England, that still-pristine park is where they'll find it—minus the crowds of other areas. At least, that is, for now.

CHATHAM TO ORLEANS

Relatively quiet compared with many of Cape Cod's larger and towns, this area has plenty of year-round residents who are deeply involved with its conservation and upkeep. A number of clean, well-kept public beaches are in the area, though be warned that even in the less tourist-swarmed areas parking in summertime can seem nearly impossible. Your best bet: Follow the beach-going rule of thumb and rise as early as you can to claim spots for both your car and your towel.

Food

Routinely named one of the best restaurants on Cape Cod by publications that tend to decide these things, ◖ **Abba** (89 Old Colony Way, Orleans, 508/255-8144, www.abbarestaurant.com, 5 P.M.–10 P.M. Mon.–Sat.; 5 P.M.–9 P.M. Sun., 5–10 P.M. daily year-round, $18–35) dishes up an unusal combination of Thai and Mediterranean cuisines, with a bit of Moroccan décor and an Israeli chef thrown in for good measure. If the thought of grilled filet mignon with green curry pasta or grilled tuna in balsamic miso doesn't set your mouth watering, one bite will. On a more casual note there's **Sir Cricket's Fish & Chips** (Rte. 6A, Orleans, 508/255-4453, 11 A.M.–8 P.M. daily, $7–19)—also open year-round—for fried clams and oysters that are hot and tender inside, crispy out.

Information

Drop by the **Chatham Chamber of Commerce** (533 Main St., Chatham, 508/945-5199, www.chathamcapecod.org) for information on parking in the area, hotels with current vacancies, and beaches and boat landings. The **Orleans Chamber of Commerce** (44 Main St., Orleans, 508/255-1386, www.capecod-orleans.com) has notably less information to hand out, but offers several pamphlets on activities in the town; the staff can answer most questions off the tops of their heads.

CAPE COD AND THE ISLANDS

EASTHAM TO TRURO

Provincetown might be the fat boy in the canoe—drawing much of the area's attention, day-trippers, and spending dollars—but for natural beauty alone, Eastham, Wellfleet, and Truro have their own spotlight. Wellfleet is home to arguably the best bivalves (clams and oysters in particular) in the nation. And Eastham, historically a farming community, provides easy access to the breathtaking National Seashore (plus several exceptional beaches that are open to non-residents).

Highland Light and the Highland House

Part museum, part working lighthouse, this 18th-century structure (27 Highland Rd., Truro, 508/487-1121, www.trurohistorical.org, 10 A.M.–5:30 P.M. mid-May–Oct., tours are $4 adults) is full of exhibits on sea memorabilia, with exhibits on shipwrecks, 17th-century weapons, and whaling gear. The observation deck of the adjoining lighthouse is one of the highest vantage points on all of Cape Cod. Children must be at least 51 inches tall to climb the lighthouse stairs.

Eastham Windmill

The oldest windmill on Cape Cod is Eastham Windmill (Rte. 6 and Samoset Rd., Eastham, 508/240-5900), built in the mid-17th century in Plymouth, moved to Provincetown in the latter part of that century, and finally moved to Eastham in 1793. Tours are offered in summertime.

Entertainment

Raw bar and oceanfront restaurant by day, music venue and bar by night, the **Beachcomber** (1120 Cahoon Hollow Rd., Wellfleet, 508/349-6055, www.thebeachcomber.com, Memorial Day–Labor Day) is a great spot for live rock, zydeco, and rockabilly bands. The small but daring **Wellfleet Harbor Actors Theatre** (Rte. 6, 508/349-6835, www.what.org) is a point of community pride for its original political satires, modern tragedies, and whodunnits for kids.

THE OUTERMOST HOUSE

A hundred years after Henry David Thoreau spent two years in the woods at Walden Pond, another Henry – writer-naturalist Henry Beston – pulled a similar retreat among the sand dunes of Cape Cod. There he catalogued the rhythms of the sea, the lashings of the storms, and the migrations of the shore birds in his classic The Outermost House, which still stands as one of the best natural-history books of all time. A burned-out magazine writer at the time, Beston originally only meant to spend two weeks at the home he had built about two miles from the Coast Guard Station in Eastham. But he became so enamored of the little home, named the Fo'castle after the spot on a sailing ship where the deck hands live, and the wildness of the environment that he stayed for a whole year. After the house was destroyed in a storm in 1978, a small plaque was placed in front of the Coast Guard Station to mark the spot. For more information, contact the **Henry Beston Society** at 508/246-7242 or www.henrybeston.org.

Shopping

Consignment shops don't get much better than **The Emperor's Old Clothes** (354 Main St., Wellfleet, 10 A.M.–6 P.M. Mon.–Sat.; 11 A.M.–5 P.M.Sun., 508/349-1893), stocked with a mix of elegant kimonos, brocade bags, and plush hand-knit sweaters. For far above-average gifts and furnishings, pay a visit to **Whitman House Gift Shop** (Rte. 6 at Great Hollow Rd., North Truro, 508/487-1704, www.whitmanhouse.com, 10 A.M.–6 P.M. Mon.–Sat.; 11 A.M.–5 P.M.Sun.) and find handmade Amish quilts, dining tables, and painstakingly constructed chairs.

Food

Fresher-than-fresh seafood can be found at the deceptively humble-looking **Finely JP's**

(554 Rte. 6, 508/349-7500, 11 A.M.–9:30 P.M. daily, $17–29). Don't miss excellently prepared dishes like garlicky calamari and scallop fettucine. Outside of Provincetown, **The Wicked Oyster** (50 Main St., Wellfleet, 508/349-3455, 5 P.M.–10:30 P.M. Tues.–Sat.; 5 P.M.–9 P.M.Sun.–Mon., $10–30) is about as cool as Cape Cod gets. The casual spot jumps with young well-dressed patrons supping on fennel-infused oyster stew and spinach-and-scallop salads. For plain ol' simple-but-scrumptious fried fish, get on line at **Mac's Seafood Market** (Wellfleet Town Pier, Wellfleet, 508/349-0404, www.macsseafood.com, 8 A.M.–9:30 P.M. daily June–Oct., $4–40). Order up a plate of steamers (or an entire lobster clambake) and head out back to one of the umbrella-covered picnic tables overlooking the bay.

Information

The **Eastham Tourist Information Booth** (1700 Rte. 6 at Governor Prence Rd., 508/255-3444, www.easthamchamber.com) doles out information on local businesses, maps, and local tides. Find out about local events, new restaurants, and boating and fishing information at **Wellfleet Chamber of Commerce** (1410 Rte. 6, Wellfleet, 508/349-2510, www.wellfleetchamber.com). The **Truro Information Booth** (Rte. 6 at Head of the Meadow Rd., North Truro, 508/487-1288, www.trurochamberofcommerce.com) has free booklets on the town and its hotels and restaurants, plus maps and recreational information.

CAPE COD NATIONAL SEASHORE

Unquestionably one of the Cape's greatest treasures, the National Seashore is an overwhelmingly beautiful utopian swath of coast, encompassing countless warm-weather activities—from camping and swimming to hiking, bike riding, off-roading, and sunset-supervising. Start your expedition of the park's 43,000 acres at the **Salt Pond Visitor Center** (Rte. 6 at Nauset Rd., 508/255-3421, www.nps.gov/caco, 9 A.M.–4:30 P.M. daily, extended hours

in summer) to stock up on maps and information on where to find the best bike trails, lighthouses, and picnic areas.

SPORTS AND RECREATION

Home to bike paths, nature trails, beautiful lakes, and the **Highland Golf Links** (Lighthouse Rd., North Truro, 508/487-9201), the Cape's oldest golf course, lower Cape Cod has no shortage of ways to keep visitors active.

Beaches

Known around town as an excellent family spot, the clean and well-maintained **Corn Hill Beach** (Castle Rd., off Rte. 6, Truro, 508/349-3635, non-resident parking $10 per day)—named such because it was where Pilgrims had once found corn gathered by Native Americans—has easy parking, views of Provincetown, and a warm bay for swimming. The sandy ocean beach of **Cahoon Hollow** (Cahoon Hollow Rd., Rte. 6, Wellfleet, 508/349-9818, parking $15 per day), meanwhile, gets considerably more crowded, but can be counted on by parents to usually have a lifeguard on duty, by surfers to have decent waves, and by seafood lovers to have fresh specimens at its restaurant, the Beachcomber (1120 Cahoon Hollow Rd., Wellfleet, 508/349-6055, www.thebeachcomber.com, Memorial Day–Labor Day). A veritable magnet for kids in the on-season, **Oyster Pond** (1233 Main St., Chatham, 508/945-5180, free parking) also boasts waters warm enough to stay welcoming in the shoulder season, when things calm down and the sheltered pond regains some serenity.

Boating

Whether you're heading to one of the area's many lakes and rivers or straight to the ocean, almost all of the outfitting you'll need is at **Jack's Boat Rentals** (Rte. 6 at Cahoon Hollow Rd. and at Gull Pond, Wellfleet; Nickerson State Park, Brewster, 508/349-9808, www.jacksboatrental.com). In addition to small boats like kayaks and sunfish, they also offer sailing lessons and guided tours by the hour.

ACCOMMODATIONS
$100-150

With its well-maintained gardens and homey rooms, the **Nantucket House of Chatham** (2647 Main St., Chatham, 508/432-5641, $130–185), an old white Greek Revival house within easy distance to downtown Chatham and the beach, is a veritable bargain for the area.

$150-250

Nestled on the stunning marsh of a private Wellfleet beach, **Aunt Sukie's Bed and Breakfast** (525 Chequesset Neck Rd., Wellfleet, 508/349-2804, www.auntsukies.com, $195–270) is a peaceful and friendly place to stay with antiques-filled rooms (some with fireplaces and water views) and first-rate homemade continental breakfasts every morning.

$250 and Up

Arguably the premiere resort on all of Cape Cod, **Chatham Bars Inn** (297 Shore Rd., Chatham, 508/945-0096, www.chathambarsinn.com, $299–685) pulls out all the stops on subdued luxury. It's one of the area's most lauded—and with a full-service spa, a restaurant serving food that's nothing short of impeccable, and a breezy spot on gorgeous Pleasant Bay, it's easy to see why.

GETTING THERE

The **Plymouth & Brockton** (8 Industrial Park Rd., Plymouth, 508/746-0378, www.p-b.com) bus line hits every major—and just about every minor—Cape Cod town, from the tip of Provincetown all the way to Boston. Fares vary; call for schedules.

Provincetown

Jutting into the cold waters of the Atlantic, the little village of Provincetown is perched both literally and figuratively on the edge. Literally, because the tip of Long Point is the farthest fingertip of Cape Cod. Figuratively, because like many remote peninsulas, the colorful town has been a magnet over the years for visionaries, artists, and eccentrics. The town is also well known for its active gay and lesbian community, and since Massachusetts legalized gay marriage in 2004, its main drag has been alive with wedding processions. The history of the town, however, is much more complex. A heavy Portuguese influence lingers from when it was predominantly a fishing village, and the "blessing of the fleet" is still an event. Apart from that, P-Town (as it's known) is home to the oldest artists colony in the country. Painters like Charles Hawthorne and poets and playwrights like Eugene O'Neill and Tennessee Williams once painted and wrote masterpieces in shacks among the dunes. Since then, the community has resisted the "resort-ification" that has subsumed other artists colonies, giving the town a living air of creativity and anything-goes

spontaneity. If P-Town is a state of mind, it is one that is open to anything—exactly the attitude you should bring to a visit here.

SIGHTS
Provincetown Whale Watch

Just north of the tip of P-Town is a sand-and-gravel rise in the ocean named Stellwagen Bank. Nineteen miles long and six miles wide, the bank causes an upwelling of nutrient-rich currents on either side that supports an aquarium of ocean life. Among the sealife present are dolphins, sea turtles, and, of course, whales. There's nothing quite like being in the middle of the ocean and seeing the giant fluke of a leviathan crest above the blue waves—or if you are lucky, seeing a humpback or right whale breach before your eyes.

The two fleets that leave from Macmillan Wharf both guarantee sightings of these magnificent creatures. **Portuguese Princess Excursions** (800/826-9300, www.provincetownwhalewatch.com, Apr.–Oct.) bills itself as an ecofriendly whale watch, with naturalists who collect data and provide an environmental

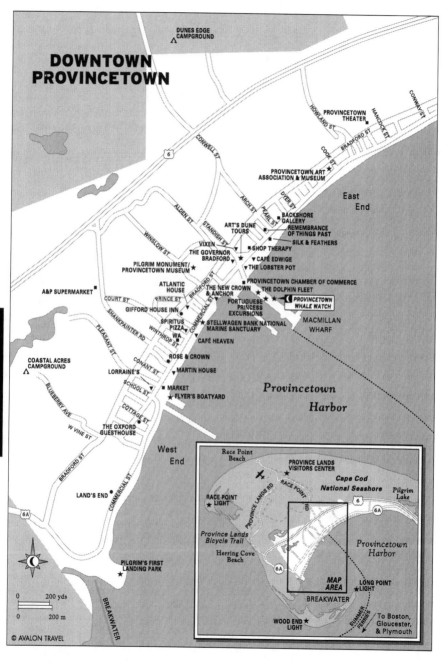

DOWNTOWN PROVINCETOWN

DUNES EDGE CAMPGROUND

PROVINCETOWN THEATER

CONWAY ST

HANCOCK ST

HOWLAND ST

BRADFORD ST

COOK ST

CONWELL ST

PROVINCETOWN ART ASSOCIATION & MUSEUM

East End

ALDEN ST

ARCH ST

PEARL ST

DYER ST

STANDISH ST

BACKSHORE GALLERY

REMEMBRANCE OF THINGS PAST

ART'S DUNE TOURS

SILK & FEATHERS

WINSLOW ST

VIXEN

THE GOVERNOR BRADFORD

SHOP THERAPY

CAFÉ EDWIGE

THE LOBSTER POT

PILGRIM MONUMENT/ PROVINCETOWN MUSEUM

BRADFORD ST

PROVINCETOWN CHAMBER OF COMMERCE

THE DOLPHIN FLEET

A&P SUPERMARKET

ATLANTIC HOUSE

PRINCE ST

THE NEW CROWN & ANCHOR

PROVINCETOWN WHALE WATCH

COURT ST

GIFFORD HOUSE INN

PORTUGUESE PRINCESS EXCURSIONS

SHANKPAINTER RD

SPIRITUS PIZZA

WA

COMMERCIAL ST

WINTHROP ST

STELLWAGEN BANK NATIONAL MARINE SANCTUARY

MACMILLAN WHARF

CAFÉ HEAVEN

PLEASANT ST

COASTAL ACRES CAMPGROUND

CONANT ST

ROSE & CROWN

Provincetown

LORRAINE'S

SCHOOL ST

MARTIN HOUSE

Harbor

BLUEBERRY AVE

COTTAGE ST

MARKET

FLYER'S BOATYARD

W VINE ST

THE OXFORD GUESTHOUSE

BRADFORD ST

West End

COMMERCIAL ST

LAND'S END

5A

PILGRIM'S FIRST LANDING PARK

0   200 yds

0   200 m

© AVALON TRAVEL

Inset map

Race Point Beach

PROVINCE LANDS VISITORS CENTER

Cape Cod National Seashore

RACE POINT RD

RACE POINT

Pilgrim Lake

RACE POINT LIGHT

6

6A

Province Lands Bicycle Trail

Herring Cove Beach

6A

Provincetown Harbor

MAP AREA

LONG POINT LIGHT

BREAKWATER

SUMMER FERRIES

WOOD END LIGHT

To Boston, Gloucester, & Plymouth

commentary. **The Dolphin Fleet** (Macmillan Wharf, 800/826-9300, www.whalewatch.com, Apr.–Oct.) is the older and more experienced outfit, touting itself as being especially child-friendly. The two companies recently merged in 2009, ensuring consistency in prices, which are $39 for adults and $31 for children 5–12. Both have regular trips in the morning, afternoon, and at sunset.

Pilgrim Monument

Before the Pilgrims touched down at Plymouth Rock, they spent five weeks in Provincetown, where they nailed down the definitive version of the Mayflower Contract and made their first "encounters" with Native Americans. Memorializing the pilgrims' stay here is a monument (High Pole Hill Rd., 508/487-1310, www.pilgrim-monument.org, 9 A.M.–5 P.M. daily Apr.–May and mid-Sept.–Nov.; 9 A.M.–7 P.M. daily June–mid-Sept., $7 adults, $5 seniors and students, $3.50 children 4–14, free children under 4) that has become a symbol of Provincetown for generations of visitors. Looking at it, you'd think the Pilgrims had come from Italy, not England, since the tower is a copy of a *torre* from Sienna, complete with crenellated top and gargoyles perched on the sides. The walk to the top utilizes 60 ramps and 116 steps. Short of a plane, it's virtually the only way to behold the geography of the Cape in its glory. On a clear day, you can see Boston. At the base of the monument is the **Provincetown Museum,** which details the Pilgrims' brief stay here as only kitschy dioramas can.

Lighthouses

Provincetown has an embarrassment of riches when it comes to lighthouses, with three real lookers. Only **Race Point Light** (Race Point Beach, Rte. 6, 508/487-9930, www.racepoint-lighthouse.net) is easily accessible. The 45-foot tower was built in 1876 and is open for tours on some Saturdays from 10 A.M. to 2 P.M. The adjoining keeper's house is also a summer bed-and-breakfast ($145–185) with the most dramatic location on the Cape. The other two beacons—Wood End Light and Long Point Light—stand sentinel on the bay side of Provincetown's curving claw. You can hike to Wood End across the breakwater at the west end of town, and from there walk the coast to Long Point. For an easier trip, take a shuttle from **Flyer's Boatyard** (131A Commercial St., 508/487-0898, www.flyersrentals.com, 10 A.M.–6 P.M. daily, $8 one-way, $12 round-trip), which also runs a pink party boat for sunset cruises.

Other Sights

It isn't everywhere you can visit and view dozens of artistic renderings of the places you've just seen. Since the 1920s, the **Provincetown Art Association and Museum** (460 Commercial St., 508/487-1750, www.paam.org) has been offering instruction to artists young and old at its P-Town campus. Over the years, it has collected thousands of paintings from artists like Charles Hawthorne and Ross Moffet, who have gone on to achieve some measure of fame. The collection, along changing exhibitions on Cape Cod themes,

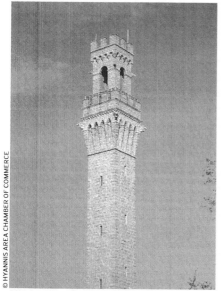

© HYANNIS AREA CHAMBER OF COMMERCE

Pilgrim Monument

© HYANNIS AREA CHAMBER OF COMMERCE

Provincetown Art Association and Museum

is displayed in a new waterfront museum. To learn more about **Stellwagen Bank National Marine Sanctuary** visit the free exhibit center (205-209 Commercial St., 781/545-8026, www.stellwagen.noaa.gov, 11 A.M.–6 P.M. daily July–Aug., plus Fri.–Sat. June and Sept., free), which explains the unique habitat with touch-screen computer exhibits and other displays. Step on the same ground that the pilgrims did at **Pilgrim's First Landing Park** at the west end of Commercial Street. A plaque there memorializes the Pilgrims' touch-down on November 21, 1620.

ENTERTAINMENT

Local thespians date the beginning of American drama to 1916, when the first Eugene O'Neill play was performed on P-Town's Lewis Wharf. The theater community was reborn in 2001 with the construction of the beautiful 200-seat **Provincetown Theater** (238 Bradford St., 508/487-7487, www.provincetowntheater.org, $20–75), which stages everything from campy musicals to heart-wrenching original dramas. On Friday nights, the shirts come off at **The Atlantic House** (4–6 Masonic Pl., 508/487-3821, www.ahouse.com), P-Town's premier gay

nightclub for two decades, with a main club and smaller "macho room" for fans of leather and Levis.

No matter what you're looking for, you'll find it (and maybe more than you bargained for) at **The New Crown & Anchor** (247 Commercial St., 508/487-1430, www.onlyatthecrown.com), an entertainment complex with a high-energy dance club, "video bar," leather bar, and cabaret that caters to a mix of queer and straight clientele. Across the street, **The Governor Bradford** (312 Commercial St., 508/487-2781) draws a mix of tourists and locals for weekend karaoke led by a caustic drag queen. Meanwhile, lesbian women and their friends head to **Vixen** (336 Commercial St., 508/487-6424) for dancing, pool, and sometimes cabaret and folk music performances.

EVENTS

Filmmaker John Waters is a regular at the **Provincetown International Film Festival** (508/487-3456, www.P-Townfilmfest.org, mid-June, $35–2000), which showcases truly independent films. The town's thriving fishing community celebrates its heritage during the weekend-long **Provincetown Portuguese**

Festival (508/487-0086, www.provincetown-portuguesefestival.com, late June, free) that culminates with the annual "Blessing of the Fleet." The **Fourth of July Celebration** (508/487-7000, www.P-Townchamber.com, July 4, free) has the best beachside fireworks on the Cape. Last but not least, **Carnival Week** (508/487-2313, www.P-Town.org, late Aug., $5–125) is a seven-day Mardi Gras that features a parade, elaborate dance parties, and performances by internationally renowned drag queens.

SHOPPING

Patchouli wafts from **Shop Therapy** (346 Commercial St., 508/487-8970, www.shoptherapy.com), a tie-dyed emporium with everything you need for the next Grateful Dead reunion. Women's clothing shop **Silk & Feathers** (377 Commercial St., 508/487-2057, www.silkandfeathers.com, 10 A.M.–7 P.M. daily May–Sept.; closed Oct.–Apr.) sells a well-edited selection of cutting-edge designs and hip, high-end dresses. Upscale **Market** (145 Commercial St., 508/487-1772, 10 A.M.–5:30 P.M. Mon.–Sat. June–Oct.; closed mid-Oct.–May) features designer men's clothing from the likes of Versace and Paul Smith. More than an antiques store, **Remembrance of Things Past** (376 Commercial St., 508/487-9443, www.things-past.com, 10 A.M.–5 P.M. daily) peddles collectibles including Betty Boop lamps and tickets to the 1940 World's Fair. **Wa** (184 Commercial St., 508/487-6355, www.waharmony.com) carries bamboo wind chimes, Tibetan altar tables, and real-life South American bugs. **Backshore Gallery** (394 Commercial St., 508/487-6870, 12 P.M.–5 P.M. daily, or by appointment), www.backshoregallery.com) sells art inspired by—and created in—the dune shacks.

SPORTS AND RECREATION
Beaches
The most stunning beach on the Cape is **Race Point Beach,** an eight-mile stretch of sand with crashing waves and sport fishing in the breakers, dominated by its eponymous lighthouse. More sheltered is **Herring Cove Beach,** a peaceful swath on the bay side

separated into straight, lesbian, and gay areas. The beach was once the province of nude sunbathers; however rangers have since quashed the practice, so disrobe at your own risk. Both beaches are accessible by public bus. Shuttles leave Macmillan Wharf for Race Point every 40 minutes 7 A.M.–8 P.M. and for Herring Cove every 20 minutes 9 A.M.–a half-hour before sunset. To get to Race Point by bike, head down Conwell Street to Race Point Road, where a bike path parallels the roadway. For Herring Cove, cyclists have two options: they can fight the traffic along Route 6, or take the longer but nicer ride along the bike path through the Province Lands. Pick up the trail at the Beech Forest Parking Area off of Race Point Road.

Province Lands
Provincetown is named for the Province Lands, a seemingly desolate area of dunes and beach grass that teems with its own unique ecosystem. Heavily forested when the Pilgrims first landed, the area was later clear cut, and erosion worked its magic to expose sand along the back side of the town. Eventually it became home to isolated dune shacks where artists and playwrights created with only the waves and wind for inspiration. **Province Lands Visitors Center** (Race Point Rd., 508/487-1256, www.nps.gov/caco, 9 A.M.–5 P.M. May–Oct.) has good exhibits on the flora and fauna, as well as guided nature walks in the area, which is now part of the Cape Cod National Seashore.

Perhaps the best way to explore the dunes is through **Art's Dune Tours** (4 Standish St., 508/487-1950, www.artsdunetours.com, $25 adults, $17 children 6–11, free children under 6), which has operated tours in 4x4 vehicles for 60 years. Now run by Art's son Rob, the tours take in a sandy moonscape where hawks ride wind currents in search of field mice and magenta petals of the *rosa rogosa* light up the beach grass. Along the way are the beach shacks, austere in their crumbling grey-shingled solitude. If you'd rather see the dunes under your own power, the paved

Province Lands Bike Trail meanders for five miles in and out of the dunes. Bikes can be rented from **P-Town Bikes** (42 Bradford St., 508/487-8735, www.P-Townbikes.com). You can also walk into the heart of the dunes along the Snail Trail, which begins on Route 6 just before the water tower. The 3.5-mile path leads to Race Point Beach. Save strength for the hike back, however, as tired legs make for slow going over sand.

Boating and Fishing

The largest selection of boats for rent on Cape Cod is at **Flyer's Boat Rentals** (131A Commercial St., 508/487-0898, www.flyersrentals.com), which has both motor boats and sailboats. If you are a lubber, lessons by expert sailors start at $80 for two hours. The 73-foot gaff-rigged schooner *Bay Lady II* (20 Berry Ln., 508/487-9308, www.sailcapecod.com, $20–25 adults, $12 children) sails several times daily for the Corn Hill bluffs and Long Point Light. Sportfishing boats lining Macmillan Wharf include the *Ginny G* (508/246-3656, www.ginnygcapecodcharters.com), which goes in search of bluefish, bass, cod, and tuna. **Venture Athletics Kayak Shop** (237 Commercial St., 508/487-9442) rents sea kayaks and leads guided tours to Wood End Light.

Camping

Located at the gateway to town, **Dune's Edge Campground** (386 Rte. 6, 508/487-9815, www.dunes-edge.com, $30–40 for basic sites) has 85 tent sites in a wooded area with hot showers and laundry.

ACCOMMODATIONS
Under $100

A painted figurehead greets guests arriving at **The Rose & Crown** (158 Commercial St., 508/487-3332, www.provincetown.com/rosecrown, $55–285), a unique guesthouse located in the center of town. Rooms are small but imaginatively designed; one is decked out with purple fabrics and Victorian antiques, another features exposed beams and a stately

brass bed. Three less-expensive rooms upstairs share a bath.

$100-150

Once the last stop for the stagecoach from Boston, **Gifford House Inn** (9 Carver St., 508/487-0688, www.giffordhouse.com, $65–282) has hosted Ulysses S. Grant and Theodore Roosevelt. The airy guesthouse features spacious guest rooms and cocktails served nightly on a wraparound front porch.

$150-250

English elegance is just the first of many contradictions at ◖ **The Oxford Guesthouse** (8 Cottage St., 508/487-9103, www.oxfordguesthouse.com, $119–329), an oasis of tranquility just steps from the hubbub of Commercial Street. The expat British owners are both hyper-attentive and delightfully deferential, and room decor is both masculine and chic, with rich colors and welcome amenities such as fireplaces and 500-count sheets.

$250 and Up

For a truly over-the-top experience, check into **Land's End** (22 Commercial St., 508/487-0706, www.landsendinn.com, $145–570), a secluded inn complete with a tower overlooking the ocean. Inside, the owner's exceptional collection of art nouveau antiques fills every conceivable nook of the common areas. Guest rooms feature skylights, interior balconies, and domed ceilings and decor from Victorian to Moroccan.

FOOD

The best brunch in town can be found at **Cafe Heaven** (199 Commercial St., 508/487-9639, $7–16), a cozy storefront with big, bold art splattered on the walls; it also serves affordable sandwiches and homemade breads and soups. At the end of a hard night of clubbing, the entire town meets at the legendary **Spiritus Pizza** (190 Commercial St., 508/487-2808, www.spirituspizza.com, 11:30 A.M.–2 A.M. daily April–Oct.; closed Nov.–March, $18–27) to gorge on steaming-hot slices and recount the night's gossip. Imagine Mexican-Continental fusion, then imagine it being delicious. That's what you'll find at ◖ **Lorraine's Restaurant** (133 Commercial St., 508/487-6074, 11:30 A.M.–10 P.M. Mon.–Sat., 5:30 P.M.–10 P.M. Sun. June–Sept.; hours vary Oct.–May., $16–26), which goes beyond burritos to offer items such as rack of lamb with roasted garlic chipotle and cognac demi-glacé. The dark-wood barroom also features 100 different sipping tequilas.

For the freshest seafood and a view of the harbor, local families crowd **The Lobster Pot** (321 Commercial St., 508/487-0842, www.P-Townlobsterpot.com, 10 A.M.–11 P.M. daily May–Oct.; 12 P.M.–9 P.M. daily Nov–April; closed Jan., $16–27), which serves fried clams, boiled lobster, and Portuguese specialties. The highly formal **Martin House** (157 Commercial St., 508/487-1327, 12 P.M.–10 P.M. Mon.–Fri.; 10 A.M.–10 P.M. Sat.–Sun. June–Sept.; 5:30 P.M.–10 P.M. Tues.–Sat. Oct.–May, $16–33) seems out of place in Provincetown, but its location in an old captain's house with a fireplace and bay view proves there is something to be said for old-fashioned romance. If popularity is any measure, P-Town's best breakfast is at **Café Edwige** (333 Commercial St., 2nd floor, 508/487-2008, 8 A.M.–9 P.M. Mon.–Fri., 5 P.M.–10 P.M. Sat.–Sun. April.–Oct; 12 P.M.–9 P.M. Mon.–Sat., 5 P.M.–10 P.M. Sun. Nov.–March, $19–29). Given the food-savvy palates in this town, acclaim like this is no small thing. Among the touches that explain the approving chorus are a choice of tabouli or home fries with the big fluffy omelets, pots of honey for tea drinkers, broiled flounder among

the usual pancake and egg options, and fresh flowers on each table. Though it's only seasonal, if you miss a table for breakfast, you can try again at dinner Thursday–Sunday. (Ask for a window table—it's one of the best people-watching seats in town.)

INFORMATION

The **Provincetown Chamber of Commerce** (307 Commercial St. at Lopes Sq., 508/487-3424, www.P-Townchamber.com) runs a visitors center just off the ferry landing. **Provincetown Trolley** (508/487-9483) offers 40-minute sightseeing tours leaving from town hall every half hour.

GETTING THERE AND AROUND

The easiest way to P-Town is by ferry. **Bay State Cruise Company** (World Trade Center, 200 Seaport Blvd., Boston, 877/783-3779, www.baystatecruises.com, mid-May–mid-Oct) runs both a 90-minute fast ferry ($49 one-way/$79 round-trip adults, $44/$69 seniors, $32/$58 children) and a three-hour slow boat ($22/$44 adults, free children). **Cape Air** (800/352-0714, www.flycapeair.com) runs daily flights from Boston. Buses by **Plymouth & Brockton** (508/746-0378, www.p-b.com) stop at the Chamber of Commerce building.

The **Cape Cod Transit Authority** runs the Breeze shuttle (800/352-7155, www.thebreeze.info), which provides transport to the airport, beaches, and town center. Travel in style with **Mercedes Cab** (508/487-3333), an actual vintage Mercedes.

Martha's Vineyard

Unlike the Hamptons or Aspen—where the beautiful people compete to see who can look more beautiful—the island of Martha's Vineyard is where the rich and the famous like to let their hair down. Titans of Wall Street walk around Edgartown with sand in their rolled-up Dockers, while Hollywood actresses don sandals and leave (most of) their makeup at home. The island really was covered with wild grape vines when explorer Benjamin Gosnold first happened upon it in 1602 and named it for either his daughter or mother-in-law (you be the judge). Many years later, the scenic island 25 miles off the Upper Cape developed a reputation as a retreat for writers and artists. Celebrities followed, and residents got used to seeing the likes of Billy Joel and Michael J. Fox at the corner market.

All that ratcheted up a notch in the 1990s, when president Bill Clinton made the Vineyard his "summer White House," and an A-list of Hollywood liberals such as Sharon Stone and Sean Penn descended on the beaches. While the celebrity wattage has dimmed since then, the island still exists somewhere between the planes of it-island and laid-back retreat. The landscape of the Vineyard is the star attraction, with endless beach roads and peaceful salt-water ponds, often lit by the stunning golden light that drew the artists here in the first place.

ORIENTATION

Residents divide the island into down-island (east) and up-island (west). The former is home to the island's three main population centers: touristy Vineyard Haven, chic Edgartown, and charming Oak Bluffs. Up-island is more rural, with the cow pastures of West Tisbury and Chilmark sharing space with the scenic fishing village of Menemsha and the cliffs of Aquinnah.

DOWN-ISLAND SIGHTS
(Oak Bluffs

Nowhere else in the world looks quite like the seaside village of Oak Bluffs, which grew from a Methodist revival camp into an African American summer enclave. In the 19th century, minister Thomas Mayhew founded a summer camp for Methodists. As pilgrims flocked here to hear religious speakers, many of them turned their tents into more permanent structures. Now the town common overlooking the beach is surrounded by literally hundreds of **gingerbread cottages**—miniature Victorians hung with decorative woodwork icing and capped with towers and turrets. Every night during the summer months, romantics bring their beach blankets and white wine to sit around the gazebo and watch the sun douse itself in the harbor.

Oak Bluffs has always had a more festive attitude than the rest of the island, dating back from the amusements and theaters founded to entertain revivalists. The **Flying Horses Carousel** (Oak Bluffs Ave., Oak Bluffs, 508/693-9481, 10 A.M.–10 P.M. Sat.–Sun. Easter–early May; 10 A.M.–10 P.M. daily early May–mid-Oct., $1.50) is still the oldest operating carousel in the United States. During summer months, throngs of children wait to ride one of 20 carved wooden horses and take turns grabbing for the brass ring. The town is also refreshingly multicultural compared to the rest of Martha's Vineyard and is home to a large African American community, particularly during the summer months when wealthy vacationers descend on the island. Many well-known African American celebrities have made their summer homes here, including Vernon Jordan and Spike Lee.

Edgartown and Vineyard Haven

The town of Edgartown has the oldest architecture on the island, including many examples of Federal-style homes built by whaling captains in the 18th century, complete with white clapboard facades and widow's walks. While the Vineyard never achieved the same prominence in whaling as New Bedford or

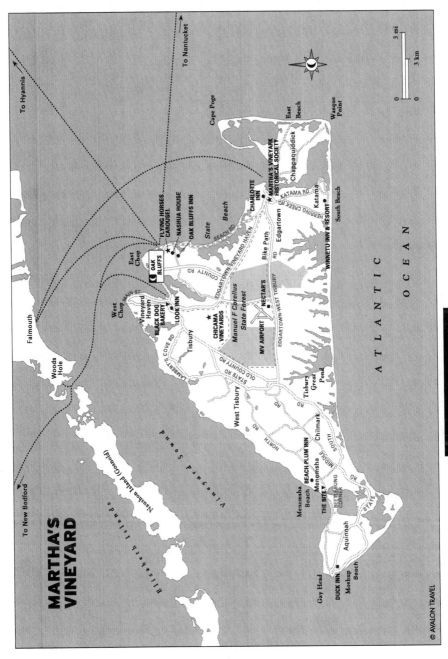

MARTHA'S VINEYARD

To Hyannis

To Nantucket

To New Bedford

Falmouth

Woods Hole

Cape Poge

East Beach

Wasque Point

Chappaquiddick

MARTHA'S VINEYARK HISTORICAL SOCIETY

CHARLOTTE INN

KATAMA RD.

Katama

WINNETU INN & RESORT

South Beach

FLYING HORSES CAROUSEL

NASHUA HOUSE

OAK BLUFFS INN

State Beach

Edgartown

Bike Path

BEACH RD

EDGARTOWN-VINEYARD HAVEN RD

HERRING CREEK RD

EDGARTOWN-WEST TISBURY RD

East Chop

West Chop

OAK BLUFFS

Vineyard Haven

BLACK DOG BAKERY

LOOK INN

COUNTY RD

LAMBERT'S COVE RD

Tisbury

STATE RD

OLD COUNTY RD

CHICAMA VINEYARDS

Manuel F Correllus State Forest

NECTAR'S

MV AIRPORT

ATLANTIC OCEAN

Tisbury Great Pond

West Tisbury

Chilmark

NORTH RD

MIDDLE RD

SOUTH RD

STATE RD

Menemsha Beach

BEACH PLUM INN

Menemsha

THE BITE

BEETLEBUNG CORNER

Gay Head

DUCK INN

Moshup Beach

Aquinnah

Elizabeth Islands

Vineyard Sound

Naushon Island (Gosnold)

3 mi

3 km

0

© AVALON TRAVEL

Nantucket, you can learn more about the history at the **Martha's Vineyard Historical Society** (59 School St., Edgartown, 508/627-4441, www.marthasvineyardhistory.org, 10 A.M.–5 P.M. Mon.–Sat. mid-June–mid-Oct.; 10 A.M.–4 P.M. Mon.–Sat. mid-Oct.–mid-June, $6–7 adults, $4 children 6–15, free children under 6), a complex of buildings filled with more than enough old artifacts to while away a rainy day. Exhibits include scrimshaw whale's teeth, Wampanoag arrowheads, models of whaling ships, and diaries of early settlers. The centerpiece of the compound, literally, is the huge Fresnel prismatic lens that used to shine from atop the Gay Head lighthouse.

The town of Vineyard Haven has its own collection of old captain's houses, though not as impressive as those in Edgartown. It is also known as the main center for the island's artists community, with galleries sprinkled throughout town. Near the ferry landing is the **Black Dog Bakery** (11 Water St., Vineyard Haven, 508/693-4786, www.theblackdog.com, $7), which has grown from a small sandwich shop supplying hungry vacationers boarding the ferry to a veritable symbol of the island. A complex of buildings now sells T-shirts, hats, beach bags, tennis balls, and every other imaginable object emblazoned with the eatery's trademark black Labrador. The symbol has long since gone from cachet to cliché, especially after Bill Clinton gave a Black Dog cap to intern-turned-mistress Monica Lewinksy.

UP-ISLAND SIGHTS

Driving through the long stretches of pastures and fields south and west of Vineyard Haven, you can quickly forget that you are on an island. The western side of the island is more "real" than the glitzy towns to the east, with sleepy corner stores and cattle barns. In the center of the Vineyard is, fittingly, **Chicama Vineyards** (Stoney Hill Rd., off State Rd., West Tisbury, 508/693-0309), the first winery in Massachusetts, which offers tours and samples of its wines, mustards, and vinegars. Nowhere is more of a throwback to the early days of the island than the pristinely crumbling

fishing village of **Menemsha,** a smattering of grey-shingled shacks and beach houses beside a small harbor of fishing trawlers and lobster boats. On the far western end of the island, Aquinnah is home to both a Wampanoag community and the breathtaking clay cliffs of **Gay Head,** which glow with orange and purple hues in the afternoon sun.

EVENTS

Summer on the Vineyard officially kicks off with the **Oak Bluffs Harbor Festival** (Oak Bluffs, mid-June, www.oakbluffsmv.com), a carnival full of live music, craft vendors, and food booths along the waterfront. Competition is fierce for the annual chalk-art contest. Every Sunday during the warmer months, local artists and craftsmen display their wares at the **Vineyard Artisans Fair** (Grange Hall, West Tisbury, 508/693-8989, www.vineyardartisans.com, 10 A.M.–2 P.M. Sun. June–Sept.; 10 A.M.–2 P.M. Thurs. July–Aug.). There is always a good selection of watercolors and photography of island scenes. One of the most anticipated nights of the summer is the **Grand Illumination** (Campground, Oak Bluffs, 508/693-0525, mid-Aug.), when the gingerbread cottages of the Oak Bluffs revival camp are all lit up with thousands of paper lanterns. Depending on your frame of mind, the effect is romantic or intensely spiritual. The week following the illumination is the annual **Martha's Vineyard Agricultural Society Livestock Show and Fair** (West Tisbury, 508/693-4343, www.mvas.vineyard.net), which for almost 150 years has celebrated the farming history of the island. Displays include sheep and cow pens, wood-chopping competitions, country bands, fireworks, and, of course, a Ferris wheel.

ENTERTAINMENT

The island's biggest nightclub, **Nectar's** (17 Airport Rd., Edgartown, 508/693-1137, www.nectarsmv.com), draws bands from throughout the northeast to its secluded up-island location. A satellite location of the Burlington nightclub that launched cult band Phish, its offerings tend towards funk and reggae. Several bars in Oak

CELEBRITY-SPOTTING

For decades, Martha's Vineyard had been the unofficial playground of everyone from legends like Jacqueline Kennedy Onassis and Walter Cronkite to singers like Carly Simon and Billy Joel. Then, in the summer of 1993, along came President Bill Clinton and family, who made the island their vacationing ground for years running, and drew the national spotlight to the resort community. In their wake came waves of Hollywood celebrities and Wall Street moguls alike: Sharon Stone reportedly bought a secluded multimillion-dollar property up-island, Mick Jagger made visits, landing on his helipad just off the beaches of Edgartown, and the late Princess Diana came to sail in its salty waters. That trend has continued – swelled, even – ever since the mid-1990s, to a point where celebrity spotting has become as much a favorite island recreation as fishing, sunbathing, and biking. Is that Ted Danson over there at the bar? Did anyone see Spike Lee eating at the Black Dog last night? Diane Sawyer was at the farmers market this morning! The island has become such a scene that it was only natural that Barack Obama would vacation on the island after becoming president in 2009 – taking at least one well-marked bike ride along Shore Rd. with a small army of secret security agents. True or not (and often they are), rumors of star sightings rumble through the island all summer long – usually spread by giddy summer and weekend visitors, while the year-round residents, by now jaded to the influx of glitz, tend to greet the gossip with nonchalant shrugs.

Bluffs also feature live music at night, including **Offshore Brewing Company** (Kennebec Ave., Oak Bluffs, 508/693-2626, www.offshoreale.com), and **The Lampost** (111 Circuit Ave., 508/693-4032), which also sports a sweaty dance floor catering to the under-30 set.

SHOPPING
Oak Bluffs

The colorful jumble of odds and ends spread throughout **Craftworks** (42 Circuit Ave., Oak Bluffs, 508/693-7463, www.craftworksgallery.com) is actually a dream team of artwork, all handmade by contemporary American artists. The highlights include nearly life-size papier-mâché cows, funky butterfly garden benches, and exquisitely carved and painted wooden plaques. Located a short drive north of town, the **Book Den East** (71 New York Ave., Oak Bluffs, 508/693-3946, www.bookden.com) is a musty old barn filled to the eaves with secondhand books; check out their collection of vintage postcards.

Vineyard Haven

Owner Carly Simon (who's also been known to sing a tune from time to time) sees to it that **Midnight Farm** (18 Water-Cromwell Ln., Vineyard Haven, 508/693-1997, www.midnightfarm.net) is stocked with a smorgasbord of high-end, quasi-bohemian wares: beaded moccasins and sequined dresses, handmade honey and soaps, etched antique cocktail glasses, and shabby-chic furniture. Opposite the Black Dog Tavern, on the dead-end lane headed toward the harbor, is **stina sayre design** (13 Beach St. Extension, 508/560-1011, www.stinasayre.com, year-round by appointment or chance), a small atelier of women's couture. If you're on the island around Thanksgiving you can catch Sayre's annual fashion show at the Mansion House, but she welcomes drop-ins, too, as she enjoys meeting potential clients in person. The very presence of **The Devil's Dictionary** (9 Main St., 508/693-0372, 10 A.M.–10 P.M. Mon.–Sat., noon–7 P.M. Sun. mid-June–mid-Sept.; off-season hours vary; closed Feb.–Mar.) on Main Street is one of those defiant gestures proving that the Vineyard is not just your parent's family resort. If you must have something emblazoned with a Black Dog, **B.D. Gear** (11B Water St., Vineyard Haven, 508/693-7381, www.theblackdog.com, 10 A.M.–5 P.M.

daily April–Dec.; 12 P.M.–5 P.M. daily March–April; closed Jan.–Feb.) sells T-shirts, mugs, backpacks, and tennis balls that sport the Labrador profile.

Edgartown

Awash in Edgartown's pink-and-green sea of preppy boutiques, **The Great Put On** (Dock St., Edgartown, 508/627-5495, 10 A.M.–6 P.M. Mon.–Sat.; 11 A.M.–5 P.M. Sun. May–Oct.; 12 P.M.–5 P.M. Mon.–Sat.; closed Sun. Nov.–April; hours vary in Jan.) is a refreshing blast of innovative women's clothing from designers like Moschino and Vivienne Tam.

Up-Island

The bluefish icon of casual clothing store **Menemsha Blues** (Basin Rd., Menemsha, 508/693-9599, www.menemshablues.com, 10 A.M.–5 P.M. daily in summer; closed Nov.–May) has replaced the black dog as the island symbol of choice. The shop also has branches in Vineyard Haven (36 Water St.), Edgartown (Dock St.), and Oak Bluffs (15 Circuit Ave.).

SPORTS AND RECREATION
Beaches

The most accessible beach on the island is **Owen Park Beach,** off Main Street in Vineyard Haven. The strip of sand at the bottom of a grassy hill affords a view of the sailboats in the harbor. Despite the two miles of pristine sand and gentle surf, you may feel nervous getting in the water at **Joseph Sylvia State Beach** along Beach Road between Oak Bluffs and Edgartown. After all, it was along this stretch that much of the movie *Jaws* was filmed. A more dramatic landscape is **Katama Beach,** a narrow barrier beach near Edgartown, with surf crashing on one side and a warm salt-water lagoon on the other. **Lobsterville Beach,** near Aquinnah, is a favorite for beachcombing, with plenty of shells and sea glass that wash up on the shore. Bring your bike, however, as there is no parking along the road.

Biking

A bike path runs alongside Beach Road from Oak Bluffs to Edgartown, so you can focus on the beautiful view, not oncoming traffic. Winds off of the waves can sometimes make for slow going, however. An easier ride is to take the ferry from Edgartown to the small island of Chappaquiddick, and bike the two miles through pitch pines and protected dunes to **Wasque Reservation.** The beach at the end is ideal for sunbathing. More challenging is the backcountry route from Vineyard Haven to Aquinnah. The hilly 20-mile round-trip offers good exercise and amazingly varied scenery. After lunch in Menemsha, you can cheat the last two miles with a bike ferry to Aquinnah.

Nature Walks

Martha's Vineyard abounds with bird life, and you can spot wood ducks, ospreys, and even nesting barn owls at the **Felix Neck Wildlife Sanctuary** (off Edgartown-Vineyard Haven Rd., Edgartown, 508/627-4850, www.massaudubon.org), a rambling preserve of salt marsh and beach meadow. If you prefer flora to fauna, island naturalist Polly Hill gathered nearly 1,000 different species of plants at the **Polly Hill Arboretum** (809 State Rd., West Tisbury, 508/693-9426, www.pollyhillarboretum.org, sunrise–sunset daily, $5 requested donation for adults), which has miles of paths through wildflower meadows and woodland of dogwood and magnolia.

Boating and Fishing

The tide ponds and lagoons around the island are perfect for maneuvering in and out of by kayak. **Island Spirit Kayak** (Oak Bluffs, 508/693-9727, www.islandspiritkayak.com) leads paddling tours that emphasize island geology and wildlife, and also rents boats ($35 for a half-day single kayak to $250 for weeklong double sea kayak), delivered to the beach or pond of your choice.

For anglers, the *Skipper* (Oak Bluffs Harbor, 508/693-1238, www.mvskipper.com, half-day trips $50 adults, $40 children 12 and under) bills itself as a "party fishing boat," which takes family-friendly trips in search of sea-bass and fluke. Serious fishermen can ride along with

Surf Master Charter Fishing (6 Mariners Circle, 508/400-9208, surfmastercharters@ hotmail.com, trips are 7–11:30 A.M. and 1–5:30 P.M., $100 deposit), which goes after bluefish, tuna, and—for *Jaws* fans—shark.

Flying

Strap on leather goggles and get a bird's-eye view of the island with a ride in a 60-year-old cherry-red biplane. **Classic Aviators** (Katama Airfield, Edgartown, 508/627-7677, www.bi-planemv.com) runs sightseeing trips that range from 15 minutes to one hour, buzzing over the island's beaches and towns in the company of an experienced guide.

ACCOMMODATIONS
Under $100

The rooms at **The Nashua House** (30 Kennebec Ave., Oak Bluffs, 508/693-0043, www.nashua-house.com, $69–219) are a bit musty, but you can't beat the view of the ocean from rooms with pastel walls and battered antiques.

$100-150

A laid-back and centrally located bed-and-breakfast, the **Look Inn** (13 Look St., Vineyard Haven, 508/693-6893, $125) has a hot tub in the backyard and friendly innkeepers who give free personalized tours of the island.

$150-250

A pink wedding cake of a house at the top of Oak Bluffs' main drag, the **Oak Bluffs Inn** (64 Circuit Ave., Oak Bluffs, 800/955-6235, www.oakbluffsinn.com, Apr.–Oct., $140–300) is appointed with a tasteful mix of modern country furniture and old English antiques. It has an informal, lived-in air that makes staying there feel like bunking at Grandma's. Up-island, the secluded **◖ Duck Inn** (10 Duck Pond Way, Aquinnah, 508/645-9018, www.gayheadrealty.com, $135–195) is located in an 18th-century home with bohemian furnishings and a knock-out ocean view. One room has a bathtub in the middle; another is swept at night with the beam from Gay Head Light. The personable owner is

oversize diversions at the Winnetu Inn & Resort

© MICHAEL BLANDING

a 30-year island resident who gives therapeutic massages and makes killer organic breakfasts.

$250 and Up

Located by the beach outside of Edgartown, the C **Winnetu Inn & Resort** (31 Dunes Rd., Edgartown, 508/627-4747, www.winnetu.com, $195–890) offers luxury without pretension. The managers pride themselves on being both kid-friendly (witness the giant-sized chessboard in the courtyard) and relaxing (a strictly enforced "quiet time" begins at 9 P.M.). All-suite kitchenettes are beach-house minimalist, many with views of the surf. Activities include oceanside tennis courts and yoga.

Your fantasies of living as a sea captain can be fulfilled at the over-the-top romantic **Charlotte Inn** (27 S. Summer St., Edgartown, 508/627-4151, charlotte@relaischateaux.com, www.relaischateaux.com, $325–795), where a personal touch is evident in every detail of plush, individually decorated rooms. The innkeepers use a collection of hand-chosen antiques to make you feel at home, for example putting an old top hat on your bed or antique looking-glass on your desk when you return at night. Behind the house, gardens are filled with a fantasia of flowers and sitting areas, and the dining room has glass walls. On the other side of the island, the **Beach Plum Inn** (50 Beach Plum Ln., Menemsha, 508/645-9454, info@innatmenemsha.com, www.beachpluminn.com, $225–450) is a secluded retreat, with six acres of hilltop property overlooking Vineyard Sound and the Elizabeth Islands. Rates include a full breakfast and a coveted pass to the residents-only Lucy Vincent Beach, one of the most beautiful on the island.

FOOD

Like everything else on the island, food on the Vineyard isn't cheap, but it does include restaurants to rival any on the mainland.

Edgartown

Taken as either verb or noun, **Lure Grill** (The Winnetu Resort, 31 Dunes Rd., 508/627-3663, 8 A.M.–10 P.M. daily May–Oct.; 9 A.M.–9 P.M.

daily Nov.–April., www.winnetu.com/dining.htm, $18–29) lives up to its name. The elegant modern nautical setting tempts diners with an equally elegant and seaworthy cuisine—whether its briny local oysters on ice dressed with pink peppercorn and pineapple, butter-poached lobster, or a simple classic grilled tuna filet. Historic sea captain's houses may be a dime a dozen in Edgartown, but you won't find many serving food like that whipped up at C **Atria** (137 Main St., 508/627-5850, www.atriamv.com, 5 P.M.–11 P.M. daily May–Oct.; 5 P.M.–9 P.M. Nov.–April; hours vary in Jan., $30–42). The globally inspired menu revolves around dishes like foie gras with vanilla French toast, prosciutto-wrapped island cod, and duck confit with spicy plum sauce. The intimate brick cellar bar is a quiet spot for dessert, a nightcap, or post-prandial flirtation.

Vineyard Haven

Reasonable prices, unpretentious but pretty decor, and the très authentic hand of a Lyon-trained French chef have kept **Le Grenier** (96 Main St., 508/693-4906, www.legrenierrestaurant.com, 5 P.M.–10:30 P.M. daily April–Nov.; 5 P.M.–9 P.M. daily Dec.–March, $23–34) going strong for more than two decades. Well-executed warhorses like *duck à l'orange*, frogs legs Provençal—not to mention a killer crème caramel—make no mystery of the spot's success. BYOB. Easily the most famous Vineyard restaurant is **The Black Dog Tavern** (21 Beach St. Extension, 508/693-9223, www.theblackdog.com, 7 A.M.–11 A.M., noon–4 A.M., 5 P.M.–10 P.M. daily June–Sept.; call for off-season hours, $14–31), next to the ferry staging area in Vineyard Haven, behind the Black Dog bakery-cum-clothing store full of Black Dog brand wearables. The T-shirts have been sighted from Patagonia to Nepal, and if you're grabbing a snack at the bakery counter, you may marvel that global fame hasn't brought about tremendous price hikes. The tavern's prices, on the other hand, are more typical of the island's best dining spots, although it isn't one of them—not for dinner, at any rate. Better to come for breakfast, when you can enjoy the harbor view and nautical mementos without breaking the bank. It's absolutely mobbed in summers; no reservations accepted.

Oak Bluffs

Crushed peanut shells litter the floor at **Offshore Ale Co.** (Kennebec Ave., 508/693-2626, 11 A.M.–12:30 A.M., Tues.–Sat., 12 P.M.–11 A.M., Sun.–Mon. June–Sept.; hours vary Oct.–May, www.offshoreale.com, $11–32), a warehouse turned brewpub in Oak Bluffs with a nautical decor and friendly atmosphere. Brick-oven pizzas and hamburgers join more substantial fare like fisherman's stew and porterhouse steak. Small and crammed with tiny tables and big baskets of wildflowers, **Slice of Life** (50 Circuit Ave., 508/693-3838, www.sliceoflifemv.com, 8:30 A.M.–8 P.M. daily, $10–22) is where tourists convene to kick back over quiche Florentine and thin-crusted pizzas, and where locals pick up takeout (pan-roasted salmon, bagels, and the day's paper) before heading to the beach.

Whatever you decide to eat for dinner, do as the locals do and skip dessert. Instead, head for one of the island's many ice cream shops or candy stores. Martha's Vineyard has more fudge and ice cream shops than you could shake a waffle cone at, but **Ben & Bill's Chocolate Emporium** (20 Circuit Ave., Oak Bluffs, 508/696-0008, 11 A.M.–6 P.M., Mon.–Sat., March–April; 10 A.M.–9 P.M. daily May–Dec.; www.benandbills.com) has some of the largest selection and richest character. Drop into the dark-walled interior for a handful of candy from the old-fashioned bins (gummy sharks, perhaps, or cashew brittle, or any of the 20-plus flavors of salt water taffy), or just grab some of the cold stuff (in flavors from chai tea to peanut butter).

Up-Island

Beach Plum Inn (50 Beach Plum Ln., Menemsha, 508/645-9454, www.beachpluminn.com, 5:30 P.M.–10 P.M. Mon.–Sat.; closed Sun.; call for off-season hours, $30–42, three-course prix fixe $50) has earned a permanent space among the island's most *amour*-inducing spots. That's largely thanks to the intoxicating sunsets seen over the abutting harbor, but also to dishes like hazelnut-crusted halibut and wild salmon napoleon with ginger-cashew glaze. BYOB. On the opposite end of the amenities spectrum sits ◖ **The Bite** (29 Basin Rd., Menemsha, 508/645-9239, www.thebitemenemsha.com, 11 A.M.–6 P.M. Mon.–Sat., closed Sun. June–Sept.; closed off-season, $5–30), doling out what may just be the island's best fried fish from what could only be described as a hut. Fried clams are succulent and greaseless; the fish-and-chips is flaky, juicy, and featherlight. Order at the door and stake your seat at the picnic tables next door.

INFORMATION AND SERVICES

Find all the maps and information you need to get around the island—plus advice on accommodations and dining—at **Martha's Vineyard Chamber of Commerce** (Beach Rd., Vineyard Haven, 508/693-0085, www.mvy.com).

The island's full-service hospital is **Martha's Vineyard Hospital** (One Hospital Rd., Oak Bluffs, 508/693-0410, www.mvhospital.com), with emergency services offered 24 hours a day. Fill prescription needs at **Leslie's Drug Store** (65 Main St., Vineyard Haven, 508/693-1010). The commercial centers of Edgartown and Vineyard Haven are home to several banks. Each also has an ATM—which are also scattered around the streets of those towns, as well as in Oak Bluffs.

Major cell phone networks function within the main towns, but can be undependable in the island's less-crowded areas. Free **Internet access** and terminals is offered at the **Vineyard Haven Public Library** (200 Main St., Vineyard Haven, 508/696-4211, www.vhlibrary.org), and **Edgartown Free Public Library** (58 North Water St., Edgartown, 508/627-4221, www.edgartownlibrary.org).

GETTING THERE

Ferries leave for the Vineyard from a variety of locations. From Woods Hole to Vineyard Haven or Oak Bluffs, take the **Steamship Authority** (508/477-8600, www.steamshipauthority.com, year-round). From Falmouth to Edgartown, take **Falmouth Ferry Service** (508/548-9400, www.falmouthferry.com, late May–early Sept.). From Hyannis to Oak Bluffs, take **Hy-Line Cruises** (800/492-8082, www.hy-linecruises. com, late May–mid-Oct.). Hy-Line also runs boats from Nantucket to Oak Bluffs (late June–early Sept.). From New Bedford to Vineyard Haven, take **Martha's Vineyard Express Ferry** (866/683-3779, www.mvexpressferry. com). During the summer, several flights a day are offered by **Cape Air** (508/771-6944, www. flycapeair.com) from Boston, New Bedford, Hyannis, and Nantucket.

GETTING AROUND

Unless you are going to be spending a lot of time up-island, a car is by no means essential.

The **Martha's Vineyard Regional Transit Authority** (508/693-9440, www.vine-yardtransit.com) runs buses between all of the towns. If you must have your own wheels, **AAA Island Auto Rentals** (196 Main St., Edgartown; Five Corners, Vineyard Haven; 800/627-6333 www.aaaislandautorentals.com) offers free pick-up in Edgartown, Oak Bluffs, and Vineyard Haven. A less expensive—and more fun—option is to rent a moped from one of several dealers around the island. Try **Adventure Rentals** (19 Beach Rd., Vineyard Haven, 508/693-1959, www.islandadven-turesmv.com) or **Ride-On Mopeds and Bikes** (9 Oak Bluffs Ave., Oak Bluffs, 508/693-2076, www.mvmoped.com).

Nantucket

Life doesn't get much more idyllic—or frankly, more preppy—than it is in the cobblestoned main streets, salt-box homes, and creaking docks of this community, renowned for its past life as the whaling capital of the world. It was that status—enjoyed from about 1800 to 1840—that brought great wealth to the community, which is to this day studded with the immense captain's homes of yore. That wealth is still readily apparent today in the form of new gargantuan mansions (sometimes complete with a helipad or two in the backyard), and boutique shopping that puts the "up" in upscale.

Not for nothing was Herman Melville's *Moby-Dick* set partially on Nantucket: This little spit of land was a major international player—in fact, *the* source of the world's whale oil—for nearly the first half of the 19th century. Nantucket was settled in 1658 by a small band of Massachusetts colonists who had their fill of the Puritans' intolerance and were looking for a solid place to raise some sheep. When the first sperm whale washed up on the beach in 1712, however, it sparked a gold rush of whaling vessels that increased Nantucket's reputation and its coffers as they sailed around the world.

By 1850, however, the whaling era was over; whales had been overhunted, and new forms of fuel were replacing whale oil. Nantucket's economy took a dive, and it wasn't until the island discovered and slowly capitalized on the appeal of its historic charm as a resort that the money started flowing back in.

As recently as two decades ago, the island was still a sleepy summer haven for bluebloods, full of family cottages, fusty country shops, and few tourist attractions. But the world has since discovered its charm, and Nantucket Town is now packed with luxury inns, high-end restaurants and stores, and bed-and-breakfasts that are as pretty as they are pricey. Its waters still teem with boats, to be sure, but nowadays they're more apt to be cruise ship–sized yachts than humble little schooners.

Outside of the main town sit two outlying communities known as **Siasconset** (or simply "'Sconset," if you summer or live here) and **Surfside.** Both are blink-and-you-miss-it small, with just one or two eateries and stores to mark them as quasi-towns. The rest of the island, meanwhile, is dotted with homes both new and historic (more than 800 houses here were built before or during the Civil War)

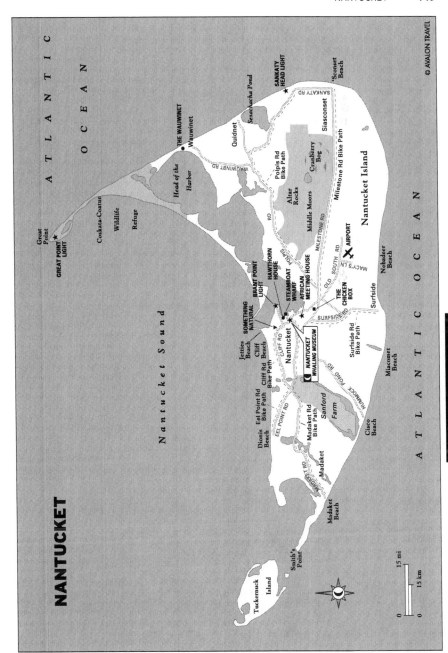

NANTUCKET

ATLANTIC OCEAN

Great Point

GREAT POINT LIGHT

Coskata-Coatue Wildlife Refuge

SANKATY HEAD LIGHT

'Sconset Beach

THE WAUWINET
Wauwinet

Quidnet

Sesachacha Pond

Head of the Harbor

Nantucket Sound

Poipis Rd Bike Path

Cranberry Bog

Siasconset

BRANT POINT LIGHT

HAWTHORN HOUSE

SOMETHING NATURAL

STEAMBOAT WHARF

AFRICAN MEETING HOUSE

THE CHICKEN BOX

Altar Rocks

Middle Moors

Nantucket Island

Milestone Rd Bike Path

AIRPORT

Jetties Beach

Cliff Beach

Cliff Rd Bike Path

Nantucket

NANTUCKET WHALING MUSEUM

SURFSIDE RD

Surfside

Nobadeer Beach

Eel Point Rd Bike Path

Dionis Beach

Sanford Farm

Madaket Rd Bike Path

Surfside Rd Bike Path

Miacomet Beach

ATLANTIC OCEAN

Madaket

Cisco Beach

Madaket Beach

Smith's Point

Tuckernuck Island

0   15 mi
0   15 km

© AVALON TRAVEL

around its beaches and large swaths of untouched land. Much of it, thanks in no small part to the ongoing efforts of the island's conservationists, is as similar to what it was in the island's yesteryear as Nantucket Town itself is now different.

SIGHTS
◖ Nantucket Whaling Museum

The history of whaling comes alive at this museum (15 Broad St., 508/228-1894, www.nha.org, 10 A.M.–5 P.M. daily mid-Sept.–Oct; call for off-season hours, $15 adults, $12 seniors $8 children 6 and over, free children under 6), which recently underwent a multimillion-dollar renovation. Peruse halls detailing the first whale killing off of Nantucket, firsthand descriptions of life on whaling boats, explanations of how the industry worked, and breakdowns of everything that the parts of whales were once used for. The new space accommodates an enormous life-size whale skeleton that hovers above visitors' heads, and a gallery of whaling artifacts—from harpoons to scrimshaw. A

movie and regularly scheduled live talks round out the experience.

Other Sights

Also recently restored, the **African Meeting House** (29 York St., 508/228-9833, www.afroammuseum.org/afmnantucket.htm, 11 A.M.–3 P.M. Mon.–Fri., 11 A.M.–1 P.M. Sat., and 1–3 P.M. Sun. June–Oct., free, donations accepted) dates to 1827, when it was used as a meeting place and schoolhouse for the island's African residents.

ENTERTAINMENT

The city that never sleeps it's not, but for a town that until only a decade ago was always shuttered by early evening, Nantucket has a respectable number of nightlife options. **The Chicken Box** (16 Dave St., 508/228-9717, www.thechickenbox.com)—named such because it's housed in what was once a fried-chicken stand—is the area nightclub, with cover and tribute bands and DJs several nights a week. Standouts among the town's cluster of

Brant Point Lighthouse at the entrance to Nantucket Harbor

© HYANNIS AREA CHAMBER OF COMMERCE

CAPE COD AND THE ISLANDS

bars and pubs are **The Ropewalk** (1 Straight Wharf, 508/228-8886, www.theropewalk. com), which has a salty-aired, wharfside setting to recommend it; **The Boarding House** (12 Federal St., 508/228-9622, www.boardinghouse-pearl.com), an upscale magnet for the perkiest bar-hoppers in the area; and **Cambridge Street Victuals** (12 Cambridge St., 508/228-7109, www.cambridgestreetnantucket.com), probably the coolest spot for a cocktail in town, and usually the least crowded.

EVENTS

Outside of the summer season, there are plenty of reasons to visit the island—not the least of which is an absence of on-season visitors. But the **Christmas Stroll Weekend** (508/228-1700, www.nantucketchamber.org/visitor/events.html) is a bona fide lure in its own right—an early December festival that sees the town's Christmas trees lit up, theater performances, concerts, and the requisite Santa arrival. Once the weather warms up, there's the **Daffodil Festival** (508/228-1700, www.nantucketchamber.org) in April, which takes over with parades of blossom-festooned antique cars and a tailgating picnic.

SHOPPING

With its crush of cute retail stores—from antiques and jam stores to art galleries and clothiers—Nantucket has made shopping a major local sport. There are the old standbys such as **Murrays Toggery** (62 Main St., 508/228-0437, www.nantucketreds.com, 10 A.M.–7 P.M. Mon.–Sat., 11 A.M.–5 P.M. Sun. June–Oct.; 10 A.M.–5 P.M. daily Nov.–May), a local institution that has been selling fragrances, shoes, and sporty duds (including the iconic "Nantucket Reds"—the faded twills synonymous with the island) for men and women since 1945. Then there are the cutting-edge ready-to-wear shops, represented on the high-fashion end by **Gypsy** (20 Federal St., 508/228-4404, www.gypsyusa. com, 10 A.M.–6 P.M. daily June–Dec.; call for off-season hours), with its beautiful big-ticket women's clothing with labels like Catherine

Malandrino, True Religion, and Chloe. Francophiles find bliss among the shelves of **L'Ile de France** (8 India St., 508/228-3686, 10 A.M.–6 P.M. daily June–Dec.; closed Jan.–March, www.frenchgeneralstore.com). The friendly French owner imports an impressive sweep of items, including authentic nautical sweaters, Provençal paintings, and weekly deliveries of the beloved Poilane bread.

SPORTS AND RECREATION

Pretty as Nantucket Town may be, it's nothing compared with the rest of the island's natural splendor. And the best way to experience it is up close and personal on a bike, by foot, or by boat.

Beaches

The first beach seen by most visitors to the island is **Brant Point Lighthouse Beach** (on Brant Point, at the tip of Easton St.), which is poised at the mouth of Nantucket Harbor and is passed by all the steamships that dock in town. It's a quiet and very small beach, about a 15-minute walk from town. As it has no facilities or lifeguard, it's frequented mostly by those looking for a brief stroll or a view of the lighthouse or town. A quick five-minute walk from town, just around the bend in the harbor toward Brant Point, is **Children's Beach** (www.nantucketchamber.org). With very few waves, a small park, a lifeguard on-duty, and restrooms, it's a perfect spot to take the tykes. On the outskirts of town, equipped with lifeguards and restrooms, is **Jetties** (508/228-5358, www.nantucketchamber.org). There's also a playground; a concession stand selling burgers, ice cream, and such; and boat rentals. Meanwhile, at the end of Surfside Road, is the extremely popular **Surfside** (www.nantucketchamber.org), named for its notoriously heavy surf.

Biking

Rent bikes or scooters (the latter, it must be noted, are frowned upon by locals) at **Nantucket Bike Shop** (with two locations on Steamboat Wharf and Straight Wharf,

508/228-1999, www.nantucketbikeshop.com). Or, if you'd rather have the wheels come to you, give **Easy Riders** (508/325-2722, www.easyridersbikerentals.com) a call. The warehouse-based operation has reasonable rates, all kinds of bikes, and free delivery to wherever you like around the island.

Boating and Fishing

One of the most peaceful ways to see the island is from the water; **Brant Point Marine** (32 Washington St., 508/228-6244, www.brantpointmarine.com), rents kayaks, canoes, and other boats as well as fishing gear, trailers, and anything else you need to get on the water. If you'd rather let someone else do all the legwork for you, find a spot on *The Christina* (Straight Wharf, Slip 1019, 508/325-4000, $25 per person), a mahogany catboat that sails regularly out of Nantucket Harbor. (The longest of the cruises, the 90-minute sunset cruise, is the best bang for your buck. For added romantic value, bring a bottle of champagne for the ride.)

ACCOMMODATIONS
$100-250

Whether your preference is toward the historic or the hip, Nantucket has a solid selection of each these days—particularly the former. Case in point: **The Ships Inn** (13 Fair S., 508/228-0040, www.shipsinnnantucket.com, $100–275), built in 1831 by local sea captain Obed Starbuck, the house was later the birthplace of Lucretia Mott. The ten sunny rooms are decorated individually in floral wallpapers, cushy duvets, and fridges. A two-minute walk from the center of town, the inn also has a commendable restaurant and a continental breakfast that includes a dynamite home-made granola.

One of the better values in town is the **Hawthorn House** (2 Chestnut St., 508/228-1468, www.hawthornhouse.com, year-round). Doubles, all with private bath, run $170–255 mid-June–mid-September (there's also a two-room suite for $275), the low end of that range representing selected rooms outside of July and August. In the shoulder season before

Memorial Day and after Labor Day rates drop up to $75. A $9 coupon is given to each guest for breakfast at either of a couple of nearby local eateries—enough to get you a hot entrée, not just muffins and juice. The premises are enlivened by an extensive collection of fine art and unique crafts, including his wife's beautiful needlepoint pillows, his own art glass lamps, and his dad's hooked rugs. The wide-ranging aesthetic brightens the 1849 house at least as much as the sunlight that so many of the rooms enjoy. The absence of phones in the individual rooms mirrors the tranquility of this little downtown block, so near to shops yet off the main path of traffic. In sum, this is an attractive and comfortable oasis.

$250 and Up

Nine miles outside of town sits **The Wauwinet** (120 Wauwinet Road, 508/228-0145, www.wauwinet.com, $380–800) designated by the prestigious Relais & Chateaux group as one of its member properties. The gray-shingled building gazes across a perfectly manicured bloom-filled lawn facing a private bay. Sound nice? That's just the beginning, from the property's luxury-laden rooms to Toppers, its world-class restaurant with the million-dollar sunset view. (Don't miss the chance to sample the house's rare wine list.)

The impeccably kept **White Elephant** (50 Easton St., 508/228-2500, www.whiteelephanthotel.com, $300–1,250) is perched directly on Nantucket Harbor. Rooms come complete with exquisite linens, high-speed Internet, CD players, personal patios, and plush bathrobes and beach towels. Many have fireplaces as well. The hotel's suite-style freestanding garden cabins are ideal for families.

FOOD

While seafood clearly tops the wish list of many Nantucket visitors, the island has also developed a healthy stable of other cuisines as well, from Italian and New American to Japanese and fusion fare. Of course, wherever seafood plays a major role in those cuisines here, it's bound to be excellent. Global-meets-coastal cuisine can be found at **The Pearl** (12 Federal St., 508/228-9701, 5 P.M.–11 P.M. Tues.–Sat., closed Sun. May–Oct.; 5 P.M.–9 P.M. Tues.–Sat., closed Sun. Nov.–April; www.boardinghouse-pearl.com, $35–44), a blue-cast room as luminous as its name. Dress your snazziest and come to dig into grilled whitefish tacos with spicy mayo, salt-and-pepper wok-fried lobster, and sea scallops with buckwheat risotto.

True food lovers—that is to say, those who relish eating the dishes rather than being seen in the right place eating them—make a beeline for ◖ **Black Eyed Susan's** (10 India St., 508/325-0308, www.black-eyedsusans.com, 5:30 P.M.–10 P.M. Tues.–Fri.; 10 A.M.–3 P.M. and 5 A.M.–9 P.M. Sat.–Sun.; call for off-season hours; $18–29). From the counter (the chandelier-topped eatery's set in a former dining car) flames jump and skillets sizzle as chefs expertly whip up sophisticated, simply scrumptious dishes like chile-revved tuna tartare and, at brunch, sourdough French toast with orange Jack Daniels butter. No reservations are taken, but you can arrive early and put your name on a list to come back later in the evening.

If **Something Natural** (50 Cliff Rd., 508/228-0504, www.somethingnatural.com, 10 A.M.–5 P.M. daily April–Oct.; closed Nov.–May, $4–7) were based in a city business district, it would have made a mint and spawned thirteen offspring by now. But as it is, the country-style bakery/store serves locals and biking visitors quietly on the outskirts of town. The draw? Homemade sandwiches like chicken salad with extraordinary chutney on thick-sliced still-warm oatmeal bread.

INFORMATION AND SERVICES

Get the lowdown on where to stay, where to eat, and how to get there from the centrally located **Nantucket Chamber of Commerce** (0 Main St., Nantucket, 508/228-3643, www.nantucketchamber.org).

The island's only emergency medical facility is **Nantucket Cottage Hospital** (57 Prospect St., Nantucket, 508/825-8100, www.nantuckethospital.org), which offers 24-hour care. Fill prescription needs at **Pharmacy-Valu-Rite** (122 Pleasant St., Nantucket, 508/228-6400, islandrx.com).

Nantucket Town's Main Street is home to two banks, **Nantucket Bank** (104 Pleasant St.; 2 Orange St., Nantucket, 508/228-0580, www.nantucketbank.com) and **Pacific National Bank** (61 Main St., Nantucket, 508/228-1917). Both have ATMs—as does the nearby **A & P** (Straight Wharf, Nantucket, 508/228-1700) grocery store. Be aware each charges a fee of $2–3 if you are not on their network.

Major cell phone networks function within town, but can be spotty beyond. Paid **wireless Internet access** is offered to patrons with laptops at the **Even Keel Cafe** (40 Main St., Nantucket, 508/228-1979) and to guests at numerous hotels on the island. Faxing and shipping services can be found at **The UPS Store** (2 Windy Way, Nantucket, 508/325-8884, www.theupsstore.com).

GETTING THERE

Ferries leave for Nantucket Town from Hyannis on both the **Steamship Authority** (508/477-8600, www.steamshipauthority.com) and the **Steamship Authority Fast Ferry.** Also leaving from Hyannis: **Hy-Line Cruises High Speed Ferry** (508/778-2600, www.hylinecruises.com). You can also get to Nantucket from Oak Bluffs on Martha's Vineyard (late June–early Sept.).

During the summer, several flights a day are offered by **Cape Air** (508/771-6944, www.flycapeair.com) from Boston, Hyannis, and Martha's Vineyard.

GETTING AROUND

Several of the usual national agencies rent vehicles from Nantucket Airport, but unless you're visiting in winter, a car isn't really necessary, given the close proximity of everything in town and the excellent bike paths running over the island. The **Nantucket Regional Transit Authority** (508/228-7025, www.shuttlenantucket.com) does continuous loops between Straight Wharf in Nantucket Town and Madaket, Surfside, Siasconset, and the airport.

WESTERN MASSACHUSETTS

In both topography and attitude, Western Massachusetts has a dramatically different character than the eastern part of the state. If the area around Boston looks toward the ocean, then Western Mass. is all about the mountains. The Berkshire range defines the region, with blue-tinted hills rising out of river valleys, and highways snaking through gorges capped with brilliant foliage in the fall. At the same time, the flat valley area along the Connecticut River has the area's richest farmland—with its loamy topsoil supporting a diverse range of crops in contrast to the hardscrabble glacial soil of much of New England.

Historically, the western part of the state has always had somewhat of a pioneer mentality, thumbing its nose at the effete ways of the city in favor of more honest pursuits of farming and manufacturing. A trace of that remains in the political independence of the people here, who skew wildly between college-town liberals and flinty hill-town conservatives, united in the common belief that the state government is unduly tilted towards Boston. This is, after all, the area of Shays' Rebellion—the last hiccup of the American Revolution, in which farmer Daniel Shays led a misguided revolt against the new federal government, only to be put down months later by Washington's army.

As the cities of New York and Boston grew in industrial might, however, they looked to the hills of Western Mass. as both a sobering refuge for their children and a summer playground for socialites. As a result, the area nowadays is known especially for its colleges and artistic attractions. In the summer, especially,

© KINDRA CLINEFF/MOTT

HIGHLIGHTS

◖ **Naismith Memorial Basketball Hall of Fame:** Chamberlain, Bird, and Jordan all get their due at this temple of ball (page 157).

◖ **Emily Dickinson Homestead:** The poet's former home is a mandatory pilgrimage spot for her devotees (page 161).

◖ **Shelburne Falls:** The Bridge of Flowers is just the beginning in a delightful town frozen in time (page 165).

◖ **Massachusetts Museum of Contemporary Art (MassMoCA):** The former mill buildings this museum inhabits are just as impressive as the modern art within them (page 170).

◖ **The Sterling and Francine Clark Art Institute:** One of the best small museums in the country specializes in Monet and Renoir (page 171).

◖ **Berkshire Athenaeum:** The Melville Room is chock-full of artifacts of the *Moby-Dick* author (page 173).

◖ **Tanglewood:** The summer home of the Boston Symphony Orchestra is the region's premier attraction (page 176).

◖ **Norman Rockwell Museum:** The man who immortalized small-town America is himself immortalized in a small town (page 178).

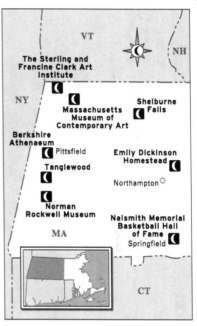

LOOK FOR ◖ TO FIND RECOMMENDED SIGHTS, ACTIVITIES, DINING, AND LODGING.

the hills are alive with the sounds of music (and art and dance), while fall signals the annual influx of youth.

PLANNING YOUR TIME

For most visitors, Western Mass. means the Berkshires, where most of the region's cultural attractions can be found. The southern Berkshires are focused more on performances and shopping, while the northern mountains have art museums and outdoor pursuits. If you have more than a few days to spend, it's well worth spending time in the Pioneer Valley as well, where the college towns of Amherst and Northampton perfectly blend big-city culture with small-town charm.

Ideally, a visit to this area in its entirety would last about a week. That kind of time provides two to three days to explore the antiques stores, theater, and arts of the Southern towns; approximately three days to take in art exhibits, galleries, and to hike several of the trails in the mountains; and two more days to soak up the funky culture of the Pioneer Valley's coffee houses and shops around campuses like Smith and Amherst Colleges. The best time to see the entire region is in autumn, so that you can take in brilliant foliage at nearly every turn. If you visit during the summer, however, plan to spend at least an extra day or two in the Berkshires, where the ongoing outdoor

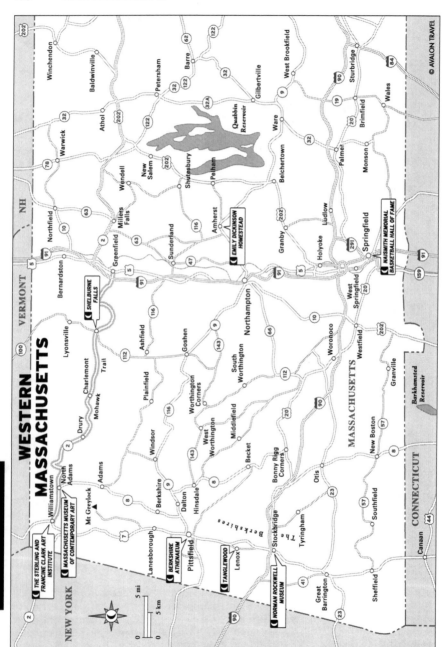

concerts at Tanglewood and summer theater festivals could keep you happily busy for weeks.

The area is a year-round destination, with hotels, restaurants, and attractions staying open throughout the seasons. Note, though, that many restaurants do not offer all meals; many higher-end spots serve lunch and dinner (and sometimes dinner) only. Always call ahead to be safe.

Pioneer Valley

The Connecticut River cuts a swath through the middle of Massachusetts, drawing a line between the gentle hills of the east and the rising Berkshire Mountains to the west. In between is a fertile bread basket of vegetable and livestock farms that seems more like the Midwest than the Northeast. Adding to the surrealism are acres of tobacco plants, which are dried in barns by the roadside. In the midst of the farmland is the mini-metropolis of Springfield, along with the vaunted "five colleges": the University of Massachusetts–Amherst, Smith, Amherst, Hampshire, and Mount Holyoke.

SPRINGFIELD

Even though it is the second-largest city in Massachusetts, Springfield has nowhere near the appeal of Boston. The city grew up as a manufacturing town, in a broad valley straddling the banks of the mighty Connecticut River, a location that gave it enviable access to natural resources and the means to get them to rich ports in Connecticut and New York. (A macho town to be sure, guns and motorcycles were its two main exports.) As the city entered the 20th century, however, the frontier moved further west, leaving it a backwater that declined slowly, but surely, into decay.

The architecture downtown still gives a nod to the city's manufacturing heyday. Most of the city, however, is abjectly poor. In recent years, migrant workers from Mexico and Puerto Rico who work the nearby tobacco fields have been settling here, adding a touch of salsa music and Latin food to the neighborhood of West Springfield. Despite a general air of depression, however, Springfield has quite a few attractions worth visiting, including the national shrine to

basketball, which was invented here by schoolteacher James Naismith in 1891; and a memorial to children's author Dr. Seuss.

◖ Naismith Memorial Basketball Hall of Fame

Whether you are a fan of the game or not, it's impossible not to get caught up in the high-energy excitement of this museum (1000 W. Columbus Ave., 413/781-6500, www.hoophall.com, 10 A.M.–4 P.M. Sun.–Thurs.; 10 A.M.–5 P.M. Fri.–Sat., $17 adults, $14 seniors, $12 youth 5–15, free children under 5), which was completely redesigned in 2000 to provide even more interactive exhibits on the sport. In addition to the predictable cases of players' uniforms and really big shoes, the hall has a circular gallery with the names and faces of all its members, and a large central court where you can practice your own ball-handling skills.

Other Sights

One of two national munition factories created after the Revolutionary War, the **Springfield Armory National Historic Site** (1 Armory Sq., 413/734-8551, www.nps.gov/spar, 9 A.M.–5 P.M. daily, free) churned out muskets, rifles, pistols, and even machine guns for almost 200 years. Unless you are a gun nut, the rows of rifles on display here are apt to look quite monotonous; there are, however, some unusual exhibits—such as one that shows what happens to guns when they are struck by lightning or gnawed by porcupines.

Before there was Harley, Ducati, or anything else, there was Indian, the original motorcycle, which dominated the industry from 1901 until

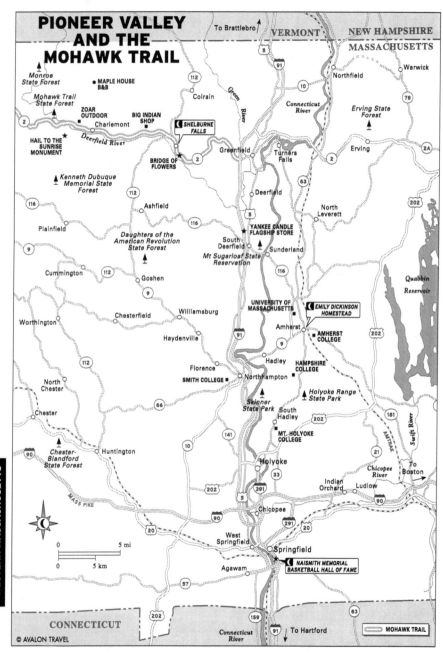

PIONEER VALLEY AND THE MOHAWK TRAIL

To Brattlebro

VERMONT   NEW HAMPSHIRE

MASSACHUSETTS

Warwick

Monroe State Forest

MAPLE HOUSE B&B

Northfield

Colrain

Green River

Connecticut River

Erving State Forest

Mohawk Trail State Forest

ZOAR OUTDOOR

BIG INDIAN SHOP

SHELBURNE FALLS

Charlemont

Deerfield River

HAIL TO THE SUNRISE MONUMENT

BRIDGE OF FLOWERS

Greenfield

Turners Falls

Erving

Kenneth Dubuque Memorial State Forest

Deerfield

North Leverett

Quabbin Reservoir

Ashfield

YANKEE CANDLE FLAGSHIP STORE

Plainfield

Daughters of the American Revolution State Forest

South Deerfield

Sunderland

Mt Sugarloaf State Reservation

Cummington

Goshen

UNIVERSITY OF MASSACHUSETTS

EMILY DICKINSON HOMESTEAD

Worthington

Chesterfield

Williamsburg

Amherst

AMHERST COLLEGE

Haydenville

North Chester

Florence

Hadley

HAMPSHIRE COLLEGE

SMITH COLLEGE

Northhampton

Chester

Skinner State Park

Holyoke Range State Park

Chester-Blandford State Forest

Huntington

South Hadley

MT. HOLYOKE COLLEGE

Holyoke

Chicopee River

Indian Orchard

Ludlow

To Boston

AMTRAK

Swift River

MASS PIKE

Chicopee

West Springfield

Springfield

Agawam

NAISMITH MEMORIAL BASKETBALL HALL OF FAME

0   5 mi

0   5 km

WESTERN MASSACHUSETTS

CONNECTICUT

Connecticut River

To Hartford

MOHAWK TRAIL

© AVALON TRAVEL

DR. SEUSS NATIONAL MEMORIAL SCULPTURE GARDEN

From there to here, from here to there, funny things are everywhere! That's certainly true of Springfield, where you can find some of the most beloved children's characters – the Lorax, Horton, and of course the Cat in the Hat – immortalized in bronze on the grassy lawn of Springfield's **Museum "Quadrangle"** (21 Edwards Street, Springfield, 413/263-6800, www.catinthehat.org, 9 A.M.-8 P.M. daily Apr.-mid-Oct., 9 A.M.-5 P.M. daily mid-Oct.-Mar.). Sitting in the center at his drawing board is their creator, "Dr. Seuss" himself, whose alter ego Theodor Seuss Geisel was born in Springfield in 1904 and lived here until he was a teenager. The author actually incorporated many of Springfield's sights and architecture into his fanciful kids' books. There actually is a Mulberry Street that served as inspiration for *And To Think That I Saw It On Mulberry Street* (though don't expect to find an elephant pulling a brass band there). Seuss also grew up only a few blocks from the Forest Park Zoo, where his father was keeper for a time, giving *If I Ran the Zoo* an interesting Oedipal twist. Inside the park is a monument with three stories of twisting stairs similar to those that find their way into the architecture of many of Seuss's books. An exhibit nearby at the **Connecticut Valley History Museum** (11 A.M.-4 P.M. Tues.-Sun., $10 adults, $7 seniors and college students, $5 children 3-17, free children under 3) shows how other landmarks around Springfield made it into his books. It also has an eclectic collection of Seuss ephemera, including the illustrator's Boy Scout badges and banjo.

the company's implosion half a century later. The **Indian Motorcycle Museum** (21 Edwards St., 413/263-6800, www.springfieldmuseums. org, 11 A.M.–4 P.M. Tues.–Sun., $12.50 adults, $9 seniors and students, $6.50 children 3–17, free children 2 and under) contains dozens of exhibits in leather and chrome, including the first motorcycle made of wood and a 1940 Indian Junior Scout owned by famous trickrider Louise Sherbyn.

Landlocked Springfield might seem an unusual place to pay homage to the greatest oceangoing disaster in history. However, the **Titanic Museum** (208 Main St., Indian Orchard, 413/543-4770, www.titanichistoricalsociety.org, 10 A.M.–4 P.M. Mon.–Fri.; 10 A.M.–3 P.M. Sat., $4 adults, $2.50 children under 12, free children under 6), however, boasts the world's largest collection of memorabilia from the HMS *Titanic*, bringing alive the fateful night of April 14, 1912, better than a Leonardo DiCaprio movie ever could.

Events

Known as the "Big E," the **Eastern States** **Exhibition** (1305 Memorial Ave./Rte. 147, W. Springfield, 413/737-2443, www.thebige.com, mid-Sept.–early Oct.) brings farmers, breeders, and trainers from around New England for the region's largest agricultural fair. When the fair isn't in town, events are often held at the fairgrounds on weekends.

Food

If your idea of culinary heaven involves lederhosen, then you'll find nirvana at **The Fort** (8 Fort St., 413/788-6628, www.studentprince. com, 11 A.M.–9 P.M. Mon.–Wed.; 11 A.M.–10 P.M. Thu.–Sat.; noon–8 P.M. Sun., $10–23), a Springfield institution that has been serving bratwurst, schnitzel, and sauerbraten for more than 70 years. Its dining room, on the original 1660 site of Fort Springfield, is decorated with stained-glass windows and hundreds of beer steins.

Italian pride is on the menu at **Mom & Rico's Specialty Market** (899 Main St., 413/732-8941, 8:30 A.M.–5 P.M. Mon.–Sat., $5–10), a lunch counter that serves sandwiches with imported cold cuts and pastas with sauces made

WESTERN MASSACHUSETTS

on the premises. The owner, Rico Daniele, is also president of the Wonderful World of Bocce Foundation, and literally wrote the book on the lawn bowling sport.

For special occasions, Springfielders spring for **Lido's Ristorante** (555 Washington St., Springfield, 413/736-9433, 11 A.M.–11 P.M. daily, $9–23), a stylish Italian-American spot with down-home but lovingly created pasta dishes and an Italian stone-lined dining room tended by ultra-friendly servers.

Information

Springfield has a large and helpful **Visitor Information Center** (1441 Main St., 413/787-1548, 9 A.M.–5 P.M. Mon.–Fri., www.valleyvisitor.com), which offers information on not only the city but also the surrounding Pioneer Valley and Berkshires regions.

NORTHHAMPTON

The brick downtown of Noho, as it's called, is an urban oasis for hipsters lost in the country. Goth kids roam the streets with brightly painted hair, while students from the all-women's Smith College pore over books in the many bars and cafés lining Main Street. The town has a progressive and active lesbian community that adds to the diverse culture of the area.

Sights

The 150-acre campus of **Smith College** (413/584-2700, www.smith.edu) is a particularly beautiful place for a stroll, incorporating botanical gardens with over 10,000 plants. Many of them are grown in the **Lyman Conservatory** (College Lane, behind Admissions Office, 413/585-2740, 8:30 A.M.–4 P.M. daily, free), the campus's star attraction. The glass-covered hothouses of the conservatory showcase plants from all over the world, from Asian bamboo to African coffee.

Entertainment

Ultracool cocktail lounge **◖ Tunnel Bar** (125A Pleasant St., 413/586-5366, www.unionstationrestaurant.com) is literally located in a 100-foot-long tunnel that once connected the train station to nearby streets. At the opposite end of the spectrum, **Ye Ol' Watering Hole** (287 Pleasant St., 413/585-0990, www.yeolwateringhole.com) boasts a "beer can museum" of hundreds of rusting cans hanging over grungy pool tables. Music lovers have an embarrassment of options. The **Iron Horse Music Hall** (20 Center St., 413/586-8686, $8–55) has two levels of tables arranged around a stage. Acts run to national indie rock and folk performers. More formal is the **Calvin Theater** (19 King St., 413/586-8686, $21–85), a restored grand movie theater that books big names in jazz and folk such as Bela Fleck and Joan Baez. Local rock bands take the stage at the intimate **Pearl Street Nightclub** (10 Pearl St., 413/586-8686, $8–35). For all three venues, check out the website for the Iron Horse Entertainment Group (www.iheg.com).

Events

Each Memorial Day and Columbus Day weekend, the country's top artisans and craftspeople descend on Northampton for the **Paradise City Arts Festival** (Three-County Fairgrounds, Route 9 and Old Ferry Rd., 800/511-9725, www.paradisecityarts.com, 10 A.M.–6 P.M. Sat.–Sun., 10 A.M.–4 P.M. Mon., $12 adults, $10 seniors, $8 students, free children under 12) to hawk and gawk over Shaker furniture, art nouveau pottery, and funky glass jewelry.

Shopping

Northampton is heaven to thrift store fans. The proprietor of **Sasha's Psychedelic Clothing and Ethnic Bling** (Mill River Marketplace, 375 South St./Rte. 10, www.gypsyheartboutique.com, Sun. 8 A.M.–3 P.M. or by appointment), Sasha Berman, describes her clothes as "funky-sexy-psychedelic," meaning paisley dresses and burlesque bikini tops. Would-be punks make the pilgrimage to **Sid Vintage** (18 Crafts Ave., 413/582-9880, www.sid-vintage.com, noon–6 P.M. Mon.–Thu.; noon–7 P.M. Fri.; 11 A.M.–7 P.M. Sat.; noon–5 P.M. Sun.) sells a bewildering assortment of counterculture T-shirts.

Food

Befitting its urban ambience, Northampton has a wide range of food options. Brightly painted Mexican art fills the walls at **La Veracruzana** (31 Main St., 413/586-7181, www.laveracruzana.com, 11 A.M.–10 P.M. Mon.–Sat.; noon–8 P.M. Sun., $4–18), a taqueria that offers authentic south Mexican dishes and Berkshire Brewing Company beers on tap. Vegetarians fill the tables at **The Haymarket Cafe** (185 Main St., 413/586-9969, www.haymarketcafe.com, 7 A.M.–9:30 P.M. Mon.–Thu.; 7 A.M.–11 P.M. Fri.–Sat.; 8 A.M.–9:30 P.M. Sun., $5–7), which serves pan-fried tofu sandwiches and cheap rice dishes in an ambience best described as the Italian Renaissance on an acid trip. On Smith's parents weekend, its near-impossible to score a table at **Spoleto** (50 Main St., 413/586-6313, www.spoletorestaurants.com/spoleto_northampton.html, 5 P.M.–9:30 P.M. Mon.–Thu.; 5 P.M.–11 P.M. Fri.–Sat.; 10 A.M.–9 P.M. Sun., $15–26), an upscale Italian restaurant with regional dishes spiced with the surprising tastes of ginger, cardamom, and even jalapeños. Speaking of spicy, the raw fish creations at **Osaka** (7 Old South St., 413/587-9548, www.osakanorthampton.con, 5 P.M.–10 P.M. Mon.–Sat.; 5 P.M.–9 P.M. Sun., $12–22) are the perfect foils for the house-made wasabi-lined sauces.

Information

The **Northampton Chamber of Commerce** (99 Pleasant St., 413/584-1900, www.explorenorthampton.com) runs a visitors center downtown.

AMHERST

The quintessential college town of Amherst is always finding its way onto those "best small town" lists—and with good reason. The immaculate town center overflows with colonial architecture around a town center that melds with the campus of its namesake Amherst College, where poet Robert Frost once taught. The town also has a vibrant commercial center that circles around its *other* institution of higher learning—the gargantuan University of Massachusetts–Amherst.

(Emily Dickinson Homestead

The Belle of Amherst spent her fifty-some years in or around the homestead where she was born (280 Main St., 413/542-8161, www.emilydickinsonmuseum.org, 11 A.M.–4 P.M. Wed.–Sat. Mar.–Dec., $10 adults, $9 seniors and students, $5 youth 6–17, free children under 6). The perception that she was a recluse who never showed her poems, however, is a myth. The newly opened Evergreens, the mansion of her sister and brother-in-law, gives a more accurate portrayal of the drawing-room society that Dickinson moved in during her life. For many devotees, however, the prime attraction is still Emily's simple bedroom, where she composed her work and where a "certain shaft of light" still inspires pilgrims to her chamber.

Other Sights

For such a small museum, Amherst College's **Mead Art Museum** (Amherst College, 413/542-2335, www.amherst.edu, 9 A.M.–midnight Tues.–Thurs. and Sun. and 9 A.M.–5 P.M. Fri.–Sat. Sept.–May; 9 A.M.–5 P.M. Tues.–Sun. June–July, free) has a first-rate collection of American and European art. A more unusual museum is the **Eric Carle Museum of Picture Book Art** (125 West Bay Rd., 413/658-1100, www.picturebookart.org, 10 A.M.–4 P.M. Tues.–Fri.; 10 A.M.–5 P.M. Sat.; 12–5 P.M. Sun., $9 adults, $6 seniors, students, youth under 18), which features work by the local creator of *The Very Hungry Caterpillar* and other beloved children's books. On the nearby campus of Hampshire College, the **Yiddish Book Center** (1021 West St., 413/256-4900, www.yiddishbookcenter.org, 10 A.M.–4 P.M. Mon.–Fri.; 11 A.M.–4 P.M. Sun., free) tells the history of this little-known subculture.

Shopping

Grab both a sense of the town's history and its academic tradition at **A.J. Hastings, Inc.** (45 South Pleasant St., 413/253-2840, www.ajhastings.com, 7 A.M.–8 P.M. Mon.–Sat.; 6 A.M–5 P.M. Mon.; closed Sun.), which got its start by providing school supplies to the local college market way back when. These days it peddles a slew of Amherst College and UMass-decorated items, alongside clever stationery, calendars, and anything else required to keep your life well documented.

Atkins Farms Country Market (1150 West St., 413/253-9528, www.atkinsfarms.com, 7 A.M.–8 P.M. daily Apr.–Aug.; 7 A.M.–7 P.M. daily Sept.–Mar.) offers up the region's agricultural bounty with gift assortments of apples, jellies, and bakery items.

Food

On the lighter side, **The Black Sheep** (79 Main St., 413/253-3442, www.blacksheepdeli.com, $2–8) is a country deli that serves New York–quality foodstuffs and sandwiches that cry out to be taken for a picnic. The Northampton burrito joint **La Veracruzana** (63 S. Pleasant St., 413/253-6900, www.laveracruzana.com, 11 A.M.–10 P.M. Mon.–Sat.; noon–8 P.M. Sun. $4–18) also has a branch here.

Information

The **Amherst Area Chamber of Commerce** (28 Amity St., 413/253-0700, www.amherstarea.com) runs an information booth on the common, as well as a larger office down the street from the Dickinson Museum.

DEERFIELD AND GREENFIELD

The small town of Deerfield has a split personality, with one of the area's most prestigious historical attractions and some of its schlockiest tourist traps. To call the gritty crossroads of Greenfield the gateway to the Berkshires is perhaps giving it too much credit. Located at the intersection of Route 2 and I-91, it is nevertheless a good place to stock up on gas and sundries before heading up the Mohawk Trail.

Historic Deerfield

When Henry Flynt took his son to Deerfield Academy in the 1930s, he was amazed to see how well-preserved the center of the town of Deerfield was. Over the years, he set about buying and restoring the old homes and putting them into a trust. The result today is an

Historic Deerfield

open-air museum (84B Old Main St., 413/774-5581, www.historic-deerfield.org, 9:30 A.M.–4:30 P.M. daily Apr.–Nov., $12 adults, $5 youth 6–17, free children under 6) that provides one of the best introductions to early New England history. Thirteen houses built between 1730 and 1850 contain 25,000 antique items from around New England, while museum exhibits tell the story of the early settlers of the area. Innovative hands-on history classes allow you to learn skills from sheep-shearing to open-hearth cooking.

Other Sights

Like the world's largest ball of twine, the **Yankee Candle Flagship Store** (25 Greenfield Rd., S. Deerfield, 877/636-7707, www.yankeecandle.com, 9:30 A.M.–6 P.M. daily Jan.–Jul; free) grew from humble beginnings into a tourist trap of epic proportions. At its center is a warehouse-sized candle store, an alphabetized assault on the nostrils from apple cider to white zinfandel. That is just the beginning, however, of a complex that includes countless home-goods stores, a candle-making museum, and even a Bavarian Christmas village complete with model trains and gondolas. Even on the coldest days, the **Magic Wings Butterfly Conservatory** (281 Greenfield Rd., S. Deerfield, 413/665-2805, www.magicwings.com, 9 A.M.–6 P.M. Memorial Day–Labor Day; 9 A.M.–5 P.M. Sept.–May, $12 adults, $10 seniors, $8 children 3–17, free children under 3) is a doorway into a tropical vacation, with walkways through lush vegetation and 3,000 butterflies of all shapes and colors flitting past. "Flight attendants" are available to help identify species.

Shopping

Dinosaurs leap from the brush behind **The Rock Fossil and Dinosaur Shop** (213 Greenfield Rd., Rtes. 5 & 10, S. Deerfield, 413/665-7625, www.georgesrocks.com), a deliciously cheesy gem and fossil store that features its own mini–Jurassic Park and "mines" where kids can go spelunking.

Food

Why should meat-eaters get all the beer? **The People's Pint** (24 Federal St., Greenfield, 413/773-0333, www.thepeoplespint.com, 4 P.M.–midnight Mon.–Fri.; noon–midnight Sat.–Sun., $6–16) melds a vegetarian ethos with finely crafted drafts. Meals of blackened veggie burgers and cheese plates are apt to please vegetarians and carnivores alike; the restaurant offers discounts for bike riders.

With food so beautifully plated you almost don't want to eat it, **◖ Sienna** (6-B Elm St., S. Deerfield, 413/665-0215, www.siennarestaurant.com, 11 A.M.–2 P.M. and 5–10 P.M. Mon.–Sat., 11 A.M.–2 P.M. and 5–9 P.M. Sun.; $17–20) is a culinary gem that could hold its own anywhere in the world. Eat it you should, because the delicate flavors of chef Richard Labonte's roast duck breast and pan-seared beef tenderloin virtually melt on the tongue. The decor of bamboo stalks and burnt-sienna walls strives to be as elegant as the food.

Information

The **Upper Pioneer Valley Visitors Center** (18 Miner St., I-91, Exit 26, 413/773-9393) has information about Deerfield, Greenfield, and the Mohawk Trail.

SPORTS AND RECREATION
Six Flags New England

New England's premier amusement park (Rte. 159/1623 Main St., Agawam, 413/786-9300, www.sixflags.com, hours vary Apr.–Oct., $42 adults, $31 youth under 5'3", free children under 3) has more than 100 rides and thrills, including the must-ride Bizarro roller coaster and a gargantuan water park with a "rocket-propelled" water coaster. Be forewarned, however, that the park can get both pricey and crowded. The best strategy is to pick either the theme park or the water park, and invest in the quick pass that helps you beat the lines.

Walking and Hiking

The 157-acre **Look Park** (Northampton, 413/584-5457, www.lookpark.org) is a beautifully sculpted Victorian park that really does have something for everyone. In addition to walking trails, paddle boats, and picnic shelters, it has a small zoo, train ride, and mini-golf course.

A few miles west of Northampton is the trailhead for **Chesterfield Gorge** (River Rd., W. Chesterfield, 413/532-1631, www.thetrustees.org), a half-mile trail that traces the seventy-foot-high cliff walls of a chasm over the Westfield River. The gorge is the entrance to an expansive recreation area that features catch-and-release fly-fishing for trout.

Biking
The 10-mile **Norwottuck Rail Trail** (Damon Rd., Northampton, 413/586-8706, ext. 12) provides a pleasant afternoon ride along the Connecticut River between Northampton and Amherst. The trail offers diverse scenery of farmland, tobacco barns, and swampy conservation area frequented by birds, turtles, and other critters. Bicycles can be rented at the Damon Road entrance in Northampton, and at **Laughing Dog Bicycles** (63 S. Pleasant St., Amherst, 413/253-7722, www.laughingdogbicycles.com).

Camping and Canoeing
You can rent canoes and kayaks at **Barton Cove** (Rte. 2, Gill, 413/863-9300, late May–early Sept., boat rentals: $25 up to 2 hours, $40/day, tents: $22/night), a campground on a bend in the Connecticut River within easy paddling distance of the scenic French King Gorge. The camp also provides a shuttle for longer river trips.

Cross-Country Skiing
The **Northfield Mountain Cross Country Ski Area** (Rte. 63, Northfield, 800/859-2960, $12 adults, $11 seniors, $6 children 8–14, free children under 8, rentals: $14 adults, $9 children under 14) provides 25 miles of groomed and sculpted trails including backwoods jaunts and grueling mountain climbs.

ACCOMMODATIONS
Under $100
West Springfield has many budget hotels, including an **Econo Lodge** (1553 Elm St., W.

Springfield, 413/734-8278, www.econolodge.com, $65–109). The **Five College Bed & Breakfast Association** (www.fivecollegebb.com) lists many small bed-and-breakfasts in the area. One of the most popular is the **Lupine House** (185 N. Main St., Florence, 413/586-9766 or 800/890-9766, www.lupinehouse.com, $80–90), where hosts Evelyn and Gil Billings go out of their way to make guests feel at home. In addition to a fireplace, VCR, and computer access, the house provides convenient access to the bike path.

$100–150
For a touch of the old grandeur of Springfield, check into the **Lathrop House B&B** (188 Summer Ave., Springfield, 413/736-6414, www.lathrophousebandb.com, $100–175), an 1899 columned mansion that had previous lives as both a Jewish temple and an art school. The multilingual innkeeper tends a rose garden and outdoor swing, and cooks breakfast in a kosher kitchen. Looking like the gingerbread house right out of the Brothers Grimm, the surprisingly affordable ◖ **Allen House Inn** (599 Main St., Amherst, 413/253-5000, www.allenhouse.com, $75–195) sports art, antiques, and wall coverings meticulously chosen to evoke Emily Dickinson's day. A five-course breakfast is included.

Black walnut trees dot the acre of grounds at the **Black Walnut Inn** (1184 N. Pleasant St., Amherst, 413/549-5649, www.blackwalnutinn.com, $120–170), a luxurious Federal-style brick mansion. The rooms are individually decorated with sleigh beds and lace and organza canopy beds; the largest has a gas fireplace and whirlpool tub. Children are welcome—and will appreciate the hot apple pie served with breakfast.

$150–250
The grand brick **Hotel Northampton** (36 King St., Northampton, 413/584-3100 or 800/547-3529, www.hotelnorthampton.com, $205–270) is a 1927 colonial revival building overlooking a park downtown. Rooms are filled with floral prints and include wireless Internet,

HBO, and continental breakfast. You can't get much closer to history than the **Deerfield Inn** (81 Main St., Deerfield, 413/774-5587, www. deerfieldinn.com, $150–260), located within the heart of Historic Deerfield. The rooms include four-poster beds, plush mattresses, and plaques telling the story of historic town residents. In one room, a ghost named Herschel is known to throw magazines around when peeved.

INFORMATION AND SERVICES

For hospital and emergency services, turn to **Baystate Medical Center** (759 Chestnut St., Springfield, 413/794-0000, www.baystatehealth.com), and for pharmacy needs, to chains such as **Rite Aid** (198 Pine St., Florence, 413/584-0182, www.riteaid.com). Banks are found all over the area (particularly in Springfield), and ATMs are easy to find all over Springfield and Northampton at bus stations, in and around hotels, in convenience stores, and, of course, at banks.

Free **Internet access** is offered at **Springfield City Library** (220 State St., Springfield, 413/263-6828, www.springfieldlibrary.org) and on the campuses of the area's colleges. Find faxing and shipping services at **The UPS Store** (340 Cooley St., Springfield, 413/782-2277, theupsstore.com).

GETTING THERE AND AROUND

I-91 runs like a spine down the Pioneer Valley, connecting the Mass Pike (I-90) to the south and Route 2 to the north. Shuttles to the valley are available from **Bradley International Airport** (11 Schoephoester Rd., I-91, exit 40, Windsor Locks, www.bradleyairport.com), just south of Springfield over the Connecticut border. All of the major car rental companies are available at the airport. Several shuttle companies offer transport from Bradley Airport, including **Valley Transporter** (413/253-1350, www.valleytransporter.com) and **Michael's Limousine & Airport Service** (800/555-5593, www.michaelslimo.com). Shuttles to Springfield take about 15 minutes and cost around $40.

Springfield is the headquarters for **Peter Pan Bus Lines** (1776 Main St., 800/343-9999, www.peterpanbus.com), which has routes from the airport and all over Western Massachusetts, including to stations in Northampton (1 Roundhouse Plaza) and Amherst (8 Main St., 893 West St., University of Massachusetts). Trains arrive at the **Springfield Amtrak Station** (66 Lyman St., 800/872-7245, www. amtrak.com).

Buses to all locations within the valley are run by the **Pioneer Valley Transportation Authority** (413/781-7882, www.pvta.com).

The Mohawk Trail

Souvenir dinner plates and sepia picture postcards come to mind along the Mohawk Trail, which seems perpetually stuck in an era of early-twentieth-century auto-touring. The route was established as a scenic byway in 1914, and still has a retro feel, with motor-lodges, cottages, Native American trading posts, and scenic overlooks lining the roller coaster ride through the mountains.

Historically speaking, the Mohawk really did use the stretch of what is now Route 2 that bears their name. The Mohawk hiked from New York through the mountains to find prime fishing spots and, on more than one occasion, to attack enemies—including the infamous French-Indian raid on Deerfield in 1704. Nowadays the biggest threat is the lack of amenities between Greenfield and North Adams. Make sure your gas tank is full and brakes and coolant are in prime condition before tackling the scenic stretch.

◖ SHELBURNE FALLS

A short detour off the Trail, this delightful village feels stranded in time. Actually the meeting place of two towns—Shelburne and Buckland—the town is a curious blend of old-time Americana and enlightened headquarters for artisans and craftspeople. Its main street is lined with owner-occupied shops and diners, and crawling with teenagers who, aside from the Slipknot T-shirts and low-rise shorts, might have stepped out of an Archie comic.

Sights

The main attraction in town is the so-called **Bridge of Flowers,** a once-blighted trolley bridge that was transformed by the local women's club in 1928. Now the 400-foot span is a linear garden full of more than 300 varieties of flowering plants, with some trees a dozen feet high. The town's other main attraction is a natural one—underneath Salmon Falls the **"glacial potholes"** are a lunar landscape of holes up to 40 feet wide, formed by the swirling action of little stones during the last ice age. While not open for swimming, they make for picturesque viewing.

Shopping

Modern arts and crafts can be found at the many artisan shops in Shelburne Falls. At **Young Constantin & Associates Glass** (4 Deerfield Ave., 866/625-6422, http://yandc-glass.com/), you can watch artisans blow and shape stained-glass vases and ornaments in a blast furnace before purchasing them next door. By the glacial potholes, **Mole Hollow Candles** (3 Deerfield Ave., 877/226-3537, www.molehollowcandles.com) sells foot-long tapers and votive candles, as it has for more than 30 years.

Food

Bridge Street Cafe (65 Bridge St., 413/625-6345, $5–9) offers home-style cooking in a cute country kitchen, with vinyl floral tablecloths and black-and-white photos on the wall. Slightly more formal, **The Shire Restaurant** (2 State St., 413/625-2727, $13–19) serves blackened chicken sandwiches and portabella parmigiana on an outdoor deck overlooking the Bridge of Flowers. Sure, there are snacks, but

Shelburne's Bridge of Flowers

© KINDRA CLINEFF/MOTT

WESTERN MASSACHUSETTS

go for the beer (and more beer) at **Moan and Dove** (460 West St., 413/256-1710, Mon.–Fri. 3 P.M.–1 A.M. Mon.–Fri.; 1 P.M.–1 A.M. Sat.–Sun., $9–21), home of more on-tap selections than you can shake a bottle at. Meanwhile, those who proudly claim membership to the cult of the popover will find utter bliss at **Judie's Restaurant** (51 North Pleasant St., 413/253-3491, 11:30 A.M.–10 P.M. Sun.–Fri., 11:30 A.M.–11 P.M. Sat., $14–22, www.judiesrestaurant.com). The funky, centrally located spot (overlooking downtown square) serves sandwiches, light daily specials, homemade soups, and (of course) killer popovers at hand-painted tables—and on the way out, sells apple butter and poppy seed salad dressings, to boot.

Information

The **Village Information Center** (75 Bridge St., 413/625-2526, www.shelburnefalls.com) has information about the town and the rest of the Mohawk Trail.

CHARLEMONT TO NORTH ADAMS

As the Mohawk Trail continues, it quickly becomes one of the most scenic drives in all of New England, playing tag with the Deerfield and Cold Rivers and opening up on stunning vistas of the surrounding hills.

Sights

The most recognizable symbol along the trail is the **"Hail to the Sunrise" Memorial,** a half-ton bronze statue of a praying Mohawk man erected near the highway at the crossroads town of Charlemont to pay homage to the Mohawk Indians. A short detour up Route 8A is the **Bissell Covered Bridge,** a 120-foot-long span over the Deerfield River. The best panoramic view is at **Whitcomb Summit,** the highest point of the trail at 2,200 feet.

Events

The acoustics in the Federated Church in Charlemont are near-perfect, making it a beautiful setting for the **Mohawk Trail Concerts**

THE HOOSAC TUNNEL

Before there was the "Big Dig," there was the Hoosac Tunnel, a massive project during the 19th century that became the construction boondoggle of its day. During 20 years of construction, workers learned the hard way how to use nitroglyceride – claiming the lives of 195 men in the process – and Massachusetts was driven into debt for a tunnel made obsolete almost as soon as it was completed due to the building of the Erie Canal. Even so, those who worked on it could take pride in the fact that a 4¾-mile tunnel met in the middle of the range within 1/16 of an inch. You can view the eastern portal of the tunnel, which still carries train traffic, by taking the long winding Whitcomb Hill Road (just east of the Whitcomb Summit) down from Route 2 to the Deerfield River. Turn left on River Road and drive until you hit the train tracks. The entrance is a short walk down the tracks to the left. In addition, North Adams' **Western Gateway Heritage State Park Visitors Center** (115 State St., Bldg. 4, 413/663-6312, www.mass.gov, 10 A.M.–5 P.M. daily, free) has a film and exhibits about the construction of the tunnel, which still stands as the longest railroad tunnel in North America.

(75 Bridge St., 413/625-9511 or 888/MTC-MUSE, www.mohawktrailconcerts.org, Fri.–Sat. in late June–July, $15–20), a series that brings internationally renowned musicians to play chamber music.

Shopping

If you've ever hankered after moccasins, dream-catchers, or spirit animals enameled on jewelry boxes, you've come to the right place. Several Native American emporiums line the trail, including **Big Indian Shop** (2183 Mohawk Trail, between Shelburne Falls and Charlemont, 413/625-6817, 9 A.M.–5 P.M. daily), which boasts a 20-foot-tall statue of a

Native American man and includes a petting zoo, and the **Wigwam and Western Summit Gift Shop** (2350 Mohawk Trail/Rte. 2, North Adams, 413/663-3205, www.thewigwam.net), which offers a stunning view from coin-operated binoculars.

SPORTS AND RECREATION
Boating
The white water of the Deerfield River provides the best terrain for kayaking and rafting in southern New England. Two companies have mastered the river. The original pioneer of the Deerfield is **Zoar Outdoor** (7 Main St., Charlemont, 800/532-7483, www.zoaroutdoor.com, Apr.–Oct., rafting $78–95/day), which runs a popular 10-mile rafting trip through the raging Zoar Gap, along with other weekend and day trips on the river. It also leads canoeing, kayaking, rock climbing, and biking trips. The Maine-based **Crab Apple White Water** (2056 Mohawk Trail/Rte. 2, Charlemont, 800/553-7238, www.crabapplewhitewater.com, Apr.–Oct., rafting $40–107/day) also offers half- and full-day rafting and inflatable kayak trips on the Deerfield, as well as other rivers throughout New England. It prides itself on its riverside cooking.

Hiking
Several trailheads leave from in and around Shelburne Falls, including an easy walk to the scenic High Ledges picnic area, and a more rugged five-mile riverside footpath along the Mahican-Mohawk Trail. Maps are available at the town information center.

ACCOMMODATIONS
Under $100
This region abounds in cheap lodging, from roadside motels to family-owned bed-and-breakfasts. One of the best is **Maple House B&B** (51 Middletown Hill Rd., Rowe, 413/339-0107, www.maplehousebb.com, $60–100), an 18th-century farmhouse situated on acres of scenic grounds with a beautiful view of the mountains. Friendly hosts Rebecca and Michael Bradley provide five rooms filled with homemade quilts and wallhangings, as well as a full breakfast. Not to be confused with Maple House, **Six Maple Street B&B** (6 Maple St., Shelburne Falls, 413/625-6807, www.sixmaplestreet.com, Fri.–Sun. May–Nov. only, $90–100) is in a colonial home built by one of the original settlers of Shelburne Falls, and one of the only places to stay within walking distance of town. The low-ceilinged rooms are filled with antique bottles, clocks, and books. Baths are shared and children are not allowed.

$100-150
Set up on a hill overlooking the trail, **(The Warfield House Inn** (200 Warfield Rd., Charlemont, 413/339-6600 or 888/339-8439, www.warfieldhouseinn.com, $100–125) is the area's most unique place to stay. Part working family farm, part country resort, the bed-and-breakfast offers a chance to meet cows, llamas, and emus. Rooms in the two converted farmhouses are simply decorated, but include access to common fireplaces and hot tubs.

Northern Berkshires

The towering peak of Mount Greylock dominates the skyline from many a backcountry road here. The highest peak in Massachusetts, it is capped by a war memorial that enables viewers to pick it out from a distance, and sets the wild tone for the area's mountainous terrain. This corner of the state has always been its most remote, a fact that has led at times to economic stagnation. The combination of cosmopolitan Williamstown and the spreading influence of summer folk in the southern Berkshires, however, has given the area a new lease on life as a cultural destination, anchored by a pair of art museums worth the trip from anywhere in New England.

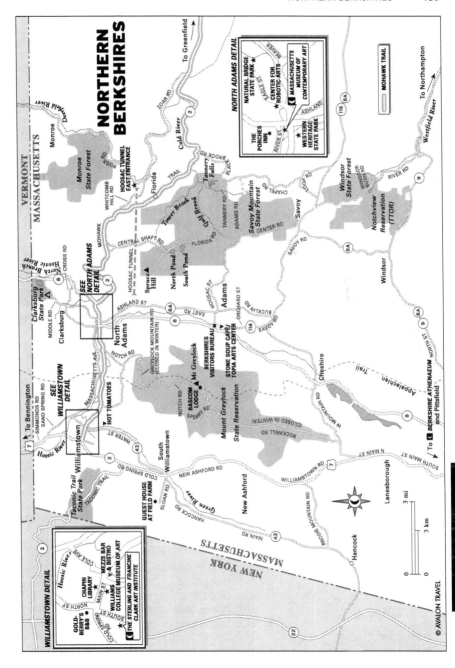

NORTHERN BERKSHIRES

NORTH ADAMS DETAIL

- NATURAL BRIDGE STATE PARK
- CENTER FOR ROBOTIC ARTS
- MASSACHUSETTS MUSEUM OF CONTEMPORARY ART
- THE PORCHES INN
- WESTERN HERITAGE STATE PARK

MOHAWK TRAIL

WILLIAMSTOWN DETAIL

- GOLDBERRY'S B&B
- CHAPIN LIBRARY
- MEZZE BAR & BISTRO
- WILLIAMS COLLEGE MUSEUM OF ART
- THE STERLING AND FRANCINE CLARK ART INSTITUTE

VERMONT
MASSACHUSETTS
NEW YORK
MASSACHUSETTS

© AVALON TRAVEL

NORTH ADAMS

It'd be hard to find a more stirring urban renewal story than North Adams, a depressed mill town that hit rock bottom in the 1990s when its main employer, Sprague Electric, took its marbles and went home. Back then, someone had the hare-brained idea to create a modern art museum in some of the old mill buildings. Fast forward a decade, and not only is the Massachusetts Museum of Contemporary Art a wild success, but its opening started a chain reaction leading to dozens of art studios, fine restaurants, and even a boutique hotel that has made this once-downtrodden town the hippest place in 100 miles. Despite its success, the town hasn't given up its working-class roots, making it a fascinating combination of opposites, with lunch-pail conservatives and blue-haired hipsters doing a daily dance of discovery with one another.

◖ Massachusetts Museum of Contemporary Art (MassMoCA)

Just the size of this museum (1040 Mass MoCA Way, 413/662-2111, www.massmoca.org, 11 A.M.–5 P.M. Wed.–Mon. mid-Sept.–late June; 10 A.M.–6 P.M. daily late June–early Sept., $15 adults, $10 students, $5 children 6–16, free children under 6) is cause for oohs and ahs. Composed of 27 red-brick former factory buildings and connected by an interlocking network of bridges, walkways, and courtyards, the galleries are of a vast size that allows artwork of an unusually epic scale—whether it's cars suspended with glowing fiber-optic cables, or a pyramid of action figures constructed by Norman Rockwell's grandson. Indeed, some say that the building is often more impressive than the artwork inside. But whatever its quality, the art is presented with a lack of pretension and an almost infectious delight in the creative process that makes the museum quite unlike any other.

Other Sights

The brainchild of local artist Eric Rudd, the Center for Robotic Arts (Historic Beaver Mill, 189 Beaver St., 413/664-9550, www.darkrideproject.org, 11 A.M.–5 P.M. Wed.–Sun. summer–fall, $10 adults, $7.50 seniors and students, children under 6 free) consists of a 15,000-square-foot immersive environment filled with robotic art creatures and moving sculptures for visitors to interact with. Rudd has also constructed A Chapel for Humanity, an overwhelming, gigantic tableau of 54 ceiling panels and 150 life-sized figures in the tradition of Rodin's *Gates of Hell,* installed in a former Baptist church at 82 Summer Street. In addition to the Beaver Mill, where the Dark Ride is located, the Eclipse Mill (243 Union St., 413/664-9109, www.eclipsemill.com) has also been converted into artists space, with 60 artists inhabiting 40 lofts, and eight galleries open to the public.

For a trip back in time, the North Adams Museum of History and Science (115 State St., Bldg. 5A, 413/664-4700, www.geocities.com/northadamshistory, 10 A.M.–4 P.M. Sat. and 1–4 P.M. Sun. Nov.–Apr.; 10 A.M.–4 P.M. Thurs.–Sat. and 1–4 P.M. Sun. May–Oct., free) is a wonderful evocation of small-town Americana, made more precious by the amateur quality of its exhibits. Three floors of old photos, clothing, Native American artifacts, and kitschy dioramas tell the story of the town from its founding.

Entertainment

In addition to its art exhibits, MassMoCA (Fri.–Sat. year-round, free–$30) serves as the cultural center of the community, staging silent movies accompanied by a string quartet, cutting-edge dance performances, and avant-garde musical performances by the likes of Yo La Tengo and Laurie Anderson.

Nightlife

In the nearby town of Adams, a Greek musician and a New York choreographer recently opened Stone Soup Cafe (27A Park St., 413/743-9600, www.topiaarts.org, 11 A.M.–2 P.M., Tue.–Sun., 6–11 P.M. Fri.–Sat.), an "art bar" with graceful nudes painted on the walls and wine tastings, music, and "aerial dance" on the schedule. The owners' eventual plan is to renovate a dormant 80,000-square-foot theater space behind the bar to offer concerts and avant-garde theater performances.

Shopping

The owner of **Persnickety Toys** (13 Eagle St., 413/662-2990, 10 A.M.–8 P.M. Thu., 10 A.M.–6 P.M. Fri.–Wed.) got so sick of driving to specialty stores for non-mass-produced toys that she opened her own shop. The one-of-a-kind folk-art objects at **Widgitz** (16 Eagle St., no phone) include country scenes painted on saw blades by a local barber. Tucked into an unassuming storefront, **Tangiers** (45 Main St., 413/664-4444, tangiersnorthadams.blogspot.com, 10 A.M.–6 P.M. Mon.–Fri.; 10 A.M.–4 P.M. Sat.) is a treasure trove of post-ironic gifts, along with a massage parlor and tanning salon.

Food

The cheapest meal in town is **Jack's Hot Dogs** (12 Eagle St., 413/664-9006, www.jackshotdogstand.com, 10 A.M.–7 P.M. Mon.–Fri.; 10 A.M.–4 P.M. Sat., $1–3), an authentic lunch counter dishing out dogs and burgers to blue-collar types who line the counter two deep at lunch time. If you are *really* hungry, you can enter the ongoing hot dog–eating competition—the record at press time was 30. Though it serves creative New American cuisine, **◖ Gramercy Bistro** (24 Marshall St., 413/663-5300, www.gramercybistro.com, 5–10 P.M. Wed.–Mon., $18–26) lives up to the "bistro" concept, with excellent food, reasonably priced.

Information

The **North Adams Office of Tourism** (6 W. Main St., 413/664-6180, tourist@northadams-ma.gov) runs an information office in town. In Adams, the **Berkshire Visitors Bureau** (3 Hoosac St., Adams, 413/743-4500, www.berkshires.org) runs a mammoth visitors center providing information on the entire Berkshire region.

WILLIAMSTOWN

A sign at the crossroads of Williamstown's small town center proclaims the town "the village beautiful"—and so it is. Completely ringed by mountains, the town is dominated by Williams College, whose green lawns and eclectic architecture makes every street corner a Kodak moment. The college is actually one of the oldest in the country, founded in 1791 through the will of Colonel Ephraim Williams, who was killed during the French and Indian Wars, but provided money for the establishment of a "free school" in the town of West Hoosac, provided it change its name to Williamstown. Just 30 years after its founding, the president and half the student body left to found Amherst College in the southeast, thus ensuring a rivalry that continues in sports to the present day. Today, the town is well known for its art museums and theater festival, which brings theatergoers from New York and Boston every summer.

◖ The Sterling and Francine Clark Art Institute

Visitors to this small mountainside museum (225 South St., 413/458-2303, www.clarkart.edu, 10 A.M.–5 P.M. daily July–Aug.; 10 A.M.–5 P.M. Tues.–Sun. Sept.–June; $12.50 adults, free students and children under 18 June–Oct.; free to all Nov.–May) are often agog that so much high-quality art is contained in a relatively obscure location. The Clark is simply one of the best small museums in the country, with a collection full of gems picked by the unerring eyes of its founders. Works by Renoir, Monet, Degas, Copley, Remington, and other well-known artists each seem hand-picked for their individual beauty or interest, often even surprising visitors familiar with a particular artist with unusual works.

Other Sights

For such a small college, Williams has an excellent art-history program, and many curators of art museums around the country are graduates of the school. That tradition is felt at the **Williams College Museum of Art** (15

Lawrence Hall Dr., 413/597-2429, www.wcma. org, 10 A.M.–5 P.M. Tues.–Sat.; 1–5 P.M. Sun., free), which has an excellent collection of 20th-century art along with a collection of underrated American Impressionist Maurice Prendergast. Williams is also the only institution outside the National Archives to have an original copy of each of the four founding documents of the United States (the *Declaration of Independence,* the *Constitution,* the *Bill of Rights,* and the *Articles of Confederation*) on view at the **Chapin Library** (temporarily located at Southworth Schoolhouse, 96 School St., 413/597-2462, www.williams.edu, 10–noon and 1–5 P.M. Mon.–Fri., free).

Events

For more than 50 years, some of the biggest names of Hollywood have descended upon the **Williamstown Theatre Festival** (413/458-3200, www.wtfestival.org, July–Aug., $15 for rush tickets, $20 for musical productions) to try out their acting chops on the stage. The festival stages a range of productions, from gala premieres to intimate play readings, allowing theatergoers a chance to see a different side of Ethan Hawke, Gwyneth Paltrow, Marisa Tomei, and dozens of other acclaimed actors.

Shopping

The main drag of Spring Street is full of art galleries and antiques shops. Owned by two Williams alumni (including a former overseer of Boston's Isabella Stewart Gardner Museum), the **Harrison Gallery** (39 Spring St., 413/458-1700, www.theharrisongallery.com, 10 A.M.–5:30 P.M. Mon.–Sat.; 11 A.M.–4 P.M. Sun.) displays artists of national standing. **LiAsia Gallery** (31 Spring St., 413/458-1600, 11 A.M.–5 P.M. Mon.–Fri.; 10 A.M.–5 P.M. Sat.; noon–5 P.M. Sun.) specializes in antique Chinese altar tables and architectural items. The overwhelming **Library Antiques** (70 Spring St., 413/458-3436, www.libraryantiques.com) has everything from Victorian-era books to mahogany beds from India.

Food

Many of the actors who have performed at the Williamstown Theatre Festival over the years are enshrined in sandwich form at **Pappa Charlie's Deli** (28 Spring St., 413/458-5969, 8 A.M.–8 P.M. daily), from Richard Chamberlain (turkey, swiss, and cranberry sauce) to Gwyneth Paltrow (eggplant parmesan). The popular student hangout has many vegetarian options. A wide variety of homemade cookies and pastries is available at **Tunnel City Coffee** (100 Spring St., 413/458-5010, 6:30 A.M.–6:30 P.M., daily), which serves coffee roasted in North Adams and abounds in comfortable couches and armchairs. Gourmet takeout-pizza joint **Hot Tomatoes** (100 Water St., 413/458-2722, http://hottomatoespizza. com, 11 A.M.–10 P.M. daily) has mastered the art of Neapolitan pizza, with cracker-thin crust and fresh, chunky tomato sauce. If the weather's nice, the adjoining park is a nice place for a picnic and a stroll. The village's culinary jewel is ◖ **Mezze Bistro + Bar** (16 Water St., 413/458-0123, www.mezzerestaurant.com, 5–9 P.M. Sun.–Thu.; 5–10 P.M. Fri.–Sat.), which blends equal parts Manhattan (leather banquettes, soft lighting, stiff martinis) and the Berkshires (birch-tree columns). A rotating menu includes such specialties as roasted skate with chanterelles.

Information

The **Williamstown Chamber of Commerce** (413/458-9077, www.williamstownchamber. com) runs a small information booth at the corner of Routes 2 and 7.

PITTSFIELD

The image of this economically depressed little city is not improved by its unfortunate-sounding name (a nod to English prime minister William Pitt, who was a sympathizer with the American colonists). In the early 20th century, the city was home to the Stanley Electric Manufacturing Company, a predecessor to electronics giant General Electric, which has long since left for greener pastures. Despite its gritty appearance, the area is now notable for several fine museums in and around the city, including two dedicated to Herman Melville, who made his unlikely home in the landlocked community from 1850 to 1863. Recently, the city has been coming back to life with the renovation of its gorgeous 1903 Colonial Theatre and the opening of several new restaurants downtown.

◖ Berkshire Athenaeum

The grand-sounding name of Pittsfield's public library (1 Wendell Ave., 413/499-9480, www. berkshire.net/PittsfieldLibrary, 9 A.M.–5 P.M. Mon. and Fri., 9 A.M.–9 P.M. Tues.–Thurs., 10 A.M.–5 P.M. Sat. Sept.–June; 9 A.M.–5 P.M. Mon., Wed., and Fri., 9 A.M.–9 P.M. Tues. and Thurs., 10 A.M.–5 P.M. Sat. July–Aug., free) doesn't quite seem to fit its blocky, concrete appearance. Inside, however, the **Herman Melville Memorial Room** is one of the region's hidden gems—a room with hundreds of artifacts from the life and travels of the author of *Moby-Dick.* The wealth of riches inside includes a case of family photos and daguerreotypes, ceremonial paddles Melville brought back from the South Seas, the desk where he wrote *Billy Budd Sailor,* and the holy of holies—a case full of quill pens and other items that were on his desk when he died.

Other Sights

After coming so close to the ephemera of the author, also visit his old home on the south side of town, **Arrowhead** (780 Holmes Rd., 413/442-1793, www.mobydick.org, 9:30 A.M.–4 P.M. with tours hourly 10 A.M.–3 P.M. daily late May–mid-Oct.; tours by appointment only mid-Oct.–late May, $12 adults, $5 students, $3 children 6–14, free children under 6), where Melville actually wrote *Moby-Dick.* Fans will appreciate the view from the room where he completed his masterpiece about the white whale, from which the ridge of Mount Greylock looks uncannily like the back of a sperm whale.

One of the most curious religious subcultures in America, the Shakers are known for their excellent furniture, their habit of shaking themselves into trances, and their strict separation of men and women, which probably led to their demise as a culture. The **Hancock Shaker Village** (1843 W. Housatonic St., Rtes. 20 & 41, 413/443-0188, www.hancockshakervillage.org, 10 A.M.–5 P.M. daily Apr.–mid-Oct., $16.50 adults, $8 children 13–17, free children under 13) provides an eye into their lifestyle in an authentic village preserved from the mid-19th century.

Chances are you have Crane paper in your pocket. The official suppliers of paper for American currency reveals the secrets of its craft at the **Crane Museum of Papermaking** (30 South St., Dalton, 800/268-2281, www. crane.com, 1–5 P.M. Mon.–Fri. June–mid-Oct., free), located in a historic old stone mill.

A great rainy-day destination for families, the **Berkshire Museum** (39 South St., 413/443-7171, www.berkshiremuseum.org, 10 A.M.–5 P.M. Mon.–Sat.; 12–5 P.M. Sun., $11 adults, $6 children 3–18, free children under 3) has a mummy, aquarium tanks, and children's toys created by modern artist Alexander Calder.

Information

The **Pittsfield Visitors Center** (111 South St., 413/4443-9186, www.pittsfield-ma.org/tourism.asp) provides information on the town and surrounding area.

SPORTS AND RECREATION
Mount Greylock
State Reservation

The 3,491-foot summit (Rockwell Rd., Lanesborough, 413/499-4262, www.mass. gov) of the highest peak in Massachusetts is a favorite for both challenging overnight hikes and scenic afternoon drives. Several trails lead to the summit—from Pattison Road in North Adams, the 6.7-mile trail offers terrific views from the summits of Mount Prospect, Mount Williams, and Mount Fitch, before the strenuous climb on the Appalachian Trail to the summit. From the Hopper Road in Williamstown, the challenging 4.1-mile Hopper Trail climbs along brooks and rocky rises in a steep climb to the top, with a campsite halfway. The (slightly) easier 6.9-mile Appalachian Trail up Saddle

© DEB SQUIRES, SUNBEAM IMAGES

cabin atop Mount Greylock

Ball Mountain begins at Outlook Avenue in Cheshire and ends with the steep Misery Hill pitch up to the summit. For gain without the pain, a scenic auto-road (May–Oct.) climbs from Notch Road in North Adams to the summit, from which you can climb to the top of a 100-foot-high war memorial for fantastic views of virtually all of the Berkshires (and some of New York besides). Also at the top is a snack bar and visitors center with information on short hikes and nature activities, as well as accommodations in **Bascom Lodge** (413/743-1591, bascomlodge.net, May–Nov., bunks $35, private rooms $100–125).

Hiking

The region abounds with shorter hikes. A favorite of Williams students is **Pine Cobble Trail** (413/458-2494, www.wrlf.org), a 2.1-mile all-season climb beginning on North Hoosac Road and rising 2,000 feet to a quartzite outcropping with fantastic views of the valley. In North Adams, **Natural Bridge State Park** (413/663-6392 or 413/663-8469), at the intersection of Routes 2 and 8, has a short hike from a rock quarry to a pint-sized natural bridge.

Biking

Running 11 miles from Adams to Lanesboro, the **Ashuwillticook Rail Trail** (413/442-8928, www.mass.gov) offers up excellent scenery of Mount Greylock and the Hoosac Range, as well as the salt marsh habitat of the Hoosic River. The trail starts at the Adams visitors center and ends at the Berkshire Mall. Bicycles can be rented at **Berkshire Outfitters** (169 Grove St., 413/743-5900, www.berkshireoutfitters.com, $21/day).

Sculling

If you've ever envied those collegiate rowers skimming the water in their sculls, take a lesson from the **Berkshire Rowing and Sculling Society** (43 Roselyn Dr., Burbank Park, Pittsfield, 413/496-9160, www.berkshiresculling.com, May–Oct., lessons $50/hr, rentals $25/hr), which rents boats on the beautiful mountain-ringed Onota Lake.

Skiing

While just a molehill compared to the big mountains in New Hampshire and Vermont, the best small-mountain skiing in the area can be found at **Jiminy Peak** (Hancock, 413/738-5500, www.jiminypeak.com, $54–64 adults, $46–57 teens 13 to 19, $40–47 seniors and children 12 and under, $19 children 6 and under), which has a good set of steep summit trails and a half pipe for snowboarders.

ACCOMMODATIONS
Under $100
The cheapest accommodations are at once the most scenic and least convenient. Overlooking North Adams, the **Wigwam and Western Summit Cottages** (2350 Mohawk Trail/Rte. 2, 413/663-3205, www.thewigwam.net, $70) offer bare-bones cottages from May to October.

$100-150
Named after a character in Tolkien's *Lord of the Rings,* **Goldberry's Bed & Breakfast** (39 Cold Spring Rd., Williamstown, 413/458-3935, www.goldberrys.tripod.com, $80–125) aspires to be a place of refuge for "weary hobbits." Genial host Mary Terio provides high-speed Internet and homemade breads and muffins in a homey Greek Revival house a short walk from Williamstown's center. Located at the crossroads of North Adams, the **Holiday Inn Berkshires** (40 Main St., North Adams, 413/663-6500, www.ichotelsgroup.com, $91–180) offers reasonable accommodations along with inoffensive art and polyester bedspreads.

$150-250
The tiered, cubist exterior, painted in hues of teal and mauve, is your first sign that the **Guest House at Field Farm** (554 Sloan Rd., Williamstown, 413/458-3135, http://guesthouseatfieldfarm.thetrustees.org, $150–295) is not your ordinary bed-and-breakfast. A Bauhaus-inspired modernist masterpiece, the home is full of modern art and design-conscious period furniture. A heated outdoor pool, private decks, and terry-cloth robes create a sense of peaceful refuge that melds with the natural setting of 300 protected acres that surrounds the house.

In a world of techno-and-neon boutique hotels, **The Porches Inn** (231 River St., North Adams, 413/664-0400, www.porches.com, $130–335) stands out for channeling the spirit of North Adams—both old and new. Workmen's rowhouses from the 1890s have been transformed into luxury guest rooms, with DVD players and ultra-soft sheets. The design sensibility, however, comes right out of blue-collar Americana, with paint-by-numbers paintings, vintage lamps scrounged through eBay, and breakfast delivered in steel lunch pails.

GETTING THERE AND AROUND
The closest airport to the region is **Albany International Airport** (737 Albany Shaker Rd., Albany, NY, 518/242-2200, www.albanyairport.com). Taxi service from the airport is available from a variety of limousine services, including **Advantage Transportation Services** (518/433-0100, www.albanycarservice.com), which charges $75 to Williamstown and $80 to North Adams. Buses to Williamstown are run by **Peter Pan Bonanza** (www.peterpanbus.com) and stop in front of the Williams Inn at the corner of Routes 2 and 7. The company also runs buses to **Pittsfield Bus Terminal** (1 Columbus Ave., Pittsfield, 413/442-7465).

Buses throughout the region are run by the **Berkshire Regional Transit Authority** (413/449-2782 or 800/292-BRTA).

Southern Berkshires

Compared to the northern Berkshires, the towns along the southern half of the mountain chain have a more sophisticated feel. The mountains themselves are smaller and have a smoother, gentler appearance than their northern neighbors, and the area has long been a country-getaway destination for wealthy urbanites from New York and Boston. Starting in the late 1900s, robber barons and socialites established summer "cottages" in the area, ranging from stone Victorian homes to sprawling manor houses with acres of grounds. Many of these homes have found a second life as spa resorts or hotels, adding grandeur to the season of art and music that fills the hills each summer.

LENOX

During the so-called Gilded Age, Lenox was ground zero for the barons of industry who made their homes here. Much of the character of the time is preserved in the green sculpted lawns and mammoth trees overhanging the roads, with an occasional mansion poking out of the greenery. The Boston Symphony Orchestra's summer presence at Tanglewood has spawned a cottage industry of other arts series and diversions, including a vibrant (if overpriced) gallery scene, and spas where the rich and famous come for respite from the spotlight.

◖ Tanglewood

Music lovers head west from Boston every summer to the warm-weather home of the Boston Symphony Orchestra (297 West St., 413/637-1600, www.bso.org, late June–early Sept.). The tradition dates back to the 1930s, when a classical music–crazy Berkshire family offered their 200-acre estate to the BSO as a gift, and legendary conductor Serge Koussevitzky gave his first all-Beethoven concert outdoors. The close feeling of nature and the outdoors imparts a languid feel to the music, often accentuated by visitors who bring picnic blankets and thermoses full of white wine. In addition to the full orchestra, the program features smaller chamber music concerts and an annual performance by singer-songwriter James Taylor.

Jacob's Pillow Dance Festival

Stars of the dance world invigorate the tiny town of Becket every summer with this internationally renowned festival (358 George Carter Rd., Becket, 413/243-0745, www.jacobspillow.org, mid-June–Aug., free–$55) founded

THE LAWN AND THE SHORT OF IT

Believe it or not, the first-rate musical performances are only part of the allure of Tanglewood, the Boston Symphony Orchestra's outdoor summer home. The other draw? The lavish picnics that concertgoers bring with them to devour on the perfectly manicured lawn during shows. These are no mere paper-bag affairs: Visitors are known to go to great lengths to outdo one another's fixings with intricate, gourmet spreads of multiple courses, wine, real glasses, and fine china and flatware. Many even tote along elaborate lawn furniture and canopies, though those outfits are relegated to the sidelines, so as not to block other guests' views of the stage. For your own picnic supplies, try **Loeb's Foodtown of Lenox** (42 Main St., Lenox, 413/637-0270, www.loebsfoodtown.com, 7 A.M.-6 P.M. Mon.-Thu. and Sat., 7 A.M.-7 P.M. Fri., 7 A.M.-4 P.M. Sun.) or better yet stop by **Nejaime's Wine Cellars** (60 Main St., 413/637-2221, www.nejaimeswine.com, 9 A.M.-9 P.M. Mon.-Sat.), which offers picnics packed and ready to go.

Edith Wharton's former mansion, The Mount

by modern-dance pioneer Ted Shawn. Every style from hip hop to ballet gets its time in the spotlight during the two-month celebration, which includes dozens of free performances and gallery talks. The main draw, however, is the showcases of artists from around the world, featuring both established companies such as Mark Morris and Alvin Ailey and emerging choreographers like Aszure & Artists.

Other Sights

You can practically hear the gossip whispering through the corridors of **The Mount Estate & Gardens** (2 Plunkett St., 413/551-5100, www.edithwharton.org, 10 A.M.–5 P.M. daily May–Oct., $16 adults, $13 students, free children under 12), *House of Mirth* author Edith Wharton's palatial home. Though much of the author's furniture was spirited to Europe following her husband's descent into mental illness, top designers have re-created the feel of the estate with antique furniture and artwork. The highlight for most visitors, however, is a stroll along the magnificent gardens, which have been meticulously sculpted with 3,000

flowers to re-create the vision of Wharton—who once famously contended she was "a better landscape gardener than novelist."

Part of the movie *Cider House Rules* was filmed at **The Museum of the Gilded Age at Ventford Hall** (104 Walker St., 413/637-3206, www.gildedage.org, 10 A.M.–3 P.M. daily, tours hourly, $12 adults, $5 children), a celebration of all things Victorian. The restored mansion was once owned by J. P. Morgan's sister, and tours bring alive the 1890s, when the Berkshires was the playground of the super-rich.

Events

Some of the best summer Shakespeare in the country is performed by **Shakespeare & Company** (70 Kemble St., 413/637-1199, www.shakespeare.org, free–$60), which performs in an air-conditioned scaffold-and-canvas theater. In addition to plays by the Bard, the company also stages premieres by area playwrights and special events, such as one-acts by Edith Wharton or interpretations of Edgar Allen Poe stories by actor F. Murray Abraham. The company is in the process of an ambitious plan to build a replica of the 1587 Rose Playhouse, surrounded by a mock-Elizabethan village.

Shopping

The main street of Lenox features many high-class boutiques and art galleries to occupy the rich during their idle time. One of the least pretentious is the **Wit Gallery** (27 Church St., 413/637-8808, www.thewitgallery.com), which features whimsical sculptures and surrealistic paintings that pop from the frames. Meanwhile, one of the most unabashedly fun is **The Gifted Child** (72 Church St., 413/637-1191, 10 A.M.–6 P.M. Mon.–Sat.; closed Sun.), a mishmash of games and books for toddlers, kids, preteens, and teens, plus cooler-than-cool clothing for all of the above ages. In nearby Lee, **Prime Outlets** (50 Water St., Rte. 20, Lee, 413/243-8186, www.primeoutlets.com, 10 A.M.–9 P.M. Mon.–Sat.; 10 A.M.–7 P.M. Sun.) features discounted clothing and housewares from dozens of name brands, including Bass, Coach, and Liz Claiborne.

Food

It's always summer at **Betty's Pizza Shack** (26 Housatonic St., 413/637-8171, http://bettyspizza.com, 11:30 A.M.–9:30 P.M. daily, $6–20), a tin-roof eatery with surfboards hung from the ceiling and some of the only cheap eats in town. A teenage and twentysomething crowd is drawn to the unlikely combination of burritos, pizza, and sandwiches.

A yellow-and-white striped awning overhangs the coveted outdoor patio at **Café Lucia** (80 Church St., 413/637-2640, www.cafelucialenox.com, 5:30 P.M.–10 P.M. Tue.–Sat., open Sun. during summer, $18–39), a bright and sophisticated Italian restaurant serving classics such as osso buco con risotto and veal parmigiana. The food is consistently good, and the wine list first-rate. **◖ Bistro Zinc** (56 Church St., 413/637-8800, www.bistrozinc.com, 11 A.M.–1 A.M. daily, $18–30) has earned a sterling reputation for unerring renditions of French bistro food, subtly tweaked for the modern palette by chef Michael Stahler. Expect dishes like organic chicken breast with crispy prosciutto or lobster with herb gnocchi and Pernod sauce, served in a dining room of blonde wood and circular marble tables.

Information

The **Lenox Chamber of Commerce** (12 Housatonic St., 413/637-3646, www.lenox.org) runs a visitors center in town.

STOCKBRIDGE

The quaint little town of Stockbridge doesn't just feel like a Norman Rockwell painting—it is one, as you can see from the ubiquitous reproductions of *Main Street, Stockbridge,* the artist's rendition of his adopted hometown. Rockwell painted here for the last 25 years of his life in a 19th-century carriage–barn-turned-studio behind Stockbridge center, and the museum dedicated to the master of small-town Americana is one of the region's most popular attractions. The town has gone to great lengths to preserve its Rockwellian character, with white picket fences shining in the sun and few visible relics of life after 1950 on Main Street. Of course, the tiny Main Street is just about all there is to the town, making it a quick study to say the least. But the busloads of senior citizens and tourists who book themselves in at the Red Lion Inn looking for a slice of nostalgia like it that way just fine.

◖ Norman Rockwell Museum

For such a supposedly vanilla artist, Norman Rockwell elicits strong reactions from viewers, who swoon at his vision of small-town life that never was, or hold their nose at his saccharine depictions of school kids in ponytails, stern but grandfatherly cops, and ubiquitous soda fountains. This large and comprehensive museum (9 Rte. 183, 413/298-4100, www.nrm.org, 10 A.M.–5 P.M. daily May–Oct.; 10 A.M.–4 P.M. Mon.–Fri. and 10 A.M.–5 P.M. Sat.–Sun. Nov.–Apr., $15 adults, $13.50 seniors, $10 students, free children under 19), however, may surprise viewers who think they know the artist from his *Life* magazine covers. Among the many paintings on exhibit is the serious series that Rockwell did on civil rights, including a haunting depiction of the three civil rights workers killed in Mississippi. Behind the museum is the artist's barn studio (open May–Oct.), preserved almost identically to the time when Rockwell painted here, and containing the artists' chair, brushes, and palette, along with his humorous collection of old military rifles and helmets.

Other Sights

Sculptor Daniel Chester French called his Berkshire home **Chesterwood** (4 Williamsville Rd., 413/298-3579, www.chesterwood.org, 10 A.M.–5 P.M. May–Oct., $15 adults, free children) his "heaven." The creator of the seated Lincoln Memorial in Washington, D.C., was one of the leading sculptors of an art period called the American Renaissance, during which a growing concentration of wealth found its outlet in patronage of parks, museums, and monuments. Tours take visitors through his elegantly appointed house, intimate studio, and 122 acres of grounds designed by the artist.

The first resident of Stockbridge, Rev. John Sergeant, came as a missionary to convert the native Mahican Indians in 1739. His home is preserved as **The Mission House** (19 Main St., 413/298-3239, www.thetrustees.org, 10 A.M.–5 P.M. late May–early Oct., $6 adults, $3 children 6–12, free children under 6), now a museum furnished with period items and containing exhibits on early colonial and Native American life.

Entertainment

At the Red Lion Inn, **The Lion's Den** (30 Main St., 413/298-5545, www.redlioninn.com) has live music nightly, ranging from Celtic to jazz to rock, along with pub grub.

Shopping

True to its name, **Country Curtains** (Red Lion Inn, 30 Main St., 800/937-1237, www.countrycurtains.com, 9:30 A.M.–8 P.M. Thu., 9:30 A.M.–6 P.M. Fri.–Wed.) carries a full selection of floral and checkerboard patterns, along with bedding, pillows, and everything else you need to turn your home into Avonlea. The trip

to West Stockbridge is worth making just to visit **Charles H. Baldwin & Sons** (1 Center St., W. Stockbridge, 413/232-7785, www.baldwinextracts.com, 9 A.M.–5 P.M. Mon.–Sat.; 11 A.M.–3 P.M. Sun.), a family-owned country store that dispenses homemade syrups and extracts, including the best vanilla extract you're ever likely to taste.

Food

An intimate bistro located on Main Street, **Once Upon A Table** (36 Main St., 413/298-3870, www.onceuponatablebistro.com, 11 A.M.–3 P.M. and 5–8:30 P.M. daily, $18–27) puts a creative American twist on continental cuisine—potpie of escargot, anyone? The chef-owned restaurant has an unpretentious but romantic atmosphere.

A rarity in the country, authentic Vietnamese cuisine is served up at **Truc Orient Express** (3 Harris St., W. Stockbridge, 413/232-4204, 11 A.M.–10 P.M. daily, $11–19), a white-tablecloth eatery originally started by two Vietnamese refugees in the 1970s. The *pho* is particularly good, as are salads, spring rolls, and seafood dishes.

Meat and potatoes figure heavily on the menu at **The Red Lion Inn** (30 Main St., 413/298-5545, 7:30 A.M.–9:30 P.M. daily, $23–34), which caters to leaf-peepers and bus tours with a heavy menu of New England classics served in a formal dining room.

Information

The **Stockbridge Chamber of Commerce** (413/298-5200, www.stockbridgechamber.org) has a small visitors booth on Main Street.

GREAT BARRINGTON

As soon as you cross the border into Great Barrington, the landscape changes, with trees and picket fences giving way to mill buildings along the Housatonic River and rusting trains on disused railroad tracks. The influx of summer guests to the Berkshires has put a new shine on a delightful downtown, making it reminiscent of what downtowns used to look like before Wal-Mart and shopping malls forced mom-and-pop stores out of business. Upscale restaurants and shops cater to the symphony and theater crowds.

Entertainment

Pronounced muh-HAY-wee, **The Mahaiwe Performing Arts Center** (14 Castle St., 413/528-0100, www.mahaiwe.org) is located in a restored 100-year-old theater and presents a first-rate, if eclectic, line-up of music, spoken-word, and theater performances. The 2005 season included a tribute to W. E. B. Dubois' "Souls of Black Folk," Cuban jazz pianist Omar Sosa, and a play reading with actress Marisa Tomei.

Events

What Tanglewood is to symphony music, the **Aston Magna Festival** (Daniel Arts Center, Alford Rd., 413/528-3595, www.astonmagna. org, $35 per concert) is to chamber music. During weekends in July and early August, both vocal and instrumental masters of the form perform at Simon's Rock College.

Shopping

A number of boutiques makes Great Barrington a great place to while away a few hours of shopping. Wistful Italian linens, robes, and hand towels are on sale at **La Pace** (313 Main St., 413/528-1888, www.lapaceinc.com, 10:30 A.M.–5:30 P.M. Mon.–Sat.; 11 A.M.–4 P.M. Sun.). Top-name women's clothing as well as spangly Indian kurta-style dresses and embroidered tapestry coats perfect for Tanglewood are on sale at **Gatsby's** (25 Railroad St., 413/528-9455). **Rubiner's Cheesemongers & Grocers** (264 Main St., 413/528-0488, 10 A.M.–6 P.M. Mon.–Sat.; 10 A.M.–4 P.M. Sun.) is Zabar's in the Berkshires, with imported cheeses from English cheddars to Italian gorgonzola. **Yellow House Books** (252 Main St., 413/528-8227, 10:30 A.M.–5:30 P.M. Mon–Sat; noon–5 P.M. Sun.) is a rambling farmhouse full of used and rare books, with a particularly good children's section. Outside of Great Barrington, the stretch of Route 7 down to Sheffield is known as **antiques alley** for its many fine antiques stores.

FROM GREAT BARRINGTON TO THE GROUP W BENCH

Every Thanksgiving, radio stations around the country play "Alice's Restaurant," an 18-minute-and-20-second talking blues satirical tour de force by folk singer Arlo Guthrie, about, among other things, his arrest for illegally dumping garbage and his subsequent rejection for service in Vietnam because of it. In fact, there actually was an Alice and she did actually own a restaurant. But at the time the song was written in 1967 she served her famous Thanksgiving dinners at the former church in Great Barrington where she lived and where much of the drama of the song takes place. Years later, in 1991, Guthrie purchased the very same church to create the **Guthrie Center** (4 Van Deusenville Rd., 413/528-1955, www. guthriecenter.org), a performance space that draws folkies from far and away for appearances by Arlo Guthrie himself as well as regular open-mic "hootenannies." The lobby of the center has photos and paintings of three generations of musical Guthries – Woody, Arlo, and Arlo's daughter Sarah Lee. Incidentally, the "Group W Bench" where Guthrie said he was banished with the other criminals and disqualified from service actually never existed. Guthrie was declared fit to serve in Vietnam, but escaped the draft because his lottery number wasn't called, not because he was arrested for illegally dumping garbage. But *that* song wouldn't have been nearly as long – or as funny!

One particularly worth a stop is **The Painted Porch** (102 So. Main St., Sheffield, 413/229-2700, www.paintedporch.com, 10 A.M.–5 P.M. daily Jun.–Dec.; 10 A.M.–5 P.M. Thu.–Mon. Jan.–May), whose owners scour the English and French countrysides for rare furniture.

Food

You can smell the garlic from the street outside

of **Baba Louie's** (286 Main St., 413/528-8100, www.babalouiessourdoughpizzacompany.com, 11 A.M.–3 P.M. and 5–9:30 P.M., $10–18) half Indian *dhaba,* half pizza cave that makes the best pizza around. The casual eatery uses a special recipe for its sourdough crusts, then piles on gourmet toppings including roasted red pepper, portabella, and chevre. A dark barroom with exposed brick walls and wooden booths, **20 Railroad Street** (413/528-9345, 11:30 A.M.–midnight or 1 A.M. daily, $8–10) serves buffalo and ostrich burgers in addition to sandwiches and pub fare. Meanwhile, bistro gets done right at **Once Upon a Table** (34 Main St., 413/298-3870, 12 P.M.–9:30 P.M. Mon.–Thurs.; 11 A.M.–10 P.M. Sat.; 11 A.M.–9 P.M. Sun., www.onceuponatable.com, $22–28). Berkshire regulars are understandably addicted to the Alaskan salmon burger with guacamole, as well as the gnocchi with roasted red pepper.

Summer reservations are made in the spring for the acclaimed **Verdura Cucina Rustica** (44 Railroad St., 413/528-8969, 5–9 P.M. Thu. and Sun.; 5–10 P.M. Fri.–Sat., $22–28), which uses the finest imported ingredients for "rustic" Tuscan cuisine of meat and seafood dishes. A happening bar menu ($7–10) at the *enoteca* next door includes a signature aged-balsamic martini.

Information

The **Southern Berkshires Chamber of Commerce** (362 Main St., 413/528-1510, www.greatbarrington.org) runs a visitors center with information on the town as well as the rest of the region.

SPORTS AND RECREATION
Spas

When the beautiful people find life too hard to bear, they book themselves in at **Canyon Ranch** (165 Kemble St., Lenox, 800/742-9000, www.canyonranch.com, 3-night packages start at $1,690), an offshoot of the original Arizona spa that takes a holistic approach to health, including exercise, bodywork, nutrition, and even lab work to get your chakras humming again.

Less intense but more relaxing, the **Cranwell Resort** (55 Lee Rd., Lenox, 413/637-1364, www.cranwell.com, 3-night packages start at $615) puts its world-class golf course front and center, along with a full range of beauty treatments, body wraps, and massages. East meets Western Mass. at the **Kripalu Center for Yoga & Health** (297 West St., Lenox, 413/448-3152, www.kripalu.org, 2-night packages start at $328), recognized as the best "yoga spa" in the country. For the rest of us, inexpensive à la carte massages and spa services are available at **Lenox Fitness Center** (90 Pittsfield Rd., Lenox, 413/637-9893, www.lenoxfitnesscenter. com), which charges $65 for a one-hour massage, and also offers reflexology, hot-stone massages, and yoga classes.

Hiking

Named by Herman Melville, October Mountain is particularly noted for its brilliant fall foliage. **October Mountain State Forest** (256 Woodland Rd., Lee, 413/243-1778, www. mass.gov) is the largest in Massachusetts, offering miles of backwoods trails and 46 campsites on a sun-drenched hillside. In the far southwestern corner of Massachusetts is one of the state's best hikes—the 20-minute ramble up to Bish Bash Falls. The waterfall tumbles through a mountain gorge down 80 feet to a sparkling pool. The hike is within **Mount Washington State Forest** (3 East St., Mt. Washington, 413/528-0330, www.mass.gov), which has more than 30 miles of trails through mountainous terrain.

Fishing

The **Berkshire Fishing Club** (Becket, 413/243-5761, www.berkshirefishing.com) runs fishing trips aboard a 16-foot bass-fishing boat on a private 125-acre lake.

ACCOMMODATIONS
Under $100

The stretch of Route 7 between Lenox and Pittsfield has many low-priced motels. The **Wagon Wheel Motel** (Rtes. 7 & 20, Lenox, 413/445-4532, www.bestberkshirehotel.com,

$45–195) is both cheery and cheesy—some of the rooms actually have heart-shaped whirlpool tubs. In Great Barrington, **The Lantern House Motel** (256 Stockbridge Rd., Rte. 7, Great Barrington, 413/528-2350, www.thelanternhousemotel.com, $45–200) has a heated outdoor swimming pool and rustic rooms set back from the road.

$100-150

The hills around Stockbridge and Great Barrington are alive with small bed-and-breakfasts. For listings, contact the **Berkshire Lodgings Association** (888/298-4760, www.berkshirelodgings.com). The **C Arbor Rose B&B** (8 Yale Hill, Stockbridge, 413/298-4744, $115–185) actually has a rose arbor on the front path that blooms in mid-June. Proprietor Christina Alsop is as laid-back and unfussy as the rooms are overflowing in rich details, including four-poster beds and dramatic window treatments. Full breakfasts include Alsop's "famous" homemade muffins. A Federal-style country inn located on ten acres, **Windflower Inn** (684 S. Egremont Rd., Great Barrington, 413/528-2720, www.windflowerinn.com, $100–225) is one of those special properties where every detail feels plucked from a romance novel. Fires blaze in a stone fireplace in one room, while perennial gardens surround an outdoor swimming pool.

$150-250

The closest you'll get to a Norman Rockwell painting is a stay in the **Red Lion Inn** (30 Main St., Stockbridge, www.redlioninn.com, $95–490), an "olde New England" inn featured in Rockwell's famous painting of Stockbridge.

A wrap-around verandah with rocking chairs provides the perfect setting for an afternoon of reverie, while rooms are simply decorated in period style. For more privacy, the inn owns several detached houses in the block behind. (Pass up the "cat suite," however, as Wilbur can be a bit temperamental.)

$250 and Up

To capture the luxury of the Gilded Age, book yourself at the **Blantyre** (16 Blantyre Rd., 413/637-3556, www.blantyre.com, $675–1,300), a Tudor-style manor modeled after a Scottish castle. Living rooms are decked out with brocade chairs, dark woods, and fireplaces, while guest rooms feature four-poster beds and sweeping views of the 100-acre grounds. The crisp staff seems to anticipate guests' needs.

GETTING THERE AND AROUND

The Southern Berkshires are easily accessible from the Mass Pike (I-90) and Route 7. **Bonanza Bus Lines** (888/751-8800, www.peterpanbus.com) runs buses to the region. In Lenox, they stop at Village Pharmacy (5 Walker St.); in Stockbridge, at the visitor booth on Main Street, and in Great Barrington, at the visitors center at 362 Main Street. **Peter Pan Bus Lines** (800/343-9999, www.peterpanbus.com) also runs buses to the Village Pharmacy in Lenox.

Buses throughout the region are run by the **Berkshire Regional Transit Authority** (413/449-2782 or 800/292-2782, www.berkshirerta.com).